HAUNTED OBJECTS

Literature and Cultures Series

General Editor: Greg Dawes
Series Editor: Ana Forcinito
Copyeditor: Audrey Hansen

Haunted Objects

Spectral Testimony in the
Southern Cone Post-Dictatorship

❧

Megan Corbin

acc

Raleigh, North Carolina

Library of Congress Cataloging-in-Publication Data
Names: Corbin, Megan, author.
Title: Haunted objects : spectral testimony in the Southern Cone
post-dictatorship / Megan Corbin.
Other titles: Literature and cultures series.
Description: [Raleigh] : Editorial A Contracorriente, 2021. | Series:
Literature and cultures series | Includes bibliographical references.
Identifiers: LCCN 2020048517 | ISBN 9781469664293 (paperback) | ISBN
9781469664309 (ebook)
Subjects: LCSH: Disappeared persons—Southern Cone of South America. |
Personal belongings—Southern Cone of South America. | Material
culture—Southern Cone of South America. | Political prisoners—Southern
Cone of South America. | Collective memory—Southern Cone of South
America. | Victims of state-sponsored terrorism—Southern Cone of South
America. | Prisoners as artists--Southern Cone of South America.
Classification: LCC HV6322.3.S63 C67 2021 | DDC 362.87098—dc23
LC record available at https://lccn.loc.gov/2020048517

ISBN: 978-1-4696-6429-3 (paperback)
ISBN: 978-1-4696-6430-9 (ebook)

This is a publication of the Department of Foreign Languages
and Literatures at North Carolina State University. For more information
visit https://uncpress.org/books/?publisher=editorial-a-contracorriente

Distributed by the University of North Carolina Press
www.uncpress.org

ACKNOWLEDGMENTS

As I reflect back on the ten years that led to the publication of this project, the words "thank you" seem profoundly inadequate to express the gratitude I feel toward all those who contributed to its completion. This book began as my doctoral dissertation at the University of Minnesota, where I spent ten years studying as an undergraduate and graduate student. Early in my studies there, René Jara opened my eyes to the power of literature and, in so doing, changed my path from one headed toward law school to one focused on studying *testimonio* and human rights. I am thankful for the support of all of the faculty with whom I took courses; without their multidisciplinary perspectives the book's theoretical framework would not exist. I want to particularly thank Amy Kaminsky, Ofelia Ferrán, and Nicholas Spadaccini for their comments.

I have been very fortunate, dare I say extremely lucky, to have Ana Forcinito as a mentor throughout the course of this project. I am grateful to her for having confidence in me when I was a graduate student and letting me run with the idea of analyzing objects in testimonial texts—I will never forget her comment early on that she saw I was thinking about something and to just keep thinking. Her support, especially during the last year of my graduate career, went above and beyond that which can be expected of an advisor and for that I am more appreciative than words can express. I hope that I can act in the same capacity for my own students one day.

I am very grateful to Alberto Ribas Casasayas and Amanda Petersen for organizing a panel at the American Comparative Literature Association's Spring 2012 conference where I received a number of comments and suggestions on an initial version of the main theoretical argument that informs this project. I am also grateful to Stacey Schlau for her mentorship on putting together a book proposal, to Jason Bartles for always sharing his perspective on the process, and to all my colleagues at West Chester University whose support in various ways helped me navigate finishing this manuscript while teaching four classes a semester.

A special thank you to all who shared their stories with me, revisiting what have to be painful memories in order to contribute to the building of this project. In Chile, thank you to Verónica Sánchez at the Museum of Memory and to Anahí Moya Fuentes, José Danor Moya Paiva, Maria Alicia Salinas, and Marcela Andrades Álfaro for helping me find information about the *artesanías carcelarias* that I could not have found on my own. In Montevideo, thank you to those at Crysol, as well as Antonia Yañez, Pedro Giudice, and Stela Reyes who invited me into their homes for conversation and to view and photograph the craftwork that they kept from their time in the political prisons.

The research for this project was made possible by the generosity of the College of Liberal Arts at the University of Minnesota, which granted me a fellowship that allowed me to travel to Chile, Argentina, and Uruguay and to discover much of the information that now forms the basis of this study. During that summer, I was generously welcomed into the homes of a number of individuals who helped me navigate the cities where I conducted my research. María Eugenia, Sebastián, Belén, Guadalupe, Patricia, Elena, Saúl, Marili and Alexis, Fernando, Mariana, Zoraya, Johan, and Saira—thank you all for opening your homes to me, and to Sebastián, a special thank you for giving up easy access to your toys and lending me your room for a month in Santiago. In addition to that funding, a Doctoral Dissertation Fellowship for the academic year of 2013–2014 gave me the time to immerse myself completely in the project. Additionally, the support of the College of Arts and Humanities at West Chester University allowed me to make subsequent trips to each country to refine my understanding of the sites of memory and incorporate more pinpointed examples into the book's argument. I also want to thank the Office of Research and Creative Activities at WCU for supporting production costs for the book.

Thank you to my family for their constant support, to my husband, Michael, for his patience with my propensity to put work before all else, and a special thank you to my son, Corbin Michael, whose impending arrival was just the push I needed to finally finish revising. Thank you for waiting until all the writing tasks on "the baby list" were completed to make your entrance into this world.

CONTENTS

The Absent Witness—The Enduring Material

🜨

Skeleton #33: We find signs that it was a woman.
A hair pin.
A bra.[1]

It is harder to find these objects associated with the skeletons
than it is to uncover the remains.[2]

We have always lived off the splendor of the subject and the poverty of the object.[3]

IN THE FAR-RIGHT CORNER of the *Parque por la Paz* (Park for Peace), the former space of the Villa Grimaldi/Cuartel Terranova detention center in Chile, there remains a seemingly inconsequential tree. One of many on the grounds, it stands largely hidden by the grandiose monument of names, built in homage to those who disappeared from the grounds of the center. This tree is easy to pass by without notice. There are no markers in this area of the park to signal to the visitor a special significance, the area stands at a distance from the rest of the grounds, a mere alternative path to pass through on the way to the next stop of the guided audio visit. However, if one looks up into the branches of the tree, they will see a loop of barbed wire that hangs around one of the branches and may wonder if it is a quiet, yet lasting testament to the atrocities of a space that was meant to be destroyed and forgotten forever [Image 1].

One small, yet durable, loop of wire, smooth but for a single, menacing barb, encapsulates humankind's potential toward cruelty, a potential fully re-alized in this space's past. This object gestures to a violence that removed

1. Barbed Wire Hanging in a Tree at Parque por la Paz: Villa Grimaldi.
Photograph by the author.

voices and eliminated subjects, impeding the historical reconstruction of a carefully targeted sector of lives. *This* remnant remains in *this* tree, frozen in the past, yet emphatically in the present. More than a symbol, it is a testament to a hand that purposefully placed it in the tree. For what purpose? By what means? At what time? On what date? The questions are numerous and remain unanswered.

The frustration of confronting this vestige from the past is evident. The barbed wire could be a remnant of the violence perpetrated during the cruel past of one of the most brutal torture centers of the Pinochet dictatorship. Or, it could be a byproduct of the work of recovering this space for the purpose of preserving the memory contained in the site. For the visitor who wonders, this doubt will remain and these questions will, of necessity, go largely unanswered—our collective curiosity just one more desire that will be left unsatisfied in the quest to rebuild the pieces of what was lost along with the lives of those beings who simply (yet monumentally) disappeared.

Claudia Bernardi is a member of the renowned Equipo Argentino de Antropología Forense (Argentine Forensic Anthropology Team). In the epigraphs above, she describes her reactions to her work at the site of the massacre of El Mozote in El Salvador, where she and her team worked to uncover the buried remains of women and children. Bernardi has also remarked that "skeletons in a mass grave give me a profound tenderness . . . I am touching history with my hands."[4] An internationally-known visual artist who uses art to promote human rights, Bernardi points to the same power identified by Marjorie Agosín in her claim that "memory speaks from dead bodies."[5] The declaration that the dead can speak appears counter-intuitive (and illogical), but begs the important question of whether a body itself can have a postmortem agency. If so, what type of capacity to speak is this? And, if objects like a hair pin or a bra are emotionally harder to find than the skeletal remains themselves, do other material *things* also hold this power?

As Baudrillard identifies in the final epigraph above, humanity tends to privilege the subject over the object. Indeed, scholarship on Latin American *testimonio* and on the periods of the dictatorships in Chile, Argentina, and Uruguay most often rests on a concern for the subject's experience, image, and voice as they are represented in narrative, art, and on film. However, the often neglected material object poses a unique possibility to the scholarship of memory; in much the same way that Francine Masiello observes that "art and literature [. . .] force us to think of interpretive strategies of resistance, interrogating the past and leading to a politics of cognition with which to move toward the future,"[6] the importance that recently has been given to objects from the past—both by survivors and in archival spaces of memory—asks us for a reconsideration of their interpretative power. Mentions of such material items abound in descriptions of the space of the concentration camps, the political prisons, and the clandestine detention centers of the Chilean, Argentine, and Uruguayan dictatorships during the second half of the twentieth century. In Alicia Kozameh's *Pasos bajo el agua*, the narrator describes how an iron is used to transmit crucial knowledge from one area of a detention center to another; carefully dismantled by one set of prisoners, it is filled with messages written on small scraps of paper, then reassembled and sent to another area of the prison, where the process repeats. This iron, no longer serving a purely utilitarian function, facilitates the expression of human subjectivity, making possible the communication of both information and sentiments of caring that became crucial to the building of solidarity amongst prisoners. An iron, a simple tool for smoothing out the fibers of rumpled clothing, in the space of the detention center breaks with its traditional meaning and becomes something else entirely, but what exactly?

In this book, I reconsider a variety of material remainders from the past, in an effort to reveal the interpretive power that memory work in the present can gain from them: the everyday object of the detention center, the prison craftwork made as an important form of survival and resistance in the Chilean and Uruguayan detention centers, the personal items that belonged to the victim prior to his/her becoming victim, the bodies that emerge from mass graves, the bodies of the second generation that carry the material copies of the DNA of their disappeared parents, and the object that was once present at the scene of torture or detention and currently occupies the role of witness in the space of the museum.

The role of the material has not been entirely ignored in critical considerations of the Latin American post-dictatorship period, nor in the field of memory studies. However, though some have discussed the power of the memory space/site of memory in transitional justice and in the healing of a traumatized society,[7] only now are scholars beginning to contemplate the plain things,[8] the tough-to-find objects, the belongings of the past whose residues haunt the present. To date, only one published study considers the craftwork of the Chilean concentration camps,[9] and none consider this phenomenon in the Uruguayan political prisons. In this study, I seek to explore and reevaluate the function of such objects, both during the temporality of the dictatorships—while victims fought for survival—and after the return to democracy, in memory projects that seek to record and transmit the violence of the dictatorships. I assert that such material objects in the present speak a truth about the past, revealing aspects of the experience of political prisoners during the dictatorship, and, especially in the cases where the object's owner did not survive the repression, giving what I call "spectral testimony" in lieu of the voices of their disappeared owners, a type of testimony that at once satisfies our quest for information about the events of the past and calls attention to the impossibilities of our understanding of such monumental atrocity.

Central to my project is the question of how objects from the past are perceived as bringing people in the present to a realm of shared sentience in which experience can be transmitted and the labors of memory[10] can take place. Not everyone (and thankfully so) has suffered the circumstances of political repression, unlawful detention, or torture. The importance of and difficulties inherent in relating such events to those who have not fallen victim to such crimes have been extensively studied and documented, both in terms of the Southern Cone dictatorships and the Jewish Holocaust. However, I ask: can visiting, viewing, and contemplating the physical evidence of mistreatment, the vestiges of the evil of the past, or the handcrafted objects of resistance transmit this knowledge? Does encountering the material of this past access a realm of shared objectification, rehumanizing those who suffered, resisting the dismissal of subjects of the past by re-contextualizing their actions through a material compilation of their former selves, of their personalities, of their having been more than the sum of their actions? By leaving a testimonial material legacy, can objects bypass the subject's need to articulate his/her lived trauma, yet still create the change in the overall political climate sought by the testimonial voice that speaks? I contend that projects that highlight the possessions of the disappeared and the craftwork made by former political prisoners serve to restitute the subjectivity stripped of these persons at the moment of detention, fostering encounters between the past and the present, and creating new and productive experiences with still largely hidden histories.

To embark on an analysis of the memory power held by material objects in the post-dictatorship, we must first return to the past moment of violence and determine the importance the material world held for those who were kidnapped, tortured, detained, incarcerated, and/or disappeared. To even begin to consider the importance of the object and its ability to bear witness to the past from the present place of the museum of memory, the family home, from texts, cinema, or the digital platform, we must first understand the history and the significance of the object in the past.

The military dictatorships in Southern Cone Latin America purported to re-establish political and social "order" in their respective countries, discouraging dissent and rigidly controlling the actions of the citizenry, doing so via the dissemination of a regime of terror, employing torture, unlawful detentions, murder, and enforced disappearance of persons. In Chile, the democratically-elected Socialist government of Salvador Allende was systematically undermined by influences from both inside and outside of the country, and was violently overthrown in a coup d'état on September 11, 1973, led by CIA-backed General Augusto Pinochet. Pinochet then installed himself as the head of the country, beginning a seventeen-year reign of state repression and massive human rights violations. In Argentina, after the death of General Juan Domingo Perón and the subsequent political chaos that plagued

the weak presidency of his successor—his wife Isabel Perón—the Argentin-
ean armed forces took control of the government in a coup d'état that would
be billed as the "Proceso de Reorganización Nacional" (Process of National
Reorganization), signaling the beginning of a military dictatorship packaged
as a necessary political change in order to rid the country of armed groups
that threatened a Communist takeover of the government. Lasting until 1985,
what ensued would come to be justified by the repressive forces as a "dirty
war," with the government—in the name of restoring order—systematically
violating the rights of its people through unlawful detentions, torture, murder, and enforced disappearance of persons.

The Uruguayan context differs somewhat from the histories of the other
two countries, in that its military dictatorship arose out of increasing eco-
nomic problems and the rise of unionizing efforts and an urban guerrilla
movement (the Tupamaros) that battled police and governmental "ineffi-
ciency, corruption and failure to enact meaningful reforms."[11] Gradually, the
country militarized and by 1973, the armed forces took over and proceeded
to impose, as Paul Sondrol has phrased it, "their own vision of political life."[12]
While in Uruguay enforced disappearance of persons was not nearly as widespread as in Argentina or even Chile, authoritarian control of the citizenry
occurred through widespread and seemingly permanent incarcerations of citizens who demonstrated politics incongruent with the vision of the military
government, along with the brutal use of torture as a method of spreading
terror.

All three dictatorships formed a part of the coordinated Operation Condor. An arrangement orchestrated in the 1960s and 1970s among Chile, Argentina, Uruguay, Bolivia, Paraguay, Brazil and, later, Peru and Ecuador that
sought to prevent the spread of Communism through the region in the wake
of the triumph of the Cuban Revolution, Operation Condor coordinated the
police and military efforts of all member countries, along with support from
the United States. This coordination meant that the tactics used by the different dictatorships often mirrored each other, even though, as always, some
differences remained—for instance, Uruguay "exported" a lot of its violence
to Argentina, resulting in fewer "disappearances" in Uruguay and a larger
number in Argentina. On the whole, though, a striking number of similarities
exist between these three Condor countries of the Southern Cone, especially
in the use of material objects by prisoners and in memory projects in the period after the transition back to democracy.

Material Proof: The Threat of the Object

The dictatorships, in attempting to exercise complete control over the populace, needed to exercise complete control over the material world. One of the most haunting examples of this desire for control over the material are the disappearances of the detained themselves, the absenting of not only subjects, but all traces of their corporal existence post-kidnapping. The term disappearance, used strategically by the dictatorships, was a way of evading legal documentation of the detention of individuals, thus avoiding the denunciation of political kidnappings by families and friends who sought answers regarding the whereabouts and conditions of their loved ones and companions. In addition, disappearance was a way to avoid international scrutiny of the methods being used by the governments in their quest to restore order to a chaotic political environment. Disappearance proved to be both a strategic and systematic means of covering up the violations of human rights that occurred during the dictatorship. As Emilio Crenzel notes: "In this way, no traces would be left, the bodies of the abducted would become invisible to the public, their captivity could be denied, and nobody would be held accountable for their death."[13] Such a policy sought to evaporate all material signs of having existed, all corporal traces of the disappeared.

However, as I explore in the second half of this study, in focusing on the bodies of the detained, the dictatorships missed the elimination of other, material signs of the existence of the disappeared, such as their personal belongings and, in the cases where they had children, the attempts to erase the identities of the second generation neglected to realize that the body is an archive that cannot be fully transformed. At the heart of disappearance is a lack, constituted not only by the loss of life and the inability to determine information, but by the impossibility of access to facts, and to materials (here, corporal; the absence of the body) that could help establish those facts. As has been extensively studied, disappearance was not only a means by which to control the population's access to information, it was also a focused effort at the destruction, elimination, and ultimate control over the circulation of peoples and goods in the realm of society—reinforcing power during the dictatorship and assuring impunity in the post-dictatorship.

Yet, little by little, the traces, the spaces, and even some of the remains of the disappeared are being recovered. In 1978, in a Chile still under the control of Augusto Pinochet, fifteen bodies burned and covered in lime were

recovered and identified in Lonquén; in 1991 a forensic anthropology team
exhumed 126 bodies from Patio 29 of Santiago's Cementerio General; and for
years bodies washed up on the Uruguayan coast of the Río de la Plata. The
files on these bodies—which were photographed by Uruguayan officials, although never officially investigated—reemerged in Daniel Rey Piuma's *Un
marino acusa: juicio y castigo a los culpables: informe sobre la violación de derechos humanos por la Marina uruguaya* (*A Marine Accuses: Justice and Punish-
ment for the Guilty Ones: A Report on the Violation of Human Rights by the
Uruguayan Navy*), and in December of 2011 were turned over as proof to be
used in the third mega-trial of ESMA, which "hasta el momento sólo contaba
con pruebas testimoniales de los 'vuelos de la muerte'"[14] (up to that moment
had only counted on testimonial proof of the 'death flights'). In Argentina, as
seen in the documentary *Encontrando a Víctor* (*Finding Victor*, 2004), Natalia
Bruschtein embarks on a search for her disappeared father. Her grandmother,
Laura, remarks to her: "Las personas . . . viste . . . no desaparecen como si
fueran cosas"[15] (People . . . you see . . . don't disappear as if they were things).
Since 1986, the Argentine Forensic Anthropology Team has worked to identify and interpret the pasts of exhumed human remains.[16] The reemergence of
bodily remains actively defies disappearance with their ability to relate facts,
fill gaps, and eliminate doubt, exhibiting the threat of the body object. However, material *things* don't seem to disappear so easily either.

The re-emergence of the material of the past does not limit itself to corporal remains. At the former Chilean detention center Londres 38, the team
that works at the site, along with the Dirección de Bibliotecas Archiva y Museos (Directorate of Libraries, Archives and Museums) and the Centro Nacional de Conservación y Restauración (National Conservation and Resto-
ration Center), carried out a biological and cultural analysis of the structure,
arriving at what they termed an "análisis testimonial" (testimonial analysis)
via an examination of the material—the objects and structure—of the space
of the building.[17] Similarly, in Argentina, the former Navy School of Mechan-
ics (ESMA) underwent its own forensic architectural analysis, the findings
of which have been presented in the "Megacausa ESMA" trials. The excava-
tions done at the Argentine site of the former Clandestine Detention Center
(ex CDC) Club Atlético (Athletic Club) unearthed the structural remains
of entire rooms, which provided survivors of that particular center with the
information necessary to pinpoint where they had been held captive. In the
summer of 2013 similar investigations were conducted at the ex CDC Virrey

Cevallos in Buenos Aires, unearthing (among other material evidence) the words "Todavía vivo" (I'm still alive) written on a wall. This slow, but sure, reappearance of material vestiges of the past points to the perhaps only rational premise that the dictatorship had in its ideology of destruction: the fear of the potential threat posed by things.

Why Spectral Testimony?

Many encountering this book may question the use of the term testimony to refer to the memory work done by material objects; *things* do not possess speech and are therefore incapable of producing narratives that articulate their experience. This use of "experience" may also seem odd—objects are not living, so how can we describe their history as an "experience"? However, in my research to try to understand the importance of objects during the dictatorship for political prisoners and the detained-disappeared, I found that survivors often speak of the object as a quasi-person, as a "being" capable of lending a form of help and/or resistance. Relying on Graham Harman's rereading of Heidegger's tool analysis, which posits that *things* have a type of being of their own ("tool being"),[18] I will make the case in the first two chapters of this book that an object can be a witness with an experience to "tell," and I will argue that objects especially should be considered as witnesses if we are to honor the testimonies already given by survivors, in which many speak of objects in this way. In order to honor this new order of *things* in the post-dictatorship, I propose that we, as readers looking for information about that past, reconsider the object's capacity to give testimony.

Simultaneous to seeing this new value of objects within existing written testimonies, I also observe a shift over the last decade whereby written testimonial production by first-generation witnesses seems to have waned, yet projects that seek to recover the past via a focus on the material—such as the recovery of former sites of violence and their conversions into spaces of memory, many of which are filled with objects of the past that help narrate the crimes of the dictatorships—are emerging with increasing frequency. Numerous projects, including *Vestigios* by Memoria Abierta, *Proyecto Tesoros* by Colectivo de Hijos, displays of prison craftwork and recovered remnants of the past at the Museum of Memory and Human Rights in Santiago, Chile, the Museum of Memory (MUME) in Uruguay, and at various former detention centers that are now sites of memory, as well as the play *Mi vida después*

(*My Life After*) by Lola Arias, all award a privileged place to the object, valued for its capacity to explain a truth about the past. This suggests that the labors of memory are taking place increasingly in the sphere of the material, which therefore merits consideration.

As Kimberly Nance observes, current testimonial scholarship seems to suggest that the moment for testimonio has passed.[19] Indeed, critical attention to the genre arguably reached a culmination around the turn of the new millennium, fueled by the controversy surrounding David Stoll's 1999 critique of Rigoberta Menchú's *Me llamo Rigoberta Menchú y así me nació la conciencia,*[20] and the subsequent publication of the canonical collections *The Real Thing: Testimonial Discourse and Latin America* (1996) (compiled by Georg M. Gugelberger, with essays by many of the formative scholars of the field[21]) and *The Rigoberta Menchú Controversy* (2001), edited by Arturo Arias.[22] These discussions, however, focus mostly on the Central American testimonial context, while (as the projects I mentioned above seem to evidence) the work of memory in the Southern Cone continues, and the need to recover voices and advocate for recognition of the personal experiences of survivors as legitimate and a part of these nations' histories still exists.

Arguably, such work will always exist, especially if the work of testimonio (as Nance suggests in her study) is to reach the reader, animating him/her to fight ongoing injustice. If the work of testimonio in the Southern Cone is to denounce state terrorism and ensure that such injustice never again occurs in the future, then that work will always extend into the future. Thus the moment for testimonio will never have passed, and critical considerations of it must simply continue to evolve.

In terms of this evolution of the field, Louise Detwiler and Janis Breckenridge identify three key moments for testimonio in the period since the publication of Arias' collection.[23] In the first, a collection devoted to woman-authored testimonio, *Woman as Witness: Essays on Testimonial Literature by Latin American Women*, editors Linda S. Maier and Isabel Dulfano identify an absence of consideration of gender and genre particular to these narratives.[24] The second moment—the publication of Joanna R. Bartow's *Subject to Change: The Lessons of Latin American Women's Testimonio for Truth, Fiction, and Theory*[25]—advocates for an ongoing consideration of the trajectory of testimonio, sustaining that the "testimonial informant . . . will evolve over time."[26] The third moment the authors identify as paramount for Testimonio Studies, is Kimberley Nance's *Can Literature Promote Social Justice? Trauma*

Narrative and Social Action in Latin American Testimonio. Nance's study re-
visits testimonio, interrogating its efficacy in exacting social change and advo-
cating for "a fundamental shift in expectations from both the instant gratifica-
tion of the poetics of celebration and the self-abasing fantasy of the poetics of
mourning—a shift from fantasy relationships with testimonio—to a harder,
less glamorous, and less ideologically pure alternative."[27] Detwiler and Breckenridge themselves, in agreement with Hans M. Fernández Benítez, declare
that "a new decade is upon us,"[28] and that their own collection, *Pushing the
Boundaries of Latin American Testimony*, "fulfills the notion of a renovated
testimonial episteme."[29]

I agree that Detwiler and Breckenridge's collection appropriately expands
the genre, considering "eco-testimonios, novel witnesses, anti-testimonios,
meta-testimonios, and graphic testimonios"[30] in oral, written, and visual
forms from a diverse array of arenas: their contributing authors consider testimonial production from India, the Spanish Civil War, Guatemala, Argentina,
and Mexico. Detwiler and Breckenridge argue that "there is no one way to 'do
testimonio,'"[31] but acknowledge the difficulties that such a stance poses for
defining the genre. In keeping with Debra Castillo's notion of a "subjunctive
mood" in women's writing, they offer that the defining characteristic of the
texts considered in their collection is the existence of a "testimonio mood."[32]
The authors "envision, in fact, that testimonio scholarship of the future will
scrutinize and embrace entirely different realms of subjectivity, such as that
of the cyborg, the nonhuman, or some other cognitive, referential, or linguistic arena not yet articulated as of this writing."[33] In agreement with their
vision, I propose that if we look at recent projects of memory in the Southern Cone, we observe that many attempts to create memory about the past
indeed encapsulate a "testimonio mood," asking for a critical consideration
of Testimonio Studies as a field even for projects that are not written texts.
Indeed, "a new decade is upon us," and, in agreement with Bartow, I believe
this new decade also merits a reconsideration of the testimonial informant,
which, as Detwiler and Breckenridge suggest, need not be human. If recent
projects attempt to translate the past of objects, we must critically engage the
object as a testimonial subject and attempt to create a theoretical framework
that describes how that subject tells its story.

In turning to the particularities of Southern Cone testimonio (here I mean
specifically Chile, Argentina, and Uruguay), it is clear that there are important differences that must be considered. In contrast to the Central Ameri-

can and other Latin American contexts—I am thinking primarily of Cuba, Bolivia, and Brazil, where a largely unlettered population required a lettered (and privileged) writer/ethnographer to convey their testimonies—most of the survivors of the political repression in Chile, Argentina, and Uruguay possessed these skills and were able to write for themselves. Indeed, in some cases (particularly those of Hernán Valdés, Jacobo Timerman, and Mauricio Rosencof) the testifying subjects were already accomplished authors before publishing their testimonial narratives. The proliferation of the genre itself in the Southern Cone is tethered to the journalistic production of accomplished authors like Rodolfo Walsh, whose documentary-style writing was the earliest to denounce the Argentine state's use of violence against its own citizens. Additionally, in the Southern Cone, the focus on the subject's status as "other" is informed by considerations of Holocaust testimony, focusing on the immense task the testifying subject encounters when searching for an adequate form of representation through which to communicate "limit" experiences (traumatic events whose magnitude often defy representation), rather than the subaltern status of the testifying voice germane to the Central American context.

Another particularity within Southern Cone testimonio is the impact of the confines of juridical testimony on the genre. As has been studied extensively by Emilio Crenzel, the report by the CONADEP truth commission, *Nunca Más,* created a narrative or frame which impacted the Argentine transition period and the memory work that could be done during that time.[34] Hugo Vezzetti also notes this impact of the *Nunca Más* report on testimonio in Argentina, arguing that the "two demons" narrative produced by the report limited the type of testimony that could be given, particularly in relation to the history of the militant groups, observing that:

> ha creado un problema muy característico en los testimonios: las dificultades para articular memorias privadas, familiares o de grupos, con el pronunciamiento de un testimonio público que habla por y para la sociedad [...] también impuso [...] un límite. En los comienzos de la democracia, cuando algunos testigos querían hablar no de los crímenes y de las víctimas sino de los objetivos que perseguían, de la razón de sus luchas, es decir, cuando quisieron inyectar una coloración política e ideológica en los testimonios, una buena parte de la sociedad mostró que no quería escuchar.[35]
>
> (It has created a very characteristic problem in testimonies: the difficulties in articulating private memories, of relatives or groups, with the pro-

nouncement of a public testimony that speaks through and on behalf of society [...] also imposed [...] a limit. At the beginning of democracy, when some witnesses wanted to speak not about the crimes or the victims, but about the objectives they had pursued, the reason for their struggles, which is to say, when they wanted to inject a political and ideological color into the testimonies, a good part of society showed that they didn't want to hear it.)

However, even with these confines, the "narrative void"[36] left by political disappearance meant survivors still felt the pressure to give their stories as a representation of a collective experience, to speak for those who had not survived. The conditions of production of testimonio are encased in this dichotomy of self and others. Indeed, for Vezzetti, testimonio does not only consist of the enunciating "I," but always of an "other," usually collective, in which testimonio is enveloped:

> los testimonios siguen capturados por esas condiciones de producción y emisión que se refieren al grupo familiar o al grupo político. Sea la trama familiar, sea la de grupos replegados sobre las amistades, los afectos y los proyectos comunes, lo característico es que en la rememoración se entrecruza la dimensión personal, privada con un espacio de significados y de acciones políticas.[37]

> (testimonio continues to be captured within those conditions of production and transmission that refer to a familial group or a political group. Whether it's the storyline of a family, or of groups enfolded in friendships, affects, and common projects, the common characteristic is that the recollection of the personal, private dimension is crossed with a signifying space and with political actions.)

This tension between the individual and the collective impacts how the representative witness speaks on behalf of a larger group, hoping to accomplish a political task.

By revisiting the material legacy of the dictatorships—by which I mean the relationship between the subject and the object during the period of violence—I hope to highlight the importance of considering the use of "object witnesses" in projects of memory within the "testimonio mood" that Detwiler and Breckenridge advocate for in their collection of essays. To date, no such study exists, and given the growing number of examples of museum ex-

14   *Introduction*

hibits and sites of memory associated with the Southern Cone dictatorships that display such objects in an attempt to transmit to present and future generations the memories of the political violence of the past, such objects are meritorious of our critical attention.

My attempt to highlight how such objects give testimony is encompassed in the term "spectral testimony." I recognize that the testimony given by objects is not equivalent to the testimony offered through written or oral language in the type of texts traditionally considered as testimonio. However, I reject the notion that such use of language is the defining characteristic of testimonial production. For an example of testimonial artwork, one need only consider Guillermo Nuñez's drawings of torture to see how a visual rhetoric may be employed to transmit an understanding of the survivor's experience in the past. The engagement with a visual aesthetic, rather than a linguistic one, does not erase the power to transmit an understanding about the past. Both Katherine Hite and Jill Bennett have made the case that an empathic understanding of the victims' plight can be achieved through such art. I contend that the object witness has a similar capability.[38] However, I reiterate my recognition that the testimony offered by such objects is not the same as that offered by written testimonio. For that reason, I insist that such object witness testimony is unique in that it is more of a ghostly testimony from the past that haunts the present.

In terming such testimony "spectral," I seek to pinpoint the way in which the present approaches these objects from the past and how the past of these objects impacts the present, regardless of the limitation of the lack of language. These objects encountered within the museum are placed in a narrative that attempts to translate a piece of their history. I see the museum context as a translator that does the work of conjuring central to the hauntology outlined by Jacques Derrida in *Specters of Marx*.[39] In placing the object witness in the museum, the curators begin the process of translating its history for the visitor in the present. The placards that offer contextualizing information further aid in this process of conjuring. However, a significant amount of the interpretative work of speaking with the ghost is left for the visitor to undertake for him/herself, for the context given is never a complete explanation of the object's past (as such a complete explanation is an impossibility). Therefore, the encounter with the object is essentially an encounter with the limits of representation, for the object cannot put its entire past into words that we can understand; it cannot speak to us on its own. Without this system for understanding, we are left to contemplate the object, to think with it, to analyze its materiality, to look for signs of the past we know it holds—signs beyond that which has been translated for us. The need for this work forces the visitor to engage in the labors of memory, to be, as Dori Laub describes, "at the same time witness to the trauma witness and a witness to himself."[40]

As Ana Forcinito has argued, those (human) survivors who give their testimony bring us to a threshold (*umbral*) through which

> Nos vienen convocando, como lectores y testigos indirectos, no tanto al orden de lo real, sino al de su representación como umbral, zona de contacto, mundo intermedio, espacio en el cual deben lidiar con las expectativas (de verdad, de legitimidad, de ética, de coherencia narrativa, de "normalidad," de heroicidad, de protagonismo, de memoria indeleble) de quienes desde afuera y desde el presente escuchamos, leemos, juzgamos e intentamos comprender sus testimonios."[41]

> (They come to convene us, as readers and indirect witnesses, not so much to the order of the real, but to their representation as a threshold, a zone of contact, an intermediary world, a space in which they must deal with the expectations (of truth, legitimacy, ethics, of narrative coherence, of 'normality,' of heroism, of protagonism, of indelible memory) of those who from outside and from the present listen, read, judge, and attempt to understand their testimony.)

Spectral testimony as a term attempts to extend that which the term *testimonio* is traditionally understood to encompass, describing the type of testimony a material object can offer in the moment of the encounter with the object. A communion on the threshold between the past and present, between the living and the dead, it delineates the simultaneous presence and absence/inaccessibility of information about the past. An object that gives spectral testimony is an object that is a witness to a past limit event: it was there, it is authentic. The information we receive from the object at the threshold of our contact with it has the capacity to have a political impact in the present. The impact of the ghostly past derives from the interpretative work required to commune with the object, a work that makes this encounter analogous to the reading of "deliberative testimonio"[42]—the written form that Kimberley Nance argues is effective at creating social change.

Part One: Subject/Object Relations During Detention

The first half of this study (Chapters One and Two) examines the temporality of the dictatorship, approached by examining narratives left by survivors in order to re-evaluate the threat posed by things and the importance the material world held for the detainee. In an effort to contextualize the theoretical arguments I develop in the second half of the book around the testimonial capacity of objects in the post-dictatorship, I start from an exploration of how the detainee's relationship to the material world changes during the course of his/her detention and scrutinize how s/he turns to the material as a quasi-human ally in the fight for survival.

To do this, the first chapter, "Loss and Reconstruction in a Still-Material World—A New Noticing of *Things*," begins with an analysis of the unmaking and remaking of the world of the subject who suffers, which I contend awakens him/her to the possibilities contained in the material objects surrounding him/her—to what Graham Harman, re-reading Martin Heidegger's tool analysis in *Being and Time*, terms their "tool-being."[43] I contend that the subject who suffers torture experiences a break with the world around him/her, and that this changed subject can't help but notice the potential of the material items that order the detention center, a noticing that results in their turning to those items as allies in the struggle for survival. Creating a bridge between Harman's "tool-being" and Elaine Scarry's analysis of the making and unmaking of the world,[44] I discuss how, for the subject who was detained and tortured during the dictatorship, a break in the tool was not required for the interior agency of the object to become noticeable, but rather that the subject's relationship to the world experiences a break (is unmade and remade, to use Scarry's terms), producing a constant state of noticing the tool-being of things. To illuminate these processes and examine the potentiality of the object for the human subject's survival, I explore the narrative voices of five people who survived the repression and reappeared: Alicia Partnoy, Alicia Kozameh, Jorge Tiscornia, Mauricio Rosencof, and Marcelo Estefanell. Beginning from Elaine Scarry's analysis of the unmaking of the world during the scene of torture, I analyze how the crimes perpetrated during the dictatorships produced a break with the material world for tortured and detained subjects, a break which (as is demonstrated in the second half of this project) remains present in memory narratives generated in the temporality of the post-dictatorship. Placing Scarry's text in dialogue with emerging theories of object-oriented ontology, I argue that this break produced a heightened awareness regarding the potential for survival and reconstruction offered to the subject by the objects that surrounded him/her in the space of detention, and gave way to a new noticing of, valorization of, and relationship to the tool-being of material things.

Chapter Two, "Material Escape—*Manualidades* and *Artesanías carcelarias* as Artifacts of Imagined Agency and Resistance," moves the discussion of the importance of the material world for the prisoner forward from an examination of found objects in detention to a consideration of the process of imagining and making-real undertaken as a form of material resistance by the prisoners themselves, focusing on two traditions of prison craftwork (objects that were produced by the hands of "incarcerated" subjects from within the confines of detention): the *artesanías carcelarias* in Chile and the *manualidades* in Uruguay. In this chapter, I contend that the constant state of noticing things that I explored in Chapter One produced an awareness in the incarcerated subject to the potential of all materials within the detention center, and I maintain that craftwork in the prisons was used as a means of amplifying the self (again, following Scarry's analysis) through the creation of an exterior artifact capable of relieving interior pain. At the same time, this exercise constituted the crafting of a testimonial object that would relay an aspect of life in the concentration camp to the generations of the future.

In the prisons, craftwork was a means by which the suffering subject imaginatively created an artifact that could relieve a facet of his/her pain. Like a chair relieves the body's pain (the classic example Elaine Scarry includes in her analysis), artifacts were imagined that moved outside and beyond the confines of incarceration. At the limits of the ordinary, extraordinary objects were imagined in order to help the subject make real the very items s/he lacked. The mental reasoning and the productive work of taking scant materials and turning them into imaginative pieces of art was a way by which the prisoner both created and expressed his/her individual agency. These items, preserved today, are therefore an important material legacy of resistance, a resistance that forms part of the basis of the material testimony being employed within spaces of memory in the present day.

Part Two: Toward a Testimonial Theory of Objects

The second half of this project (the final three chapters) introduces the concept of spectral testimony and explores the implications this concept has for the consideration of three instances of the use of objects from the past: first, by examining the singular object itself in the space of the memory museum; second, by revisiting the body as a material object capable of relaying a spectral testimonial truth from the past to the present; and third, by examining collections of everyday objects and material belongings (such as those one might find in a childhood bedroom) of the disappeared and their use in memory projects intended to transmit knowledge about the victims of the dictatorship.

With the premise of this second half of the project in mind, the third chapter of this project moves from the temporality of the violence to the post-dictatorship period of democracy, in which each country continues to grapple with how to approach the legacy of the traumatic past, and the survivors in each context struggle to relay their memories to present and future generations. In Chapter Three, "After Detention or Disappearance—Spectral Testimony in the Museum of Memory," I first re-examine classic scholarship on testimonio as a genre in an effort to highlight already existing examinations of the testifying voice's productive ability to speak and be heard. Next, I scrutinize what testimonial theory might gain from a dialogue with material and spectral theory, especially in regard to the use of objects in current memory projects in the Southern Cone. And lastly, I argue that when we reconsider the everyday object—once present at the scene of torture or detention and presently occupying the role of witness in the space of the museum—and re-evaluate this material in light of testimonial and spectral theory, it becomes clear that material objects speak a truth about the past, giving what I introduce as "spectral testimony," in lieu of the voices of their disappeared owners— a type of testimony that is a form of deferred agency that lies in the realm of the just beyond. It is a concept I connect to Agamben's notion of the third state of the *Muselmann*,[45] but also to Derrida's ruminations on the specter of Marx that continues to haunt our society, along with his thoughts on the fiction of testimony, a writing that yields a phantom real that is ever-present, yet ever just beyond reach. I suggest that spectral testimony interpellates the viewer in the present with a deferred past and requires him/her to do the work of memory, to contemplate what the object offers, at the same time that the spectral nature of this process calls attention to the limitations on knowing posed by the violence of the past.

In Chapter Four ("Bodily Incarnations—Forensic Memory and Hauntings in the Everyday), I extend my analysis in Chapter Two of the made object as an externally created artifact to a material consideration of the bodies of the children of the disappeared, exploring the impact disappearance had and continues to have on society's view toward the capacity of the body to remember and to "speak" or "testify," especially those bodies that can be viewed as the living physical material remainder of the disappeared. Drawing inspiration from Judith Roof's elaboration of the concept of a "poetics of DNA" in North American cultural production,[46] I examine how the legacy of disappearance contributed to the creation of a "poetics of DNA" that promotes a hope that the truth of the past lies in the corporality of the body and which continues to inform the narrative logic of advocacy work and art related to memory activism. I examine how the belief that the truth of the past emerges via the body informs the promotional materials created by the Grandmothers of the Plaza de Mayo in their activism in locating the second-generation disappeared, those children who were appropriated at birth (or "disappeared with life," as the group terms it). Lastly, I argue that the body of the child of disappeared parents is uniquely positioned to not only contribute forensic testimony, but in its very physical existence, constitutes another type of artifact, a material that is haunted by the former activism of the child's parents and which yields a spectral material testimony that continues to sow doubt and animate action in the present day.

In my last chapter, "Reappearance—Learning to Live and Speak with Ghosts," I explore how the material narrative both created and left by prisoners and discovered in the wake of disappearance is being used to recreate and transmit memory by second-generation actors in the post-dictatorship. First, I argue that projects (such as the *Sala de Memoria* in the space of the former detention center Villa Grimaldi in Chile, and the art project *Memorias de Vida y Militancia* undertaken by the groups that inhabit the ex ESMA in Argentina) are using the former belongings of the disappeared in order to conjure forth their individual specters in an effort to rehumanize them and permit them to speak, thus resisting the emptying of their identities that lies at the core of disappearance as a systematic form of repression. Second, I consider how the virtual art exposition *Proyecto Tesoros* took these projects further in an attempt to weave together the voices and materialities of the past and present generations in the creation of memory narratives that interrupt the impersonal and collective narrative of disappearance. Lastly, I examine how the film *Cautiva* (Gastón Biraben, Argentina, 2005) and recent theatrical productions by Lola Arias further enmesh the material and the voice in an effort to dramatize the testimonial encounter with the objects of the past, depicting a scene of spectral communion in which the present experiences the ghosts of the past through an affective commingling and conversation with material belongings.

The Testimonial Splendor of the Object

In the consideration of these examples and these periods in the development of the importance of the material world, what becomes clear is that living off the splendor of the subject is not possible in the period of the post-dictatorship, as the subjects are largely missing and those who survived often experience a crisis of representation where they cannot find an adequate means through which to transmit their lived memories to the present and future generations. The object in the post-dictatorship, however, as another witness to the history of the violence of the past, survives to preserve its story. The poverty of the object, its lack of voice, dictates that in order to access its past, we must learn to speak with the ghost that inhabits it. Forensic readings as well as consideration of the symbolism contained in the object can yield a form of testimony that, upon contemplation, forces the generations of the present to confront the limits of the past, placing us one step closer to understanding the survivors.

Testimonial narratives reveal a different relationship to objects, to the potential for survival they offer to the subject with their *tool-being*. In the camp or detention center, things like the iron never break; their purpose is simply modified. The change undergone by the subject produced an entirely new order of extraordinary things, a new utility of objects largely unconnected to their understood use. These objects, though imaginable in our minds, remain inaccessible, their true meaning for the survivor or the victim perpetually just beyond reach. These objects, haunted by their pasts, bring us, the outside readers, to a place of shared sentience, but at the same time the difference between our subjectivity and that of the survivors keeps our relationship to the object separate and different. That is the meaning of spectral testimony in this project. These objects—many made by the hands of those who are no longer here to speak, others emblematic of who these individuals were before disappearance—are at once the lasting, durable remainder of the past and a conscious reminder of the inaccessibility of the "truth" of the violence of that moment. In that sense, as I will demonstrate, the spectral testimony yielded by objects is both frustrating and extremely productive.

Part One

Subject/Object Relations
During Detention

CHAPTER ONE

Loss and Reconstruction in a Still-Material World—A New Noticing of *Things*

꙰

A Marxist recognition of our journey from matter will return us, finally, to a world in which matter is truly humanized and internalized. Matter must not remain in itself, nor must it simply be wished away as already human. Recognition of matter's own dynamism—its role in the trajectory of human history—will allow us to harness matter's potentiality such that human life can live in accord with its own material nature.[1]

It is impossible to speak of either torture or war without attending to the destruction of the artifacts of civilization in either their interior and mental or exterior and materialized forms.[2]

At the concentration camp kitchen they made a list of her belongings [. . .] 'A wedding ring, a watch . . . dress color . . . bra . . . she doesn't wear one . . . shoes . . . she doesn't have any?' [. . .] When she thought the interrogation session was about to begin, they took her to a room. She walked down a tiled corridor, then an old wooden floor. After arriving at the wretched bed assigned to her, she discovered a ragged blanket. She used it to cover her feet and did not feel so helpless.[3]

THE TURN TO THE material in the search for knowledge about the past calls us to reconsider just what the object is (its being), how it retains (or is perceived to retain) information about the past, and the relationship the *thing* has with the individual. In short, as Elizabeth Grosz comments above, "its role in the trajectory of human history"—in the present study, the traumatic history of the Southern Cone's recent past. Elaine

Scarry's reading of matter in *The Body in Pain* emphasizes the process of the material "making" of civilization, originating from the interior mental state and projected outward into an external form. In Scarry's words, "independent objects, objects which stand apart from and free of the body, objects which realize the human being's impulse to project himself out into a space beyond the boundaries of the body in acts of making, either physical or verbal, that once multiplied, collected, and shared are called civilization."[4] This conceptualization of the material world emphasizes human being's relationship to the object, the utility we draw from the inanimate, the making external of an internally created idea. The final passage above is from the opening tale of Alicia Partnoy's *The Little School: Tales of Disappearance and Survival*, describing her initial arrival at The Little School (*La Escuelita*), a clandestine detention center that operated in Bahía Blanca, Argentina. Partnoy's initial account of her detention is jarringly centered on the relationship between her experience and the objects that compose it. The attempt to communicate the terror she felt in not knowing if (or, perhaps better stated, when) she would be taken from her home plays out over a comment on footwear: "She had waited for them to come at night. It felt nice to be wearing a loose house dress and his [her husband's] slippers after having slept so many nights with her shoes on, waiting for them."[5] The loss of Partnoy's freedom is accompanied by the loss of her slippers in a futile attempt to flee the men who arrive to take her to the detention center: "When the soldiers grabbed her, forcing her into the truck, she glanced down at her feet in the dry street dust."[6] At the Army Headquarters, waiting for her transfer to The Little School, she again describes her feet against the cool, "tiny black and white tiles,"[7] calling explicit attention in both instances to the lack of protection on her feet, their bare vulnerability to the changing ground she treads. Her arrival at the detention center is accompanied by an inventory of her belongings, and finally her encounter with the ragged blanket she uses to cover her feet in order to "not feel so helpless."[8] The blanket lends her its warmth and comfort, acting as an ally in the struggle for survival. Later, the guards give Partnoy a pair of slippers to wear during her detention—only one of which retains its decorative flower, a "huge plastic daisy,"[9] the absurdity of which lends Partnoy a little levity in a situation dominated by fear.[10] Partnoy describes that she often searched blindly for the daisy "between the guards' shouts and blows"[11] and that when she was moved to a prison, the "one-flowered slippers remained at The Little School, disappeared."[12]

Questions abound after reading these passages—why narrate via the material when the human suffering taking place in the space of detention is so great? What power does the description of a slipper hold? What power did *the slipper* itself hold for Partnoy in detention? Why emphasize an absurd "huge plastic daisy" amidst the descriptions of the violence inflicted by the guards? If recovered, could that daisy and slipper contribute to the understanding of the past? Would it retain its significance for Partnoy? Could it communicate this significance to others? These questions point to the importance of examining the specific and important ramifications held by the un-making and re-making of the world for the victim of torture—the prisoner, the detainee—a process that plays out across the relationship between humanity and the materiality of our surroundings. For Partnoy, the blanket is a welcoming friend, offering itself as an ally in surviving the hard times ahead, if only through the comfort of a bit of warmth on her feet. The one-flowered slipper also occupies this role, offering its own absurdity as a comic escape from the ominous confines of The Little School. More than bastions of civilization, traces of the exterior world miraculously encountered in the interior of a torture center, such objects offer up the dynamism of their own matter for use by the prisoner in resisting and surviving, hence it might just make perfect sense that Partnoy begins her collection of "tales of disappearance and survival" via a pointed observation of her commingling with objects.

Recent theories of the philosophy of objects posit that, like humans, objects have an interior being of their own: they have a "tool-being,"[13] or must be considered as "vibrant matter."[14] This being normally hides in plain view, in the ready-at-hand tools that we use in the day-to-day.[15] Yet, every once in a while, human *Dasein* encounters a broken tool,[16] the tool becomes present-at-hand, and we, if only fleetingly, become aware of a being held within the object, for "equipment is not effective 'because people use it'; on the contrary, it can only be used because it is *capable of an effect*, of inflicting some kind of blow on reality."[17] In the case of the detention center, it is not necessarily the *object* that is encountered as a broken tool, but the occupied world that undergoes this transformation. The entire reality in which the prisoner exists is altered, thus calling attention to the tool-being of not only specific objects, but *all* of the matter that occupies the space of mistreatment. The ragged blanket and the plastic daisy of the sandal are objects *capable of an effect*—they inflict a blow on the cruelty of the detention center, they reveal their interior power to the subject who suffers, a power that then marks Partnoy's reconstruction of her detention via her testimonial text.

While in general we, as subjects, don't notice the *things* around us until they break (my computer, for instance, is a tool that largely goes unnoticed by me until it stops functioning and interrupts my ability to work on this text), the unmaking and remaking of the world awakens the subject who suffers the extreme pain of torture to the possibilities contained in the objects surrounding him/her, to their tool-being.[18] S/he can't help but notice the potentiality of the material items that order the detention center, an altered state that produces a constant *noticing* of things. To illuminate these processes and examine the potentiality of the object for the human subject's survival, this chapter turns to the literary voices of five people who survived the repression and reappeared: Alicia Partnoy, Alicia Kozameh, Jorge Tiscornia, Marcelo Estefanell, and Mauricio Rosencof. Beginning from Elaine Scarry's analysis of the unmaking of the world during the scene of torture, I will explore how the crimes perpetrated during the dictatorships produced a break with the material world for tortured and detained subjects, a break which (as will be demonstrated in the second half of this project) remains present in memory narratives generated in the temporality of the post-dictatorship. Placing Scarry's text in dialogue with emerging theories of object oriented ontology, I will argue that this break produced a heightened awareness regarding the potential for survival and reconstruction offered to the subject by the objects that surrounded him/her in the space of detention, and gave way to a new noticing of, valorization of, and relationship to the tool-being of material things, a shift that is detected in the narratives these survivors use to relate their experiences in detention.[19]

Un-making the World: Torture, Destruction, and the Subject

Torture was supposedly used in the Argentine, Uruguayan, and Chilean dictatorships as an instrument by which the military forces could, little by little, uncover the structures of leftist (so-called subversive) militant organizations believed to be working to thwart the successful reorganization of their countries by the military regimes. Yet, the quest for information in many cases can be dismissed as a mere façade, the true aim of torture and disappearance being the creation of a rhetoric of fear that orders the larger environment in which the citizenry lives, thereby controlling through a culture of terror and violence.[20] Another, more immediate goal, of torture was, according to physicians Inge Genefke and Peter Vesti, to "break down a person's personality, his or her identity."[21] In both breaking down identity and fomenting fear, the use of torture by the dictatorships had at its core an alteration of the body/subject's interaction with the exterior world.

This systematic employ of torture also had its own material component. The careful design of the material space of detention by the military relied on a secondary dimension: the creation of an environment in which the use of torture could take place and perpetuate itself. Hernán Vidal posits that for mass torture to be possible, along with a general asceticism toward human dignity and a perverse conception of what it is to be a citizen, a material element is necessary:

> En lo material se requieren instalaciones especialmente habilitadas y discretamente localizadas, provistas de instrumentos adecuados, de un personal entrenado y burocratizado por estos efectos, y de la dotación, orientación y connivencia de la autoridad estatal.[22]

> (In terms of the material, specially equipped and discreetly located installations, stocked with adequate instruments and a trained and bureaucratized personnel are required, along with the endowment, orientation, and collusion of state authorities.)

In short, the material element of this schemata exhibited a specific design that assured both the immediate and future destruction of the subject. The intent to destroy the subject through torture was not only a utilitarian tool for eliminating threatening voices from the sociopolitical sphere via an erasure of their autonomy, but also a means by which to ensure that the repressive forces put into place would continue operating, supported by a band of officers whose job became the systematic physical and psychological torture of a subject dehumanized in the very process.[23] From the beginning, this task had at its core a consideration not only of the individual that was to be tortured and how best to inflict that pain, but the material design of a space and a process by which the torturer could continue his/her work without hesitation. The dehumanization of the victim, his/her reduction to the status of a *thing*, of an object, in a space specifically designed for this task, was used to facilitate this ongoing mistreatment of some humans by other humans by providing a psychological barrier that permitted the torturer to disconnect from the inhumane nature of his/her crime in order to continue carrying out brutal acts of terror.[24]

However, no matter how thoroughly planned and successfully implemented the design of a space for the sheer purposes of torture, testimonial accounts of the space of the detention centers, political prisons, and concentration camps reveal that this work of conversion always remains incomplete. This is because the prisoner him/herself undergoes a change in the scene of torture—the remaking of his/her world gives him/her a new relation to the realm of objects, finding in the least assuming of *things* an important ally in the fight for survival.

While it is true that the material world of the detention center was specifically designed to inflict pain and the destruction of the subject, objects within these spaces were also a means by which the testimonial subject retained and/or rebuilt his/her subjectivity while in detention. Objects in testimonial texts hold utilitarian value for both the testimonial subject and his/her victimizer. As Elaine Scarry observes in her analysis of the use of pain to increase the torturer's power, torture occurs largely through objects, through a changing of the relationship the subject has with his/her sentient world. This can occur through the use of one's body against him/her (as a source of pain), but also through the remodeling of an object's use, making a formerly benign object into a weapon capable of producing pain. During the period of violence, everyday items—often belonging to the prisoners themselves—were converted into objects of torture. The Argentine *Nunca Más* report recounts cases in which "the captors either brought their own blindfolds, or used the victim's own clothes—shirts, pullovers, jackets, etc., or sheets, towels and so on."[25] The turning of such personal belongings, formerly inconsequential and largely unnoticed, into producers of pain demonstrates the unmaking of the subject's relationship to his/her exterior world. It produces a new relationship to formerly present objects, revealing to the subject a newly noticed potentiality or power of the exterior world.

The change produced by detention was not just an imposed reconfiguration of the subject's world, but a shift which gave way to a new system of survival for the prisoner him/herself—a new order of *things*. Testimonial accounts from the dictatorships of the Southern Cone reveal both an exercised control over the objects that make up the world of the detention center and a fear of what potential acts of resistance such items may allow the prisoners to carry out from the space of detention. This important role of objects for both the breakdown and, later, the recuperation of subjectivity signals a fundamental change in the everyday object pre- versus post-victimization. Such a reliance on the material world demonstrates a facet of the resistance to the dictatorship (even from within the space of the scene of torture and/or detention) that has the possibility of revealing truths in the present about the past, should we choose to engage in dialogue (even if incomplete) with the object.

Before I move on to place Scarry's analysis of unmaking and remaking in dialogue with Harman's reevaluation and extension of Heidegger's tool analysis, I first will demonstrate how objects referred to in testimonial texts show that *things* were important factors for survival and resistance within the space of detention. To do this, I turn to two narratives written by survivors from the Argentine context: Alicia Partnoy and Alicia Kozameh.

Material Matters: The Role of the Object in Resistance

In survivor Alicia Partnoy's *The Little School: Tales of Disappearance and Survival in Argentina*, objects are relied on by the subject for solidarity and survival. Partnoy's text has been heavily examined by theorists of *testimonio*[26] and many analyses of it highlight the author's literary treatment of the blindfold she was forced to wear in the detention center, a consideration to which I offer to add the following analysis of the weapon, in light of its interior tool-being.

The blindfold is, technically, employed by the dictatorship as a weapon, but, as emphasized in Partnoy's text, it also can be manipulated by the prisoner into serving as an ally in survival. The blindfold's potentiality evades the total control of the guards who employ it to help them render helpless the prisoner; its vibrancy rebels against the status quo.[27] The fabric of the blindfold loosens over time, as it moves ever so slightly under the strain of the prisoner's movement. Such malleability is a property interior to the object itself—it is a feature of the fabric's being in the world. But it is precisely this feature which comes to the aid of the prisoner. The prisoner relies on this malleability to manipulate the fabric to capture visions of the space that surrounds her. The blindfold here serves not as a weapon, but, conversely, an ally in the prisoner's struggle.

In another prisoner's reconstruction of her time in detention—this time an Uruguayan political prison—the blindfold-as-ally leads the prisoner to another object: a shoe, which offers a similar structure of support. Martha Valentini states:

> Una de las mil formas de tortura fue ponernos de *plantón* sin un zapato, te desquilibrás y caés sin remedio, sobre todo las mujeres que usamos tacos. Nuestros zapatos se apilaban en un rincón. Una querida amiga que estaba en aquel *plantón*, me contó mucho después, que mi zapato, que veía por debajo de la venda, la alentaba, quería decir que no estaba sola. Fijáte los apoyos que lo afectivo puede encontrar.[28]

> (One of the thousands of forms of torture was to make us stand in place without one shoe, one lost their balance and fell without remedy, especially those of us women who used heels. Our shoes were piled up in a corner. A beloved friend who was in that stand-in-place session, told me much later that my shoe, which she saw from beneath her blindfold, encouraged her, it meant to say that she wasn't alone. Just look at the supports that the affective can find.)

The highlighting of the shoe-as-conduit for support in Valentini's testimony (and, in other testimonies, as will be explored later) shows that the object-as-ally, the *noticing* of the potentiality of things—to both harm and help—was not specific to Partnoy's personal experience, nor to the Argentine context, but rather was a phenomenon held in common to the experiences of torture and mistreatment characteristic of the Southern Cone dictatorships.

In other tales in Partnoy's text, objects function similarly to the shoe that encouraged Valentini's friend, as conduits by which to extend kindness and caring to a fellow detainee, yet also as a means by which to retain a semblance of subjectivity in a space systematically designed to deny the prisoner such autonomy. For example, food not only nourishes the body, but the soul: "I have some cheese and a small end of bread saved for tomorrow . . . If I cut them into little pieces, then put them between my toes, I can pass the bread and cheese to Benja. The blanket is covering my feet; the guard won't see me. It's too bad I didn't save the quince jam!"[29] The food passed to Benja during his first night of detention at The Little School is a medium not only for sustaining his bodily strength so that he may withstand the brutal violence inflicted on him during the torture sessions, but also a way for Partnoy to nurture Benja's spirit, as Partnoy describes: "Bread is also a means of communicating, a way of telling the person next to me: 'I'm here. I care for you. I want to share the only possession I have'" (84) and "to give a brother some bread is a reminder that true values are still alive. To be given some bread is to receive a comforting hug." [30]

Food also functions as an ally in serving as a creative outlet in Partnoy's text. In the prologue to the testimony, Julia Alvarez astutely observes: "We watch as she rolls her ration of bread into twenty-five little balls rather than eating it, desperate to *create* something, anything, in an environment where everything is being destroyed." [31] In the tale to which Alvarez refers—appropriately titled "Bread"—one of the guards discovers that Partnoy has been creating the balls of bread and asks her what they are for. She responds: "To play with." [32] In turn, he "kept silent for two minutes while he meticulously calculated the danger level of that toy," [33] then determined that "it's okay." [34] Yet Partnoy disagrees, stating the guard was "wrong." [35] Her ruminations on the way in which the little balls of bread could be used to transmit caring—thus, subverting the dominant paradigm of absolute silence and isolation amongst the prisoners—ultimately point to the small piece of bread as a tool for resistance, an act of defiance that cannot be undertaken without a self-sense of some type of subjectivity: the prisoner who resists through an act of creation has necessarily not been successfully subdued. [36] The difference between Partnoy's relationship to the bread versus the guard's (she disagrees that the bread is a benign toy, and he fails to see its potential), demonstrates how the experience of detainment, torture, and detention alter the subject's relationship to the material world around him/her.

In *The Little School* it is not only food (a non-enduring substance) that acts in this manner, but material objects as well. In "The Small Box of Matches," Partnoy describes how she has lost a tooth in the detention center, a piece of herself that she now keeps safeguarded in an empty *Ranchera* matchbox. Partnoy explains:

> This small box of matches is my only belonging. Sometimes I own a piece of bread, and once I even had an apple. But this box is my only non-edible belonging. Now I keep my box under the pillow. Every so often I touch it to make sure it is still there, just because inside that little box is a piece of myself: my tooth. [37]

The matchbox allows Partnoy to keep a secret: the possession of her tooth. The matchbox lends a determinate facet of its being to Partnoy—the capacity to hold, hide from view, to keep safe another object—and, defiantly, the matchbox permits her to keep a part of herself (of her body) for her alone, outside of the watchful and violating gaze of the prison guards. Such an act of resistance openly defies the dictatorship's objective of total domination over the detained subject; the tooth is a part of Partnoy's body that, hidden, remains beyond the torturer's control. The power of the object for Partnoy is underlined for the reader in the recognition of the danger it poses in the detention center: "The little matchbox will bring me trouble. Sooner or later a guard is going to decide that the box is a dangerous object in my hands. Right now it's my only possession."[38]

Material possessions are often the markers by which we identify the personalities of individuals, a means by which one cultivates a personal style or way of presenting him or herself to the world. The statement "right now, it's my only possession" points to this important connection with the realm of individual personality, a state of being meant to be effaced by the very design of the detention center. In this sense, the object is a tether to subjectivity, to the resistance of the total destruction sought out in the dictatorial quest for determinative control in the social (and, of course, political) sphere. Partnoy's little matchbox is a small item, but it performs a monumental task: it guards a piece of Partnoy that the dictatorship has violently removed from her—her tooth—and assures that her personhood remains intact, that the small piece that has become detached from her body remains with her, remains a part of her, remains in her possession, by virtue of the storage properties of the matchbox. Here, the object and Partnoy's subjectivity overlap via the commingling of matchbox and tooth—the matchbox's past, its having been with Partnoy specifically is emphasized.

The change of the detainee's relationship to the material world pre- versus post-detention is also demonstrated in Alicia Kozameh's *Pasos bajo el agua*. Detained and incarcerated during the Argentine military dictatorship, Kozameh expresses that she does not write *testimonio*, but rather novels and poetry, insisting on a differentiation between her voice as a survivor and the authorial voice that appears in her text. Yet, an image of a cup and spoon—which appears in the first edition of *Pasos bajo el agua*, but in none of the subsequent versions—is directly reproduced from the notebook that Kozameh was allowed to have in prison. The first edition begins with the reproduction of the official document that gave Kozameh the permission to keep the notebook. I contend that *Pasos bajo el agua*, while a novel, has a testimonial nature that lies in the material details that appear in and are described by the text, and that the removal of the images of the document and the cup and spoon (presumably used by Kozameh to eat in prison) after initial publication helped to diminish this testimonial quality, placing it further in the realm of the novel, after it forced Kozameh into exile a second time when she was threatened in Argentina for the book's publication. The drawing, the objects, augmented the novel's testimonial power (and, arguably, its subversive threat), thus pointing us to the importance of a reconsideration of their power.

The representation of objects in subsequent versions of *Pasos bajo el agua* moves out of the temporality of the dictatorship and into the immediate years that followed. The detained person's voice remains represented but is no longer speaking from the space of the prison, yet it retains the changed relationship to objects exhibited in Partnoy's case above. In a chapter added when the text was translated and republished into English, "Sara, What Does a Jacket Mean to You?", the importance of the object for the detainee after liberation is markedly evident and demonstrates that this changed relationship to the object world remains present after the end of detention. In the space of exile (in Mexico), Sara (the text's testimonial subject) remarks to her friend Chanita: "You don't know what a jacket is,"[39] marking a fundamental difference between the two. She reveals: "This jacket has an importance for me that would be very difficult for you to imagine,"[40] placing herself at a distance from the comprehensible realm of possibility that exists for Chanita. Sara's conception of jackets is fundamentally human: "The jackets tremble. They shake. They walk. They face death."[41] This humanness is further emphasized in the remark:

> That's why thinking of that denim jacket makes me sleepy. Because it humiliated itself trying to be something it wasn't. And people like that bore me. I know we're not talking about a human being. Though to tell you the truth, certain human beings are not easily distinguishable from jackets. And certain jackets seem to have attitudes. The attitudes of certain human beings.[42]

Sara goes on to conclude, "there are jackets that are part of some people."[43] I contend that more than mere allegorical personification, these comments reveal that post-detention the perceived line between subject and object becomes blurred: both exist within the same realm of being (what Harman would refer to as tool-being). These explorations in later editions of the text are echoes of the original text's testimonial charge, emanating from the materiality described in the initial version of the text.

This chapter tells the story of the jacket that belonged to Hugo, Sara's husband, prior to his detention. The blending of Hugo's subjectivity into his (and *specifically* his) jacket, this "very symbiotic relationship"[44] for Sara marks the robbery of this item and its use by a *milico* (a derogatory slang term for a member of the military during the dictatorship) as an even greater violation: "Just like that, out of nowhere, and with Hugo's jacket. Not carrying it around, but wearing it. Wearing it . . . Taking it over. Filling, invading that space which didn't belong to him. Almost like peeling off Hugo's skin and covering himself with it."[45] The allusion to the melding of flesh and leather signals a re-ordering of the material world that exists for Sara post-detention; her re-construction of the events of Hugo's kidnapping and mistreatment by the military regime occurs allegorically through the mistreatment of the jacket—the flesh being pulled off of one man, to cover another.[46] The revealing of Hugo's story via the disappearance and subsequent reappearance of a jacket signals a recognition of a testimonial capacity held by objects due to their connection to personhood, especially that of detained/disappeared subjects, a power which remains in the period after violence, in the fight for the reconstruction of memory.

Hugo's subjectivity, his personhood, remains attached to the jacket, haunting it as it goes on to circulate through society, through the space of the city of Rosario, Argentina, disappearing and reappearing from Sara's life in unpredictable ways. In part due to this residual presence, the use of the jacket by others is represented as a violation. In a similar recognition of the residual presence of past owners of the object, survivor Adriana Calvo describes the circulation of possessions amongst the prisoners:

> Recuerdo que le di a Eloísa mi hebilla para el pelo, un trofeo muy preciado, una hebilla de esas francesas que agarran bien el pelo; las dos lo teníamos muy largo. Le di mi vestido a Patricia, estaba con un camisón y la chaqueta. Me decía: 'Vas a salir, vas a salir.' Le dejé mis sandalias a Inés Ortega, que andaba en ojotas de goma. Y así salí, con las ojotas de Inés y el camisón de Patricia.[47]

> (I remember that I gave Eloisa my hair comb, a very valued trophy, one of those French combs that really holds the hair well; we both had very long hair. I gave my dress to Patricia, she was there in a nightgown and jacket.

She said to me, "you're getting out, you're getting out." I gave my sandals to Inés Ortega, who was walking around in rubber flip flops. And with that I got out, with Inés' flip flops and Patricia's nightgown.)

Even after the exchange of these objects, the previous owner's personhood remains attached to the object. Adriana is not just wearing any flip-flops as she leaves the space of the prison, but *Inés'* flip-flops. She wears not just any nightshirt, but *Patricia's* nightshirt. In much the same way that Partnoy shares food as a demonstration of caring, the exchange of objects here also highlights a nurturing gesture of camaraderie. But this moment (much like the jacket in Kozameh's text) also points to a mobility (and perhaps agency) held by the object—a mobility that supersedes the limits imposed on the detained subject. If Adriana is wearing Patricia's nightshirt as she moves out of the space of the camp into liberty/freedom, the testimonial personhood (ownership) attached to the nightshirt moves with her. The significance of the material form, its prior context, changes as it moves from the space of the camp/prison back out into the circulatory market of society. The object retains a telling significance: outside of the camp it can be used as evidence to the previous owner's family and friends that Adriana had truly seen Patricia. It lends credibility to the testimonial function; its own being affixes a stamp of authenticity to the message being transmitted.

Remaking the World: The Constant State of Noticing Things

In a testimonial story titled "La llegada" (The Arrival), Jorge Tiscornia reconstructs the details of his arrival to the Penal de Libertad, one of the main prisons used to house male detainees during the Uruguayan dictatorship. Tiscornia's narrative reconstruction of the events occurs not solely from his own interior memory, but relies on the guidance of a "pequeño almanaque que fui haciendo desde que caí preso, para recoger, desde él, el ancla de mi memoria"[48] (a small almanac that I went about making from the time I fell prisoner, to collect, from it, the anchor of my memory). The almanac is a material ally that lends its permanency to Tiscornia, to help him reconstruct the events of ten years' worth of imprisonment.[49] Tiscornia's story is prefaced by a reliance on the material world for the successful narration of his past. The *almanaque* is his memory, his past embedded into an exterior, material *thing*. In the longer collection in which this short story was later included, as well as the documentary filmed by José Pedro Charlo about the *almanaque*, Tiscornia reflects on his poor memory, such that it can be assumed that without the almanac, he would not have been able to register and later recall all of the memories contained in the material pages of this calendar.[50]

Tiscornia describes how, upon preparing to leave Punta de Rieles—which thereafter was converted into the women's prison—, he is told to collect his things. He writes: "Las historias me decían que sería difícil pasar algo en el Penal, que lo primero que hacían era quitarte todo lo que llevabas"[51] (Stories told me that it would be difficult to transport anything to the Prison, that the first thing they did was take away everything that you carried with you). Tiscornia decides to at least try and explains his plan:

> Llevaría la almohada, mi almohada. Probaría con algún libro y un poco de ropa. Dejaría el juego de ajedrez que estaba construyendo y las cosas de dibujo que me acompañaban, y el resto de la ropa; acá serían más útiles.[52]

> (I would bring the pillow, my pillow. I would try with a book and a little clothing. I would leave the chess board that I was constructing and the drawing instruments that accompanied me, and the rest of the clothes; here they would be more useful.)

It is important to note that this is not Tiscornia's first arrival to prison, but rather a transfer from one prison to another. Given these nuances to Tiscornia's story, his choice of which objects to bring and which to leave behind reveal an already reoriented relationship to things. Tiscornia's first item of choice is a pillow, but not just any pillow, *his* pillow, a lifelong companion. He explains the importance of the pillow and his choice to try to bring it with him:

> Con la almohada probaría, pues la relación con ella provenía desde mi niñez, había pasado por mi adolescencia, y por mi casamiento, donde no le permití a mi suegra más que hacerle una funda, sobre la que ya tenía. La había pedido cuando estuve en el cuartel, y había llegado pese a ser de lana y poder ser portadora de cualquier cosa adentro; había ido conmigo a Punta de Rieles y vuelto al cuartel.[53]

> (With the pillow I would try, since the relationship with it came from my childhood, had passed through my adolescence, and through my wedding, where I didn't permit my mother-in-law more than to make it a pillowcase,

which I still had on it. I had asked for it when I was in the military head-quarters, and it had arrived to me even despite being made of wool and potentially hiding anything inside of it; it had gone with me to Punta de Rieles and returned to the military headquarters.)

This transfer, as one can probably foretell, is the last moment in which the pillow remains in Tiscornia's possession. Upon arrival at Penal de Libertad, Tiscornia, one among a group of sixteen transferred prisoners, affirms his presence as his name is called by the guard taking attendance, then enters the gates of the prison. Describing the moment in which he crosses the threshold of the prison, Tiscornia writes

> Aquí quedaba nuestro nombre, nuestra identidad, congelada hasta que, para mí, aquel 10 de marzo de 1985, dentro de otra heladera, entre los mismos portones, la recobrara, y en sentido inverso, la pusiera al calor, y ahora caminando, recorriera este camino hacia mis familiares y amigos. . . . No lo supe claramente, pero en pocos metros y en pocas horas dejaría también otras cosas, la vestimenta de civil, el pelo largo, y con el tiempo la juventud.[54]

> (Here remained behind our name, our identity, frozen until, for me, that March 10th of 1985, inside another transport truck, between the same gates, I recovered it, and in an inverse sense, I gave it warmth, and then, walking, I traversed this path toward my loved ones and friends. [. . .] I clearly didn't know it at the time, but within a few meters and a few hours I would leave behind other things as well, such as civilian clothing, my long hair, and, with the passing of time, my youth.)

The next morning, Tiscornia indeed does lose his personal items, the last traces of his life prior to his initial detention. He is "processed": the guards make him undress, he is examined by a doctor, assigned a number, has his head shaved (Tiscornia is emphatic in writing that this is the last moment he ever saw himself with a full head of hair), is made to undress again, commanded to shower and shave, and finally, "sin pelo, sin barba, y de piel rosada, me tuve que calzar el mameluco gris y las alpargatas negras, que el sargento me alcanzó"[55] (without hair, without beard, and with pink skin, I had to put on the gray coveralls and black sandals that the sergeant gave me). Amidst the donning of an imposed new order of *things*, Tiscornia remembers he left his personal belongings on the other side of this process: "'Mis cosas,' le dije, intentando el rescate de la ropa, que me habia quitado, y de la bolsa"[56] ("My things," I said to him, trying to rescue my clothes, which they had taken from me, and my bag). The guard commands him to "póngalas aquí"[57] (put them here) and Tiscornia undertakes the arduous task of giving up his last possessions, the last remaining remnants of his youth, his life prior to the prison: "Aquí quedaba mi almohada, y la placidez de mis sueños. El sueño tranquilo, efectivamente, regresó con mi libertad. No así las cosas"[58] (Here remained my pillow, and the tranquility of my dreams. Calm sleep, in effect, returned with my freedom. Not so the things). While Tiscornia signals that upon entering the gates of the prison he loses his name and identity, he draws attention to the incomplete process of this loss at the initial moment of entrance; it is not until he loses his civilian clothing, his long hair, and "otras cosas"[59] (other things)—presumably the things that he has attempted to bring with him (among them his pillow)—that he suffers the total reduction/oppression imposed by the prison. The process remains incomplete while he remains in possession of his belongings.

The pillow is an important item to consider in this process. For Scarry, the making of the world, and, by extension, the object (the artifact), is an act based on a model of creation. The design of the artifact has at its core the goal of taking over the work of the body, thereby creating less pain for the individual. Scarry uses the example of a chair whose design is to relieve the subject of the discomfort imposed on the spine by having to remain standing, a creative design undone by the use of the chair to immobilize a victim, imposing pain after long durations of time. Scarry explains:

> Torture begins at precisely the point where the other has left off: it starts by appropriating and deconstructing the artifacts that are the products of creation—wall, window, door, room, shelter, medicine, law, friend, country, both as they exist in their material form and as the created contents of consciousness. Torture ends at what is the other's starting point: it 'produces' the pain that has not only been eliminated by the act of creation, but whose very existence has been the condition that originally occasioned the act of creation. In the one, pain is deconstructed and displaced by the artifact; in the other, the artifact is deconstructed to produce pain. Thus, torture not only deconstructs the 'products' of the imagination, but deconstructs the act of imagining itself.[60]

Applying this logic of the creation of the object, one understands that the pillow's design and manufacture has at its core the desire to relieve some kind of interior pain, the body's suffering. The pillow, made to relieve the pain of (to make more comfortable) the head, spine, and body while sleeping, in this case represents a means by which Tiscornia can make the space of the prison more bearable. But, *this particular pillow* also holds for him the function of memory: like the *almanaque* with which Tiscornia is able to reconstruct the story of "La llegada," the pillow serves as an amplifying device, helping him visualize the happiness of his past, of his youth, his adolescence, his marriage, and therefore providing him a tool for the self-soothing, healing power of re-calling comforting past memories. However, the pillow itself can also be con-sidered a companion, it has accompanied Tiscornia like a friend. The loss of this tool is the loss of an ability to reach out beyond the bars of the prison for help. It is a loss of an amplification or extension of the body which is capable of making that body feel less pain and resist more. The loss of the pillow is more than what it seems. It is a closing off, a limiting of the prisoner's world, the loss of an ally, a fellow subject, a tool-being on which to rely for comfort, an increase of the prisoner's sentient discomfort, and, thereby, an increase in the repressor's power. The loss of all his objects changes Tiscornia upon his arrival, and he is remade in a new material order, that of the Penal de Libertad.

My use of the term "subject" to refer to an "object" in the previous para-graph is intentional and merits explanation. The heritage of Heidegger's phi-losophy derives firstly, from the legacy of Franz Brentano who argued that every intention is an objectifying act and secondly, from Edmund Husserl's use of this term ("intention") in the development of a phenomenology, a use focused on describing how things appear to us. Heidegger develops this fur-ther, stating that intentionality "reduces things to their accessibility to hu-man thought"[61] and ignores that there is always something that remains in the *thing* that eludes our reach.[62] The "as structure" we employ to relate to objects is only ever a superficial bridge to their tool-being, which remains always present, yet unreachable to human *Dasein*. In the "as structure" by which human *Dasein* relates to the object world of which it forms a part, one observes an echo of Scarry's stance that we tether our emotions to external objects, having "feelings for"[63] in both our interactions with other *things* as *things* and in our expressions of the emotions our interior being hides. The reason I discuss the pillow as a subject is due to this complexity of the inacces-sible being/ally within the object. I argue that the prisoner who has suffered the unmaking and remaking of his/her world is uniquely attuned to the existence of this unreachable, but nevertheless existent, quality in the object. The prisoner treats the object in a way that acknowledges this presence beyond his/her reach, but that can be conceived of in terms of a recognition of a type of subjectivity in the object capable of sharing its agency with the prisoner. Heidegger pushes us to theorize objects in a way that doesn't "reduce things to their external properties," but rather grasps them "in their deeper factical reality."[64] By considering that objects act with their own subjectivities—and do so in a way that demonstrates solidarity to human subjects who are suffering—one acknowledges this deeper existence of the object. The extremity of the circumstances of deprivation, of unmaking and remaking, provokes this recognition on the part of the human subject. In the following chapters, it is important to keep in mind this new dimension and to remember that the object—recognized in its tool-being (even if the understanding of that tool-being remains just beyond reach) by the human subject rendered psychically distinct due to circumstances of torture, by the remaking of his/her world—participates in the prisoner's struggle for survival and aides him/her in the fight for resistance.

Heidegger's philosophy of objects (of being) focuses on the "veiling and unveiling of things encountered in the world by *Dasein*."[65] The distinction between tool and broken tool is really a distinction between ready-to-hand and present-at-hand. Heidegger posits that the moment at which the tool breaks is when human *Dasein* becomes conscious of its relationship to the material item. The tool is integral to our functioning as agential subjects, it facilitates our relationship not only to one another, but to the world that surrounds us. Yet, does the tool need to break in the space of detention for it to become visible to the detainee? Let's consider the following comment by Marcelo Estefanell, another former political prisoner in Uruguay:

> Con la atención sobrada que un preso en soledad puede prestar a cada detalle de sus paredes desnudas durante las largas horas de confinamiento, es posible distinguir detalles que, en otras condiciones, no merecerían ni media mirada.[66]

> (With the excessive attention with which a prisoner in solitary can give to each detail of the naked walls during the long hours of confinement, it is possible to distinguish details that, in other conditions, would not merit even half a glance.)

Estefanell's comment highlights a distinct, changed environment in which the prisoner exists in a *constant state of noticing things*. His comment reveals a break not within the object (or, a broken tool), but a break between the subject and the world, provoked by extreme circumstances of depravation and abuse. Prolonged solitude in conditions intentionally meant to produce deprivation has the secondary effect of not allowing anything to go unnoticed. For Heidegger, the functioning tool only remains functioning so long as its tool-being goes unnoticed. In the vigilant space of the prison nothing goes without scrutiny, neither the prisoners themselves under the constant watchful gaze of their guards, nor the object world. All tool-beings are constantly reflected upon by the prisoners, both for their utility and their limits. This process necessarily creates relationships between subject and object, forever bringing the object into the present-at-hand: "it is *relations* that turn objects into present-at-hand atoms [...] the tool-being withdraws into its vast inner reality, which is irreducible to any of its negotiations with the world. Only in its relations with other entities is it caricatured, turned into a unitary profile."[67]

In *El hombre numerado*, Estefanell narrates his experience arriving at the Penal de Libertad, one that runs parallel to that of Tiscornia's in "La llegada."[68] Estefanell describes how the prisoners prepared themselves upon hearing the news that they would be transferred from Punta de Rieles:

> Sabíamos que debíamos tomar ciertas precauciones como consecuencia de las severas normas que íbamos a encontrar allí, como el hecho, por ejemplo, de que con excepción de las prendas interiores nos quitarían toda la ropa y los zapatos y, en su lugar, vestiríamos un mameluco de brin color gris y calzaríamos alpargatas negras. . . Por otra parte, como no íbamos a tener ningún medio de comunicación a mano, alguien llegó a planificar el traslado oculto de una radio portátil.[69]

> (We knew that we should take certain precautions as a consequence of the severe norms we would encounter there, like the fact that, for example, with the exception of our undergarments, they would take away all our clothes and shoes and, in their place, we would wear a grey canvas jumpsuit and black slippers on our feet... On the other hand, since we weren't going to have any method for communicating at our disposal, someone ended up planning the secret transfer of a portable radio.)

The resistance that prepares the prisoners for the transfer begins prior to the arrival at Penal de Libertad and has its basis in the material. The prisoners make plans to smuggle a portable radio into the space of the prison: "¿Una radio?—le pregunté incrédulo al Pochilo durante un recreo—¿Cómo vamos a meter de queruza una radio en el Penal de Libertad?"[70] ("A radio?," I asked Pochilo incredulously during our recess time, "how are we going to sneak in a radio to the Penal de Libertad?"). Pochilo responds to Estefanell explaining that the radio will be dismantled and each piece "del tamaño de un grano de café"[71] (the size of a coffeebean) will be given to a different prisoner, each *compañero* responsible for his piece's safe arrival to the new prison. Estefanell is assigned "un diodo"[72] (a diode) which he successfully smuggles into Penal de Libertad, hidden away on his body with the money he carries in the sole of a shoe, waiting for the moment in which he will be called on to participate in the construction of the radio, the resistance, the ear to the outer world. The diode gives Estefanell a purpose, a task:

> Una vez integrado a la vida carcelaria del penal esperé durante semanas que alguien se acercara a decirme si tenía algo para pasar. Si bien era cierto que en mi piso y sector (2° B) había compañeros de confianza, ninguno provenía de mi columna y, menos aún, de Montevideo. Entonces me encontraba en una especie de limbo organizativo y estructural; dudaba qué hacer o a qué atenerme y, por otra parte, si bien era consciente de que en esas condiciones de reclusión resultaría extremadamente difícil armar una organización compleja, confiaba en que de todas maneras alguien aparecería y me diría "pasá la guita y el diodo."[73]

> (Once integrated into the routine life of the prison I would wait during a few weeks for someone to approach me asking if I had something to pass to them. If it was true that on my floor and sector (2nd B) there were comrades of confidence, none came from my column of the organization or even from Montevideo. Therefore, I found myself in a sort of structural and organizational limbo; I doubted what to do and to what to abide by and, on the other hand, even though I was very conscious that in these conditions of reclusion it would end up being extremely difficult to establish a complicated organization, I trusted that despite it all someone would appear and tell me "pass me the money and the diode.")

This passage reveals the task performed by Estefanell (to preserve the diode for its future job in the making operable of the portable radio), but it also signals a task being performed by the diode itself. The diode holds within it the possibility to make operable the rest of the pieces that compose the radio: it is one piece of a whole, existing in relation to the composition that results in a functioning machine. This distinction may appear to be splitting hairs, but it is an important difference to consider moving forward with the reading of this narrative. If one recognizes the potential for operation held in the diode, it must also be recognized, as Heidegger (via Harman) posits, that: "Things are not objects: instead, they have significance, which means they belong to a system of relation with other things in the environment."[74] The diode is significant not only to Estefanell, representing a reason for his continued survival, but to the rest of the radio of which it is destined to form a part. Like Estefanell, just one person in the resistance in Uruguay, the diode is one part of a systematic whole: the radio. They both hold an important interiority to their being and in their relationships blur the distinctive features of subject and object, bringing tool-being to the undeniable fore.

In the new prison, Estefanell patiently awaits "una señal, un mensaje, algo que me diera a entender que esa era la persona que me reclamaría lo que yo llevaba"[75] (a signal, a message, something that would make me understand that this was the person that would reclaim from me what I carried). Finally, one day Pochilo appears and Estefanell's task is completed. However, "la radio nunca se llegó a armar: faltaron piezas"[76] (the assembly of the radio never came to fruition: pieces were missing). Here, the classic dimension of Heidegger's tool analysis becomes clear. The radio, in its missing pieces, if it wasn't noticed by the prisoner prior to this moment, is impossible to not observe in its broken-tool form. Estefanell's initial reaction to the plan to bring a radio into Penal de Libertad ("¿Cómo vamos a meter de queruza una radio en el Penal de Libertad?"[77] [How are we going to sneak in a radio to the Penal de Libertad?]) reveals the new relationship to noticing that takes place in the space of detention, even prior to the state of the broken tool. Under "normal" circumstances the transport of a radio from one place to another is not one that calls attention to itself, reflecting Heidegger's assertion that the true being of things is absence (withdrawl). The dismantling of the object in order to transport it successfully, and the subsequent failure to do so, produces a broken tool that, rather than being the initial change in the relationship between subject and object that calls attention to tool-being, is a second step that further augments the already noticed state of the *thing's* tool-being.

The unmaking of the world explored earlier through Elaine Scarry's theoretical perspective, here produces a relationship between the prisoner and his newly remade object world (the prison) in which the material thing cannot go unnoticed—everything is noticed and noted for its potentiality as a form of resistance. For example, Estefanell's constant state of noticing reveals that an inconsistency in the material that makes up the wall of his cell is an electrical outlet that had long been forgotten and overlooked:

> Parecía mentira ver ese adminículo en el medio de la pared de mi celda; la tapa de plástico blanco y esas tres hendiduras que parecían los ojos de un chinito triste con nariz y sin boca.[78]

> (It seemed a lie to see that gadget in the middle of the wall of my cell; the white plastic cover and those three slots that looked like the eyes of a sad China man with a nose and no mouth).

This new relationship to the power outlet creates an agency for Estefanell. It produces a new purpose in his existence within the prison. The discovery of the outlet reanimates the lost world of electrical appliances (*electrodomésticos*), remakes them in the present, brings them forward from the realm of broken tools, from "[el] *reino* de los recuerdos"[79] (the kingdom of memories).[80] With this re-discovery, brought on by the extreme noticing provoked by the long hours of confinement, Estefanell becomes the only possessor of an outlet on his floor of Penal de Libertad. What's more, the outlet creates the "posibilidad cierta de poder ingerir la infusión gauchesca"[81] (true possibility to ingest Gaucho tea)—it falls to Estefanell to heat the water for *maté* for all of his *compañeros* and even for the guards on the fourth floor: "Esta tarea, tan prosaica si se quiere, fue para mí el reverso de mi rutina"[82] (This job, as commonplace as one may believe it, was for me the reversal of my routine).

The outlet lends Estefanell its agency—as a *thing* it is a creator of electrical energy and as such it holds the power to animate other *things*: it exercises influence over another being (even if that being is another tool-being [i.e. *un electrodoméstico*]). By its mere presence in Estefanell's cell, the outlet shares its agential power with the prisoner. The spread of its power, made perceptively present in Estefanell's relationship with the outlet, even goes so far as to liberate the locks on his cell: the guards take to using Estefanell's outlet to heat the water for their *maté* to save them the trouble of descending three sets of stairs to the other station, which meant that "con el correr de las semanas, esto último fue generando cierta complicidad entre la guardia y mi tarea, a tal punto que de noche solían dejar la puerta de mi celda abierta, entornada o a media tranca, cosa de poder entrar a cualquier hora para calentar sus propios termos"[83] (with the passing of the weeks, this last element began generating a certain complicity between the guards and my job, to such a point that at night they tended to leave the door of my cell open, half shut or at half threshold, so as to be able to enter at whatever hour to freshen their own water thermoses). Graham Harman writes, "equipment is not effective 'because people use it'; on the contrary, it can only be used because it is capable of an effect, of inflicting some kind of blow on reality."[84] The outlet in Estefanell's cell is not only effective because it is used to heat water (changing the temperature of the water from cold to hot inflicts a blow on reality), but is also effective as an unlikely tool of survival for Estefanell. The blow it inflicts on reality is also a change in Estefanell's routine, the creation of a new job for him, and, most shockingly, the opening of the locks on his cell door (even if this never results in Estefanell's escape, it is a monumental blow, to say the least). None would have happened without the *noticing* of the outlet in the first place. None would continue to take place should the outlet fail to function.

Beyond Personification: The Object's Support

Estefanell's assessment of confinement and its result of revealing things previously unseen is echoed in *Conversaciones con la alpargata* (*Conversations with the Shoe*), a collection of poems by another former prisoner, Mauricio Rosencof. Rosencof, an accomplished playwright, poet, and author of numerous novels, was one of the famous nine Tupamaro hostages (*rehenes*) taken by the Uruguayan dictatorship and held for over ten years, much of which he spent in nearly solitary confinement. This collection is a compendium of the poems that Rosencof was able to eventually sneak out of prison (once he was transferred to a prison environment in line with the typical political prisoner's experience) written on cigarette papers and hidden in his visitors' undergarments. Thus, as the cover description of the collection suggests, they represent "un caso singular de poesía carcelaria" (a unique case of prison poetry).[85] While these poems may be a unique example, they are not unique in their turn to the material as ally in an attempt to grapple with and relate the realities of detention.

The 126 poems of the collection constitute a series of conversations with a shoe, an *alpargata*, that Rosencof has with him in his cell. The first line of the opening poem ("1") declares, "he vuelto a conversar con la alpargata"[86] (I've resumed conversing with the shoe), revealing a prior act of conversation; the return to speaking with the inanimate footwear indicates that this is not the first dialogue Rosencof has had with the material being. The subsequent lines "No debo hacerlo más"[87] (I shouldn't do it anymore) and "Evitaré en lo sucesivo su mirada"[88] (I will avoid in the future his[89] gaze) tells the reader that the prisoner's intent is not to speak to this material ally anymore, and endows the shoe with a recognized subjectivity on the part of the prisoner, for the shoe is capable of looking upon Rosencof, having a gaze that must not be engaged in the future. Throughout the collection of poems, the prisoner must actively remind himself that the alpargata is not an animate subject, in many instances seeming to conflate the alpargata with a pet cat. For example, poem 20 openly declares: "Vos / no sos / gato / le digo"[90] (You / are not / a cat / I say to him), before clarifying: "Sos / alpargata, / algo / sin vida"[91] (You are / a shoe, / something / without life). Yet, even amidst this fight to not "notice" the alpargata's subjectivity, in the next line of the poem the alpargata "Medita. / ¿Y vos? / me dice"[92] (It meditates / And you? / he says to me). The alpargata responds to Rosencof and challenges his own deduction that the alpargata is an object without life, while at the same time seeming to pose the existential question to Rosencof as to whether or not his existence in prison qualifies as a life. In this poem, one observes the transformation the prisoner experiences in the extreme space of the political prison—no matter his reminders to himself that this is a shoe, he cannot help but return to the alpargata's gaze, engaging its tool-being as an ally in survival.

As the poems tell us, the alpargata "entiende todo"[93] (understands everything) and Rosencof explains "Nos llevamos lo más bien"[94] (We get along in the best way). Treating the alpargata like a cat once more, one poem explains "Me / hace / reír. / Juega / con / una / bolita / de papel, / igual / que / un niño"[95] (He / makes me / laugh. / He plays / with / a / little ball / of paper, / just / like / a child). Perhaps in order to expel doubts regarding his sanity, and to remind us of this transformation in the ability to engage the object, at one point Rosencof writes: "No me engaña. / Sé que es alpargata"[96] (He does not fool me / I know he is a shoe). The alpargata-as-ally is vigilent and helps Rosencof remain alert to possible impending danger: "Se alarma. / ¿Qué has oído? / Una voz humana / dice. / Alguien / dijo"[97] (He gets alarmed / What have you heard? / A human voice / he says. / Someone / he said). The alpargata-ally encourages Rosencof to stay in shape: "Tensa / los músculos / hace reflexiones, / salta. / ¿Para qué? /

le digo. / Puede / hacer / falta / dice. / Salta"[98] (Tense / the muscles / do reflections / jump. / For what? / I tell him. / It could / be necessary / he says. / Jump).

Finally, the last poem of the collection points perhaps most directly to
the companionship Rosencof finds in the alpargata. Dedicated to one of the
other *rehenes*, Eleuterio Fernández Huidobro (El Ñato) for his birthday, the
poem closes the collection seemingly concluding that the alpargata is a friend:
"Y si este fuera / mi ultimo poema, / insumiso y triste, / raído pero entero, /
tan solo / una palabra / escribiría: / Compañero"[99] (And if this were / my
last poem / rebellious and sad / threadbare but complete / just one / word /
I would write: / Comrade). Without changing to whom he is directing these
poems, the final poem imbues the shoe with the companionship of Rosencof's fellow prisoner, merging human subjectivity with object subjectivity
within the poems. Only having read the preface of the collection does the
reader know that this last poem was a birthday gift to Rosencof's comrade.

In his introduction to *Conversaciones con la alpargata*, Mario Benedetti
contextualizes the use of the shoe in the collection in the following terms:
"Condenado a la soledad, al silencio, a la mudez y sordera del mundo, el preso
inventa un interlocutor: la alpargata, algo que efectivamente forma parte de
su ámbito forzoso"[100] (Condemned to solitude, to silence, to the muteness
and deafness of the world, the prisoner invents an interlocutor: the shoe,
something that effectively forms part of his forced environment). However,
it is my contention that, given the changed relationship to objects the political prisoners experienced during their mistreatment, the incorporation of
objects in texts such as Rosencof's goes beyond mere invention or personification of the inanimate, instead revealing the result of the subject's break with
the world: the new and constant state of noticing things.

Literary production by former prisoners, particularly well-illustrated in
the case of this collection of poems by Rosencof, demonstrates a different
relationship to objects, to the potential for survival they offer to the subject.
In the camp or detention center, things never break, their purpose is simply modified. The change undergone by the incarcerated subject during the
dictatorship produced an entirely new order of extraordinary things, a new
utility of objects largely unconnected to their understood use. Rosencof's
alpargata—to us understood as a means of protecting our feet, facilitating
our walking—for him was a companion with whom he couldn't help but dialogue. Rosencof's case exemplifies Estefanell's contention that in prison it's
possible to see things that otherwise wouldn't merit even a sidelong glance,

for the conditions of imprisonment during the dictatorship changed the sub-ject's relationship to the material world, producing a new and constant state of noticing things.

Conclusion: The Object Ally

Dori Laub argues that a key element for survival of the Jewish Holocaust was the creation of an internal witness to which the victim could testify during the moment of trauma: "Survival takes place through the creative act of es-tablishing and maintaining an internal witness who substitutes for the lack of witnessing in real life."[101] In the case to which Laub refers, this internal witness was an identity card of the child victim's mother, to whom he talks, prays and bears witness. In literary production by former prisoners, such as Rosencof's, one sees the same process occurring in Southern Cone detention centers via the creation of a witness in the object—the object, viewed as an ally, creatively fulfills externally the role of an "internal witness" to which the prisoner can testify. The crisis of witnessing that occurs for those that were incarcerated in the concentration camps, clandestine detention centers, or political prisons during the dictatorships, produced a search: of the walls of the cell looking for inconsistencies (Estefanell), of jackets looking for infor-mation about the past (Kozameh), for the retaining capacities of matchbooks (Partnoy), for the comfort of the past held in a pillow (Tiscornia), and for the companionship offered by a shoe (Rosencof).

In one final example—from "Entrevista a una llave de agua" (Interview with a Water Facuet), in the third edition of *Diario de Chacabuco 73*, a news-paper produced by the political prisoners from within the confines of the concentration camp Chacabuco in Chile—, a man finds the witness, the sol-idarity, and the support he seeks for survival in a water faucet:

> No discutiré con aquellos compadres graves que aseguran no haber visto nunca hablar a las llaves. Estoy de acuerdo con ellos, pero me tocó una llave que al abrirla emitió el sonido de no tener agua, sino aire, le pregunté qué pasaba y después, de prudencial esfera y lanzar algunas gotas de H_2O, me contestó que el agua la habían cortado en la copa, por problemas propios del desierto y del campamento.[102]

(I won't argue with those serious comrades who swear they've never seen the faucets speak. I'm in agreement with them, but I encountered a faucet that upon opening it, emitted a sound of not having water, but air. I asked it what was happening and after, with prudential specialty and shooting a few drops of H_2O, it answered me that they had cut off his water in the tank, due to the desert and camp's problems.)

The water faucet, experiencing problems of its own, is a broken tool, its suffering mirrors the suffering of the man in the camp, and the two—companions in their suffering—reveal a recognition that under normal circumstances goes unnoticed: Harman's observation that all beings (including human *Dasein*) at their core exist as tool-beings and hold something within themselves that cannot be expressed outwardly except through an as-structure. Yet, the two commence witnessing to each other:

> Nos entretuvimos un largo interrogatorio recordando al velódromo del ESTADIO NACIONAL, muy conocido de algunos compadres. Supe que habrá venido desde Antofogasta y haber sido escogido al azar, entre muchos miles de llaves.[103]

> (We entertained ourselves a while, remembering the velodrome of the NATIONAL STADIUM, so well-known by some comrades. I found out that he had come from Antofagasta and had been chosen by chance, from among many thousands of faucets.)

The man and the water faucet remember the trauma of the violence of the *Estadio Nacional*.[104] The man finds out that the water faucet (perhaps not unlike the man himself) was taken "by chance"[105] (*al azar*) from amongst many other thousands of faucets (or, men). Once again, we must assume that, given the realities of the time period, the faucet's story parallels that of his comrade. The faucet remarks:

> "No tengo culpa de estar aquí, pero serviré muchos años hasta al último de los amigos, siempre me tratan bien. Estoy aburrida de la Pampa, porque en la noche hace ffrrío y en el día calorr . . ."[106]

> (It's not my fault to be here, but I will serve for many years up to even the last of the friends. They always treat me well. I'm bored of the Pampas, because at night it's ccoold and in the day hotttt.)

Like the men in the camp, the faucet is destined to be held prisoner for many more years, even though it is innocent of any crime. Additionally, the faucet feels for the suffering of others: "Me contó que a veces le daba lástima ver a muchos bañistas jabonados que debían secarse con la toalla por no haber agua"[107] (he told me that sometimes he felt bad watching many soaped-up bathers having to dry off with towels due to the lack of water) and reveals that he offers a bit of his subjectivity to alleviate the pain of others, acting as an ally in solidarity to the prisoners: "Yo guardo siempre algunas gotas para el amigo paciente que me junta gota a gota"[108] (I always save a few drops for the patient friend that gathers me up drop by drop); and commiserating and celebrating with the prisoners:

> "A veces me entristezco con las conversaciones de los compadres que vienen a lavar su ropa y hacen recuerdos a sus mujercitas o mamas a quienes nunca le ayudaron en el lavabo y siempre les exigían camisa limpia y bien planchada. También gozo de cuando sé que un compadre cercano a mí, ha recibido noticias optimistas, o buenas de su casa porque así no toma caldo de cabeza, que hace mucho daño con estos calores."[109]

> (Sometimes I get saddened by the conversations of the comrades that come to wash their clothes and remember their girlfriends or mothers who they never helped with the laundry yet they always demanded of them a clean and well-ironed shirt. I also enjoy when I know a comrade close to me has received optimistic news, or greetings from his home because that way one doesn't drink head soup, which does a lot of damage in this heat.)[110]

The man has to cut short his conversation with the water faucet, but not before the faucet offers him water to drink. Upon saying goodbye to the faucet, it tells the man: "Si te vas luego lloraré de alegría; pero si te quedas, me pondré triste y frustrada. De todos modos te ayudaré a pasar las penas"[111] (If you go, later I will cry of happiness; but if you stay, I will become sad and frustrated. In any case, I will help you to get through the pain).

One could read this story as the personification of an inanimate object, pure and simple. However, given the context in which the story was written (from within the space of the concentration camp Chacabuco) and the other examples I have cited throughout this chapter, I contend that the use of the faucet in this story is more than intentional. It directly illustrates the changed relationship that the subject of torture and detention has to the material world that surrounds him/her. It evidences the constant noticing of the potential of *things*. Michael Lazzara asserts: "the victim who speaks after

trauma is not the same subjectivity who spoke prior to the traumatic moment."[112] De Silva notes that for survivors of torture "the presence or absence
of social support and the perception of others' helpfulness are important vari-
ables for the reduction of the probability of full-blown PTSD."[113] In this story,
the social support the victim looks for is held in the ally status of the object.
It is more than the poetic personification of the *thing*. It refers to a noticed
internal pragmatism of the object. It acknowledges an interior being to the
object, capable of commiserating: "A thing is more than its appearance, more
than its usefulness, and more than its physical body."[114]

When we consider how each survivor discussed in this chapter speaks of
objects in his/her narrative (Partnoy—a ragged blanket, a plastic flower, food,
a matchbox; Kozameh—jackets; Tiscornia—an almanac, a pillow; Estefanell—a diode, an outlet; Rosencof—a shoe), it becomes clear that within
the space of the torture center, of the prolonged and severe mistreatment
of the prison, there occurs not only a break with the object that makes the
human aware of its relationship to it, not only a reordering of the subject's
relationship to language and therefore the material world, but a changed environment in which that object exists. The object in the space of the prison
no longer completes the simple task for which it was designed; instead it
lends a part of its subjectivity as an ally to the victim, as an aide in his/her
survival. As will become evident in the chapter that follows, the object, even
when broken, never truly breaks in the eyes of the subject who suffered torture. Because this break occurs on the side of the subject, this constant state
of noticing gives way to an entirely new order of extraordinary things. Bread
crumbs become the basis for elaborate floral sculptures, bone fragments left-
over from soup become intricately crafted rings. In an endless cycle of reuse,
the object lives on as a changed entity, yet retains an essential function, that
of maintaining and recording the link between subject and the world. It is
precisely this living on of the object as an ally for the subject in survival that
will be the focus of the next chapter, as I consider the role prison craftwork
played in the self-care of the prisoner.

Material Escape—*Manualidades* and *Artesanías carcelarias* as Artifacts of Imagined Agency and Resistance

꣠

La vida diaria se rige por normas racionales y la dictadura basa el terror en la irracionalidad. He meditado mucho sobre esto. Me costó darme cuenta que era un método y no una cuestión circunstancial. El absurdo que impone la irracionalidad te exige un esfuerzo muy grande para crear modos de supervivencia que la contravenga.[1]

(Daily life is regulated by rational norms and dictatorship bases terror in irrationality. I have meditated a lot on this. It took a lot for me to realize that it was a method and not a question of circumstances. The absurdity that irrationality imposes requires a very big effort from you to create modes of survival that counter it.)

The only state that is anomalous as pain is the imagination.[2]

Cuando estoy triste lijo mi cajita de música. No lo hago para nadie. Sólo porque me gusta.[3]

(When I am sad, I sand my little music box. I don't do it for anyone else. Just because I like it.)

I AM SITTING AT THE kitchen table in the home of Pedro Giudice and Antonia Yañez, both of whom were imprisoned for political reasons during the civic-military dictatorship in Uruguay. Over the course of our conversation, during which Pedro has been showing me the *manualidades* (prison craftwork) that he made during his incarceration, Pedro suddenly recalls the confusion he felt over the lyrics of the popular song "Cuando estoy triste" ("When I Am Sad"), sung by Mercedes Sosa, during the time of his incarceration in the Penal de Libertad, a prison for male detainees during the dictatorship. Pedro tells me that he has always wondered if the lyric was "cuando estoy triste lijo mi cajita de música"[4] (when I am sad, I sand my little music box) or if it was "cuando estoy triste elijo mi cajita de música"[5] (when I am sad, I choose my little music box) and goes in search of a laptop to Google the song, after so many years, to determine which was the actual phrase used. Upon finding "lijo" (I sand) to be the official lyric, Pedro remarks that for him, it was always "lijo," a reflection of his own actions sanding, sanding, sanding away, slowly but surely creating small pieces of art from the interminable time and cramped space of incarceration, one item of which was specifically a small box, made for his son, also named Pedro.[6]

In his own testimony, another former political prisoner from Uruguay, Roberto Herrera, explains the significance of turning to material creation in an effort to adapt to, cope with, and survive detention. Roberto explains:

> Una vez, después de una paliza, me llevaron al baño atado—te ataban con un cable largo—y pensé en matarme. Me iba a colgar de la cisterna, llegué a atar el cable a la cisterna, y ahí me puse a pensar "¿qué estás haciendo? ¿No decíamos que era una lucha ideológica? ¿Varios frentes para luchar? Bueno, ¡ahora te tocó este!" Solucionar esa contradicción fue lo que me permitió vivir. La contradicción no estaba entre la libertad y el estar preso, sino en estar preso y aprender a estar preso, porque la lucha se daba en todos los frentes y eso es central en la vida. Yo fui de hacer pocas manualidades, hacía algunas cosas, dibujitos para que otros grabasen.[7]

> (Once, after a beating, they brought me, tied up, to a bathroom—they tied you up with a long cable—and I thought about killing myself. I was going to hang myself from the toilet tank. I got as far as tying the cable to the toilet tank and then I got to thinking, "what are you doing? Didn't we say this was an ideological fight? Various fronts to fight? Well, now you're faced with this one!" Solving this contradiction was what permitted me to live. The contradiction wasn't between freedom and being a prisoner, but between being imprisoned and learning to be imprisoned. Because the fight was on all fronts and that is key in life. I started to do a few crafts, I made a few things, little drawings for others to carve.)

Roberto's means for adapting to life in prison, to coping, to surviving is to begin participating in the imaginative work of the *manualidades*. The constant state of noticing the potential of things reveals to him the creative potential of the objects to which he has access in the prison. This work permits him to learn to be a political prisoner, and ultimately to survive the dictatorship. A similar attitude is expressed with regard to the concentration camps in Chile:

> La prisión es un signo de un tiempo diferente ... Pero el hombre no muere ... las manos torpes y dañadas trabajan afirmando la libertad aprisionada ... aquí estamos, aquí somos todavía. Desde el campo de prisioneros nace un grito de hueso que trae una semilla de pan y de paz.[8]

> (The prison is a sign of a different time ... But man does not die ... the clumsy and wounded hands work affirming imprisoned freedom ... here we are in this place, here we exist still ... From the prisoners' camp is born a cry of bone that brings a seed of bread and peace.)

Written in reference to the *artesanías carecelarias* made in the Tres Álamos prisoners' camp in Chile, this passage emphasizes the collective and orderly nature of the workshops (talleres) organized by the prisoners to help them survive and resist from within the space of detention. It affirms not only the same work of resistance through adaptation that Roberto mentions, but also gestures toward a collective effort to testify from the space of detention: "aquí estamos, aquí somos todavía"[9] (here we are in this place, here we exist still). The vocal cry (grito) that the silenced prisoners did not possess, at least openly, here is manifested through the soup bones they crafted into pendants, rings, and sculptures. The object-as-artifact creates that which the prisoner lacks: a voice, a means by which to communicate, a hope for survival; as Martha Velentini contends is necessary, they create modes of survival that counter the irrationality of the dictatorship, helping the prisoner survive. Prison craftwork demonstrates a specific turn to the material world by the prisoner in resisting, in learning to cope with his/her new day-to-day reality and in the looking forward to a future freedom. For Pedro, the simple, yet productive action of sanding away at a little box was an act of comfort. For Roberto, the turn to creating through *manualidades* was a way of learning to be a prisoner, of reconstructing or remodeling his subjectivity within the confines of a new space and reality. For the prisoners in Chile, their hands worked to affirm liberty even when reality denied it to them.

In this chapter, I contend that the constant state of noticing things born out of the changed relationship with the material world explored in Chapter One produced a turn in the incarcerated subject to the potential of all material objects within the detention center. I argue that we observe this turn in the craftwork they used as a means of amplifying the self—drawing from Elaine Scarry's analysis—through the creation of an exterior artifact capable of relieving interior pain and, at the same time, as the crafting of a testimonial object that would relay an aspect of life in the concentration camp to the exterior world, and subsequently, to the generations of the future. As was briefly mentioned in Chapter One, for Scarry, a productive power lies in the making of the world that can counter the pain and hurt caused to the suffering subject by the violent unmaking of his/her world. Such objects can relate "interior facts of bodily sentience"[10] to another being and bring that person to a "realm of shared objectification,"[11] thus communicating an aspect of the suffering subject's reality to another. However, this "expressive potential of the sign of the weapon"[12] occurs only because the artifact itself performs a specific function in the prisoner's world. Revisiting Scarry's discussion of the chair (previously referenced to explain Tiscornia's valorization of his pillow), one observes that the objects that populate this world have a specific design—the chair is conceptualized and created as an object that will relieve the body of the discomfort of having to stand continuously and alleviate the strain of the spine, providing a brief respite for the subject. In the prisons, craftwork was a means by which the suffering subject imaginatively created an artifact that could relieve a facet of his/her mental anguish. Like the chair that relieves the body's pain, artifacts were imagined (and ultimately created) which moved out and beyond the confines of incarceration. At the limits of the ordinary, extraordinary objects helped the subject make real the very item(s) and abilities s/he lacked. The mental reasoning, the productive work of taking scant materials and turning them into imaginative pieces of art was a way by which the prisoner both created and expressed his/her individual agency. These items, many preserved today in museums, others kept in personal collections by the survivors themselves, are therefore an important material legacy of resistance. As will be further explored in Chapter Three, such items are more than mere art projects, they are witnesses to both terror and survival. They are the extraordinary items made on the limit of humanity, the work of the hands of those who created them as an escape from their pain, as a means for their very survival.

Fugas Materiales: Craftwork as Escape

As was argued in Chapter One, during the dictatorships, the totalitarian attempt at complete destruction of subjects deemed "subversive" found its limit in the changed relationship of that subject to his/her material world. As Pilar Calveiro contends in her study of the concentration camps in Argentina, totalitarianism is never absolute, there will always be "líneas de fuga"[13] (lines of escape).[14] For Calveiro, to study the dictatorships, one must refer not only to the specific nature of each power or what constitutes it, but also to what it excludes or what escapes from it.[15] Departing from this perspective, she bases her analysis on the testimony of persons, all of whom, as she says, "fugaron en más de un sentido"[16] (escaped in more than one sense). This comment, conceptualizing the idea of escape as possessing multiple forms, means that escape from the concentration camps is understood not exclusively in terms of a physical escape from the space, but also, as in the cases introduced above, in a momentary psychological escape from the harsh reality of the conditions of detention.

While the narratives analyzed in the previous chapter demonstrate the prisoner's changed relationship and new noticing of the potential of the *things* that make up the material world, it is in an exploration of two separate, but very much related phenomena that one observes the direct connection between the made object and the subject's self-construction of an independent agency within the confining space of detention: the *manualidades* (such as Pedro's box) in the Uruguayan context and the *artesanías carcelarias* in the Chilean context. In the only existing analysis of this phenomenon to date, Ruth Vuskovic and Sylvia Ríos consider such prison craftwork in Chile through the concept of "freedom in prison"[17] ("Libres en prisión"). In this chapter, I will consider how the turn to the material as an ally, produced by the prisoner's changed relationship to the material world, paves the way for this idea of freedom within confinement, examining how the prisoners created imaginative escapes from the concentration camps relying on *things* as allies, especially in the creative work of the *artesanías carcelarias* and *manualidades*.

The Object as Ally: Turning to the Material for Solidarity and Survival

A first step toward understanding how the material ally was used as the basis for creative escape through the creation of prison craftwork is to understand how *things* aided in resistance more generally. An important way such material *things* of the detention center served as allies for survival was by allowing prisoners to communicate with each other and build ties of solidarity within the space of incarceration, a space where such acts were carefully surveilled and controlled. Marcelo Estefanell recounts that upon arriving to Penal de Libertad, a fellow prisoner shared with him the "key" for understanding and producing the modified Morse code designed by the male prisoners to communicate (and play chess) with each other, unbeknownst to the prison guards. Estefanell practices the code on his own and then sets to attempting to communicate with a neighboring inmate:

> Mi vecino me contestó rapidamente: 'Arriba,' y luego me propuso jugar al ajedrez . . . Le contesté afirmativamente y, con un lacónico 'Esperá'—en nuestro morse—le pedí que aguardara mientras me fabricaba el tablero y las piezas: en media hoja de cuaderno dibujé la cuadrícula del tablero (8 por 8), rayé los cuadros que debían ser negros con birome y de un cilindro de cartón de papel higiénico corté las piezas burdamente. A la media hora—tack, tick-tick-tick—arranqué con las blancas: Peón 4 Rey.[18]

> (My neighbor answered me quickly: 'Let's go,' and then proposed we play a game of chess . . . I answered him affirmatively and, with a laconic 'Wait'—in our morse code—I asked him to hold on while I created the board and the pieces: on half a sheet of notebook paper I drew the grid of the board (8 by 8), scratched out the boxes that should be black with a ballpoint pen and, from the cardboard cylinder of a toilet paper roll, I crudely cut the pieces. After half an hour—tack, tick-tick-tick—I started with the whites: Pawn 4 to King.)

The truly revelatory statement accompanying this flurry of creative improvisation comes next: "Cuando me respondió mi vecino—tack, tick-tick-tick—pensé que si la cana era un campeonato, ya teníamos ganado el primer partido"[19] (When my neighbor responded—tack, tick-tick-tick—I thought that if prison were a championship, we had already won the first game). As

2. Chessboard created in a political prison on display at the Museum of Memory (MUME) in Uruguay. Photograph taken by the author.

is observed in this passage, the prisoner turns to and relies on the material as an ally in resistance. It would be easy to focus exclusively on the subjects in this scene—Estefanell and the fellow prisoner who communicate with each other—who collaborate in survival. However, there is a "third party"—the material—to consider in this equation. The Morse code would not facilitate the communication that leads Estefanell to this first victory over detention were it not for the material properties that permit the prisoners to make a sound when tapping one material against another. It is the coming together of human hand and solid material that produces the sound. And it is ultimately the sound born of this material that travels and convinces Estefanell the prisoners have won the first match of the "game" of survival. Additionally, the notebook paper, ballpoint pen, and toilet paper roll lend their tool-beings to Estefanell in allowing him to register the moves of the game in a way that will help him remember the positions while playing. Thus, the material, the *thing*, whose properties have the power to make sound and document information, lends itself to the prisoners to be used as a tool, an ally, in their survival. While this example is perhaps more recognizable than others, prisoners turned to the material for various possibilities of resistance, to imaginatively escape in multiple ways.

Another documented example of this turn to the material for solidarity and creative escape within the political prisons is a deck of cards made by a political prisoner in Uruguay whose surname was Pardal in 1972:

Entre septiembre de 1972 y abril de 1973, en la soledad de uno de aquellos minúsculos calabozos del FUSNA y con un tiempo indeterminado por delante, se me dio por pedir cartulina y algunos marcadores de colores y empezar a diseñar un mazo de naipes con figuras que simbolizaran la lucha y las costumbres de nuestro pueblo (la estrella de 5 puntas, la lanza tacuara, el mate y la guitarra).[20]

(Between September of 1972 and April of 1973, in the solitude of one of those miniscule cells of the FUSNA and with an indeterminate amount of time before me, it occurred to me to ask for some cardboard and a few colored markers and begin to design a deck of cards with figures that symbolized the fight and the customs of our people [the five-pointed-star, the Tacuara lance, the mate, and the guitar.])

Pardal explains that these cards "escaparon de los barrotes para llegar a mis familiares, como uno más de los tantos mensajes simbólicos que los presos políticos enviamos al mundo en los años de la dictadura"[21] (escaped from the iron bars to arrive to my family, as one more of the many symbolic messages that we, the prisoners, sent out to the world in the years of the dictatorship). Here, the material cards stand in as an extension of the voice. They travel out of prison in lieu of the prisoner who cannot, thereby acting as a prosthesis for that which the prisoner lacks: an ability to communicate with the outside world.

Other former political prisoners from Uruguay explain the importance of being able to express oneself during the most difficult moments of detention, especially to express solidarity to a fellow prisoner:

"Cuando la gente está incomunicada necesita hacerle llegar un mensaje, hablar; sabe que hay otros seres humanos alrededor suyo y sin embargo ellos no te dejan interactuar. El ser humano busca siempre la forma de comunicarse, somos seres sociales . . ."; "Uno de los elementos represivos más importantes fue la incomunicación y el aislamiento, entonces nació como una forma de resistencia a esa herramienta represiva . . ."[22]

("When people are in solitary confinement they need to get a message out, to speak; to know that there are other human beings around you and, despite

3. Pardal's original playing cards, on display
at the Museum of Memory (MUME).
Photograph by the author.

this, they don't let you interact. Human beings always look for a way to
communicate amongst themselves, we are social beings . . .''; "One of the
most important repressive elements was solitary confinement and isolation, so then it was born as a form of resistance to this repressive tool . . .'')[23]

Although this study, published by Castillo et al., primarily explores the birth
of the sign language invented by the female prisoners in Punta de Rieles, the
prisoners interviewed also identified an equivalent communicative value held
by the "regalitos en el baño del calabozo"[24] (little gifts in the bathrooms of
the cells), showing how material allies helped them communicate affect to
one another, thus facilitating an aspect of survival. One of the interviewed
former prisoners recalls the memory that "cuando había alguna compañera
en el calabozo y le mandábamos desde el sector ropa para cambiarse, le bor-

dábamos alguna palabrita, un número, algo para darle ánimos o datos de la realidad"[25] (whenever there was a comrade in the dungeon cell and we sent her clothes from our sector to change into, we embroidered a little word, a number, something to give her a spirit lift or information from reality). The little gifts and the material they were composed of served as a tool that lent a piece of its durable being in the world to the prisoners, facilitating the communication of solidarity in the context of the prison. Material creation stood in where the body faltered, where the prisoner was deprived of communication, of voice, of the ability to extend a kind word to a friend; needle and thread stepped in to create an imagined extension of that which was lacking. Solidarity amongst prisoners was constructed via the exchange of created material items, but the material also was a means by which the subject could affirm his/her own existence to his/herself.

One former Uruguayan prisoner, Stela Reyes, describes how in solitary confinement she would turn to the only material object she was allowed, her clothing, in search of a stray string out of which to fashion a small doll, a stick figure composed on the floor, and how she would carefully show it to the prisoner across the hall, by placing it in the small crack underneath the door of the cell, as if to say "look, look what I made."[26] She recalls how in absence of the ability to communicate by voice, the doll gave the female prisoners a way to share a piece of themselves, an accomplishment all their own, with one another. In lieu of the voice, the made object stands in and communicates encouragement and survival. Regarding such survival strategies and the guards' reactions to them, Raquel Barratta remarks: "¡Cómo les fastidiaba la unión entre nosotras! '¿Por qué se regalan?' Era pregunta corriente en los frecuentes interrogatorios que para amedrentarnos nos hacían"[27] (Oh, how the unity among us bothered them! "Why do you all give gifts?" It was the common question in the frequent interrogations they gave us to frighten us). The guards' frustration shows how access to these objects and their use as allies for survival frustrated the dictatorship's repressive apparatus. Such acts constituted a means by which the incarcerated subject expressed him/herself independently, the creative decisions of making such items were ways of overcoming not only the physical, but also the psychological torture of the detention center.

Material Creation as a Tether to Sanity:
Prison Craftwork as Productive Labor

In Uruguay, as a means of psychological torture, the prison guards would force the prisoners to do work of a fundamentally useless nature. By forcing the detainees to uselessly move a pile of dirt around the prison yard, from one place to another, the guards insulted and demoralized the largely Marxist group who believed in the power their labor accorded them. Whereas useless work was employed as a form of psychological torture, productive work was used as a form of resistance—both to keep one's mind occupied in an attempt at mental escape and as a means of providing for a family outside of the confines of the prison or concentration camp, constituting a form of truly productive labor. In terms of the former, Roberto Herrera relates:

> Nosotros teníamos el taller de dibujo, proyectos y eso. Por ejemplo, diseñábamos muebles, sillas, equipamiento para los talleres nuestros. Andábamos en eso y siempre estábamos en contacto con oficiales. Eso nos permitía movernos, hacer cosas. Y, bueno, había cierta condescendencia en el trato.[28]

> (We had the drawing workshop, projects and such. For example, we designed furniture, chairs, equipment for our workshops. We worked on this and always were in contact with the prison officials. This permitted us to move ourselves, to do things. And, well, there was a certain graciousness in the agreement.)

This productive work, the work of designing useful things, gave the political prisoners a purpose, but also served to help improve their conditions in some degree, as agreements with guards to allow the prisoners to keep their workshops functioning were often arranged as a result.

In Chile, the creation of similar workshops (to produce bags, belts, ponchos, copper engravings, and more) served to facilitate a schedule by which the prisoners could organize and break up the monotony of the day, providing a temporary mental escape from the reality of the camp. In *Dignidad hecha a mano: 30 años*, the Fundación Solidaridad documented some of the *artesanías carcelarias* (prison craftwork) and explained part of the origin of such art in Chile, linking the emergence of the phenomenon with the effort of groups like the Catholic Vicariate of Solidarity (*Vicaría de la Solidaridad*) to help free the prisoners through legal defense, denouncements of the injustice of their detainment, and the provision of medical and psychological support.[29] The organization explains that despite all of these other types of support, the

> presos y detenidos pedían algo más: 'Ayúdennos a poder trabajar, el tiempo parece interminable, queremos hacer algo con nuestras manos.' ¡Trabajo, eso era lo que pedían los encarcelados! Había que responder, aunque la tarea nos parecía casi imposible de realizar. ¿Qué se podía producir en una cárcel? ¿Qué herramientas sería posible ingresar a un campo de concentración? ¿Cómo hacer llegar los materiales? ¿Permitirían las autoridades organizar y desarrollar una actividad laboral al interior de estos recintos?'[30]

> (prisoners and detainees asked for something more: "Help us to be able to work, time seems interminable, we want to do something with our hands." Work, this was what the prisoners asked for! We had to respond, although the task seemed nearly impossible for us to achieve. What could one produce in a prison? What tools could possibly be made to reach the inside of a concentration camp? How would they send them? Would the authorities permit them to organize and develop work activities in the interior of these facilities?)[31]

In these comments, the prisoners' insistence on their desire to work, to produce, is telling. It shows the need to *create* after an experience that has unmade the subject's world. Definitively, in some of the detention centers, the prisoners, often with the help of outside support institutions, managed to establish these types of workshops and to produce goods that could be sold. In this way, the craftwork gave the prisoner not only the means to work, but also a way to have that work translate to monetary support for their loved ones, allowing the prisoner to feel like a productive member of their family (and society) from within the confines of detention.

In terms of this productive labor, in Chile, the *Vicaría de la Solidaridad* bought the craftwork made in the concentration camps and sold it abroad. In Uruguay, the craftwork was often passed to family members during supervised family visits to the prisons. The family members were then able to sell it on their own.[32] However, as is evidenced by the insistence on the work of creating with one's hands, the craftwork was not just a utilitarian means for earning money while in prison. Such creative work was an escape for the prisoner— one created in accordance with his/her own mind, making decisions about

design, rationalizing how to achieve the desired product given what scant resources were available, and problem-solving along the way. In these places, the
workshops also became a way by which to break up the day in the concentration camp, to create a sense of semi-normality—one got up in the morning,
had breakfast, and then went to work. Within the workshops that produced
items to be sold by the *Vicaría*, prisoners were often organized into small
groups, each working to produce certain parts of the items, according to their
personal strengths, thus producing collaboratively shaped products. For this
reason, Vuskovic and Ríos document that many of the examples of prison
craftwork in Chile must be viewed as collective activities, with multiple pairs
of hands participating in the process to create the final product.[33]

Individual Creation: The Object as Prosthesis for Familial Relations

While the organized workshops constituted a collective project of productive labor, the *artesanías carcelarias* and *manualidades* were also an important means for individual, personal survival. Craftwork not only served as a
collective means of producing goods that could be sold, but was also done
as individual projects by the prisoners. Some such uses of the material world
facilitated communication with family, acting as a sort of prosthesis for the
relationships that were not possible while the detainees were held captive. For
example, many of the female prisoners made dolls that they gifted to their
children during family visits, the doll allowing the mother to express her love
for her child, sending a piece of that love home with the child after the visit.
One unique example of these dolls in Chile, the *soporopo*, is particularly illus-
trative of this use of the object.

The *soporopo* is a little doll with a large head, small body, short, stumpy
arms, and large, smiling eyes. Purposefully disproportional, the unusual appearance of the doll and its funny name (*soporopo* is a play on the name of
the traditional Chilean dish "sopa de porotos" [bean soup] and was meant to
sound silly and provoke laughter) reflect the happiness the doll was supposed
to bring to anyone who received it.[34] Of the craftwork that was made in the
Chilean camps, only the soporopo and the carved wooden drawings of Chacabuco (*los tabiques de Chacabuco*) are unique to the camps. The rest have
their roots in Chilean patrimony and artistic traditions.[35] But this doll, made
by the mother's hands, often with scraps of the mother's own clothing, was

a "regalo con sentido"[36] (heartfelt gift), an object that could "play" with the child outside of the space of detention, serving as an extension of the mother, a prosthesis that "mothers" the child while the mother herself was unable to do so. Thus, again, the benign nature of the material steps in to lend a piece of itself to the prisoner, who imaginatively engages with the possibilities offered by the *thing* and uses it to facilitate an aspect—as incomplete/inadequate as it may seem—of the important work of parenting.

In the Argentine context, we also see the creation of dolls as gifts for children among the sparse examples that survived the severity of the repression. Included in the permanent exhibit at the Space of Memory Ex ESMA in Buenos Aires, is an image and the story of a doll that was made by María Elsa Garreiro Martínez, "La Gallega" [Image 4]. María Elsa's daughter is quoted in the exhibit, explaining:

> En esa visita, mi mamá nos trajo de la ESMA estas muñequitas, que te-nemos una mi hermana y una yo. Supimos después, por testimonio de los sobrevivientes, que las armó en Pañol. Mi mamá fue a escuela de monjas y por su edad, nació en el '45, obviamente sabía coser, bordar, tejer. Cosas necesarias que son importantes para la vida cotidiana de esa época.[37]

> (In that visit, my mom brought us from the ESMA these little dolls, of which my sister and I each have one. We found out after, through survivor testimony, that she made them in the Pañol. My mom attended a nuns' school and, as is typical for those her age, having been born in '45, obvi-ously she knew how to sew, embroider, and knit. Necessary things that were important for daily life in that time period.)

The visit Laura references in the explanation document in the exhibit is likely one of the supervised home visits that the female prisoners were often granted, as a part of the dictatorship's "re-education" plan for certain (primar-ily female) detainees.[38] The doll, made in the Pañol—the area of the ESMA where detainees were made to work for the dictatorship, in this case sort-ing the clothing that was taken from subversive homes—is an example of prison craftwork made out of found items within detention. The testimony of Norma Cristina Cozzi in the 2010 trials related to the ESMA (and cited within the exhibit) clarifies: "con esos trapitos hizo tres muñequitas, de las cuales traje una que la voy a mostrar. Esta muñequita fue el regalo que llevé a mi hija, que tenía un año, y que fue hecha por La Gallega, la hemos conser-

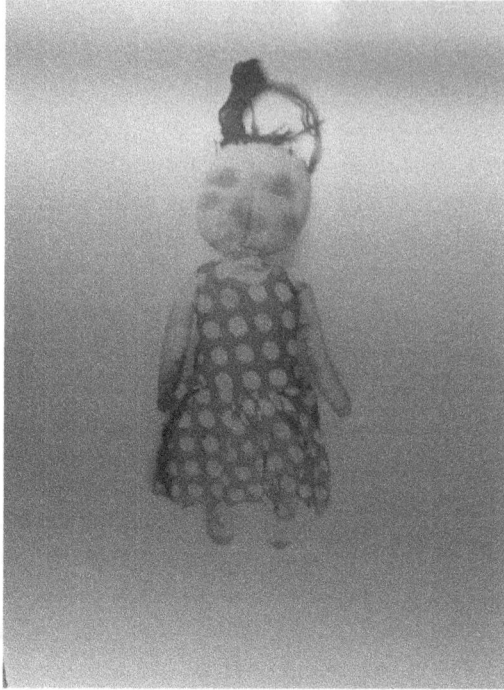

4. Image of a doll made by María Elsa Garreiro Martínez, "La Gallega,"
on display at the Ex ESMA. Photograph by the author.

vado hasta ahora. Hay otras dos"[39] (with these remnants she made three little
dolls, of which I brought one that I'm going to show. This little doll was a
gift that I brought to my daughter, who was one year old, and was made by La
Gallega. We've conserved it until now. There are two others).

In the case of this doll, of which three were made, two for María Elsa's own
daughters and one for her friend Norma Cristina's daughter, one observes
the way the material extends the mothering that is deprived of the mothers
by the dictatorship. While they cannot be physically present for their daughters, the dolls can stand in as a prosthesis for them. The exhibit clarifies that
Laura is the daughter of María Elsa and Raimundo Villaflor, both of whom
disappeared, thus the doll in this case also serves as a material remainder of
a motherhood that was not just interrupted by the dictatorship, but permanently denied. As will be further explored in Chapter Three, this imbues the
doll with an additional testimonial quality that goes beyond the material ally
as an aid for survival.

The Material Ally in Resistance: Craftwork as Creative Rebellion

So far, we have explored the "gift" aspect and the "merchandise" category of prison craftwork, but there is a third way in which these made objects served as material allies in resistance. In the Chilean context, Ignacio Vidaurrázaga, identifies these first two "categories" of prison craftwork that he observed during his time in the Chilean detention camps and adds a third, the "barretín"[40] (secret compartment). The category of *barretines* is a particularly interesting use of the object as an ally in resistance, in that it permitted the prisoner to accomplish the task of actively working against the dictatorship even while the dictatorship attempted to control that activism through overt repression and deprivation within the confines of detention. The *barretín*, which I loosely translate as "secret compartment," was an object, in any form, that was designed to hide within it information that would then be smuggled out of the camp to the outside world. It was a way for the prisoners to actively denounce their situations even while being deprived of the agency or voice with which to do so. Some of the *soporopos* actually functioned in this manner, in addition to being gifts to children and family members. Marcela Andrades Álfaro recalls that on visit days, when her mother, Eva, gave her the *soporopos* she had made in detention, she would often give Marcela certain ones [Image 5], and then give others to Marcela's father, with the instructions that those were for the *Vicaría de la Solidaridad*. Marcela explains that the *soporopos*:

> Fueron usados para extraer nombres de los detenidos en el campo de concentración, adentro del Soporopo estaban los nombres de los detenidos desaparecidos, mapas, oficiales a cargo, tácticas, casas de tortura, etc. Los nombres eran escritos en pedazos de tela y con estos se rellenaban secretamente para ser llevados a la Vicaría de la Solidaridad de la Iglesia Católica de Santiago, para luego entregar la información a la Comisión de los derechos humanos en la OEA (Organización de los Estados Americanos).[41]

> (Were used to extract the names of those who were detained in the concentration camp. Within the *soporopo* were the names of the detained-disappeared, maps, officials in charge, tactics, torture centers, etc. The names were written on pieces of cloth that they then secretly used as stuffing to be brought to the Vicariate of Solidarity of the Catholic Church of

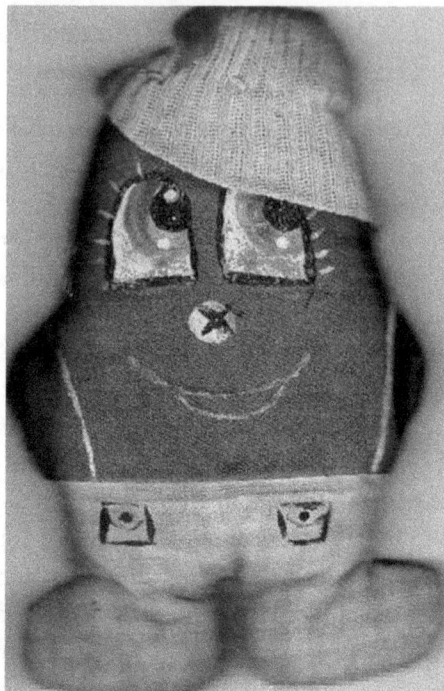

5. Soporopo made by Eva in Tres Álamos for her daughter, Marcela.
Reproduced with permission from Marcela Andrades Álfaro

Santiago, to later be given to the Human Rights Commission of the Organization of the Americas.)

Yet it wasn't only *soporopos* that provided this possibility of resistance, but, as Vuskovic and Ríos report, pots, pencils, glasses with false bottoms, miniature wooden figures, wallets, belts, money pouches, shoes, all served this function.[42] In the Uruguayan context, the film *El Almanaque* (José Pedro Charlo, 2012) documents how Jorge Tiscornia hid the calendars he secretly made to keep track of the events of each day of the ten years of his detention in a pair of wooden sandals he made, the shoes serving as a sort of *barretín* that allowed him to save the calendars from destruction by the guards during cell raids.

In addition to objects serving as *barretines*, many of the objects in Chile that were made with the intention of being sold abroad were embedded with symbols meant to serve as a mark of resistance to the dictatorship. Many carried the name "Chile" along with the year in which the object was produced and a message of resistance carried within a symbol, whether it be an upheld "puño" (fist), a "paloma" (dove), or another image of solidarity. The Museum of Memory and Human Rights in Santiago, Chile holds an extensive collection of these types of items. They carry symbols that range from these types of popular signs to more overt denunciations of violence, such as an outline of Chile's form as a country with barbed wire surrounding it.

The *artesanías carcelarias* and the *manualidades* ultimately produced a legacy of handcrafted objects with very specific and powerful prior contexts. The object, as a forensic material proof of the productive work of hands meant to be silenced and deterred from creating, is the exterior and lasting manifestation of the interior imaginative sentience of their makers. These objects, these allies for physical and emotional survival, truly escaped not only the physical confines of the prison, but—in traveling outside of the prison to places abroad, and through their preservation for the future—they activate the enduring nature of the material, and in this way (as will be explored in Chapter Three) escape the boundary of time and the limits of representation. Where the voice faltered, was dismissed, denied, or even didn't survive to speak, these objects made and continue to make themselves undeniably present.

The Artifact: Imagined Agency in Material Form

In order to explore the details of how this process of creation and the imaginative work of the *artesanías carecelarias* and the *manualidades* helped the prisoners create an "escape" for themselves, thus leaving a material object that can now be seen as a testimony to their working through or expressing their state of pain, we must first further examine the place of the object/artifact in the political prisoner's new reality. In the second half of *The Body in Pain: The Making and Unmaking of the World*, Scarry explores the intricacies of the project of "making" the world (or, "remaking," in the case of the torture victim's world). Scarry places on opposite ends of a spectrum the experience of pain as a state that "unmakes" the world and the experience of creating/imagining that "makes" the world. For Scarry, "while pain is a state remarkable for being wholly without objects, the imagination is remarkable for being the only state that is wholly its objects."[43] When one imagines, one doesn't need to have access to the physical object, the object itself can be manifested via the imagination. The objectlessness of pain when experienced by the subject is a futility that animates him/her to move to imagining as a means by which to objectify pain, to render it within language (or, in the case of expressing the pain of the political prison, within a made material):

> this objectlessness, the complete absence of referential content, almost prevents it [pain] from being rendered in language: objectless, it cannot easily be objectified in any form, material or verbal. But it is also its objectlessness that may give rise to imagining by first occasioning the process that eventually brings forth the dense sea of artifacts and symbols that we make and move about in.[44]

While the person in pain (here, the victim of torture) may find it impossible to accurately represent that pain through a material object (or even language), s/he simultaneously experiences the parallel process of turning to imagination in order to self-soothe the pain caused by his/her circumstances and to attempt to communicate that pain by creating symbols and artifacts. Scarry is quick to point out that imagination is the "ground of last resort"[45] only turned to in a crisis of representation, but she also underlines that it is the terrain in which objects can be accessed should the subject be deprived of them in his/her reality. Scarry explains this process using the example of hunger:

> Should it happen that the world fails to provide an object, the imagination is there, almost on an emergency stand-by basis, as a last resource for the generation of objects. Missing, they will be made-up; and though they may sometimes be inferior to naturally occurring objects, they will always be superior to naturally occurring objectlessness. If no food is present, imagining grain or berries will, at least temporarily, allow the hunger to be experienced as potentially positive rather than as wholly aversive, and the imagined image may remind the person to walk over the next hill to find real wheat and berries.[46]

In the case of the detainee, there are many lacks to be made up for, but perhaps the most primary lack experienced is the loss of control over his/her world. The detained subject cannot decide for him/herself, cannot provide for him/herself, and is completely at the mercy of his/her captors. In this space, just as Pedro and Roberto comment above, the detainee—predisposed to a new state of noticing the potential of things—turns to that which s/he has at his/her disposal in order to exact an impact on the exterior world. In

Chile, this turn was a new envisioning of the potentiality of bones from soup, of breadcrumbs, of pieces of wood from the walls—all materials used to create the *artesanías carcelarias*. In Uruguay, a parallel use of the found objects of the detainee's world resulted in the creation of the *manualidades*. In both instances, these small pieces of prison craftwork that use the materials found in the prisoners' camps are specific manifestations of the artifact, a making-material of the inner state of the imagination. But, they are also a making-real, making-material of the internal suffering of the prisoner, of the suffering of being in prison, of the lack of individual agency.

The prison craftwork in Chile and Uruguay helped detained persons overcome the passivity of the painful circumstances of detention, incarceration, and torture, in the way in which they facilitated an individual expression in an environment designed to eliminate this type of autonomous subjectivity. Regarding her time in Tres Álamos (in Chile), Nubia Becker states, "nunca en mi vida vi tanta creatividad, ni tanta imaginación para divertirse, para hacer teatro, y para disfrazarse, como entre las prisioneras en la dictadura"[47] (never in my life did I see so much creativity, nor as much imagination to enjoy oneself, to do theater, and dress up, as I did among the female prisoners during the dictatorship). Becker's observation that she has never seen as much imagination and creativity as in the concentration camp is perhaps the best evidence of Scarry's assertion that imagination is a limit point, a "ground of last resort," turned to when ordinary objects are found to be beyond reach: "Beyond the expansive ground of ordinary, naturally occurring objects is the narrow extra ground of imagined objects, and beyond this ground, there is no other. Imagining is, in effect, the ground of last resort."[48] By "ground of last resort" Scarry means that the imagination provides what the being cannot access. She writes, "imagining provides an *extra and extraordinary* ground of objects beyond the naturally occurring ground: it actively 'intends,' 'authors,' or 'sponsors' objects when they are not *passively* available as an already existing 'given.'"[49] While these objects were often created as a means to occupy time, they also served as a way of overcoming abject circumstances and of making decisions entirely of one's own volition:

> Pero, también al final, esto era, una superación de uno mismo. . . . Como desafíos que uno se pone—desafíos técnicos, de paciencia, de disciplina.[50]
>
> (But, in the end, this was, an overcoming of one's self. . . . Like challenges that one gave oneself—technical challenges, of patience, of discipline.)

6. Flower sculpture created in Punta de Rieles Prison.
Photograph by the author.

Pedro explains that creating these items, often from what in the everyday world would seem to be nothing, was a challenge (*un desafío*); it occupied one's mind to solve the problem of the lack of access to adequate materials, and it required active mental activity. In another example, pictured above [Image 6], is a collection of flowers Stela Reyes made during her detention. The flowers were fashioned out of bread crumbs, then painted with the dyes that seeped out of new clothing sent to the prisoners by their families (which was left to soak in water to extract the dye from the fibers so that it could then be used to paint). The flower sculpture, in documenting the profoundly imaginative ingenuity of its artist, is an *extraordinary* artifact that records the prisoner's experience. At the point where the subject has no agency, has lost his/her dignity, has been detained in the "cárcel modelo"[51] (model prison) from which there is to be no escape (and no testimony), the object stands in to fill a lack. In the Museum of Memory and Human Rights in Chile, the imaginative content of these *extraordinary* objects is explained for visitors:

7. Crayon rendering of a Matisse painting, created by Pedro Giudice in the *Penal de Libertad*. Photograph by the author.

"En el encierro, los días se hacían interminables y este tiempo luchando para darle forma a una piedra o un trozo de madera, para recuperar la dignidad que da el trabajo, los acercaba un poco a la libertad"⁵² (In confinement, the days become endless and the time spent fighting to bring shape to a rock or a piece of wood, to recover the dignity that work gives, brought them [the prisoners] a little bit closer to freedom).

In my visit to view his craftwork, Pedro shows me paintings he did with crayons during his incarceration in Uruguay and emphasizes that they were a very difficult medium to use to really render the details of the pieces effectively, but that he found innovative ways to manipulate the blunt end of the crayons to make a fine dot or a thin line as needed to complete the finishing touches on his *manualidades*. One specific crayon painting that Pedro shows me is of a young girl [Image 7], a copy of a Matisse painting Pedro found in one of the books he was able to have in his cell, on loan from the prison library. The seated girl symbolized for Pedro the daughter (the second child) that he and his partner, Antonia, were planning to have prior to both of their detentions. The girl in the painting is Pedro and Antonia's future, the daughter that they will have (and, indeed, do have) after they are freed. Thus, the painting, at the same time an act of creation, an activity that requires creative thinking in order to successfully come to fruition due to scant resources, makes symbolically real the most basic act of human creation: the birthing of an autonomous subject, a daughter. In this sense, the painting acts as an artifact that is made real through imagination when such an object is unobtainable given the circumstances of imprisonment. I read the painting as not only the imaginative birthing of Pedro and Antonia's child, but simultaneously as an imaginative making real of the possibility of a future, when the assuredness of having a future is precisely what the prisoner during this time period lacked.

Imagination, here, in the creation of *manualidades* is an act that permits the prisoner a type of (even if incomplete or inadequate) healing, a particular form of self care that would permit survival within the gross mistreatment in the concentration camps and political prisons. But it was also a means by which to leave a testimonial mark, to choose to communicate an aspect of his/her sentience to the outside/future world. This type of elimination of the burden of pain (and, perhaps, the difficulty of testifying) is reflected in Scarry's premise:

> To be more precise, one can say that pain only becomes an intentional state once it is brought into relation with the objectifying power of the imagination: through that relation, pain will be transformed from a wholly passive and helpless occurrence into a self-modifying and, when most successful, self-eliminating one.[53]

Like the chair that is an exterior object created to relieve the pain of the sitting individual, the prison craftwork in Chile and Uruguay were objects that relieved the pain of the individual in feeling helpless, without agency, without productive/creative power. As lasting remainders (and reminders) of that process, the *manualidades* and *artesanías carcelarias* are objects that signify that which language cannot transparently render: the internal and painful experience of the political prisoners. Today, in the Museum of Memory (MUME) in Uruguay, the display of the *manualidades* stands out, then, as a visual testimony that puts on display the external manifestation of the inner sentient state of the prisoner [Image 8].

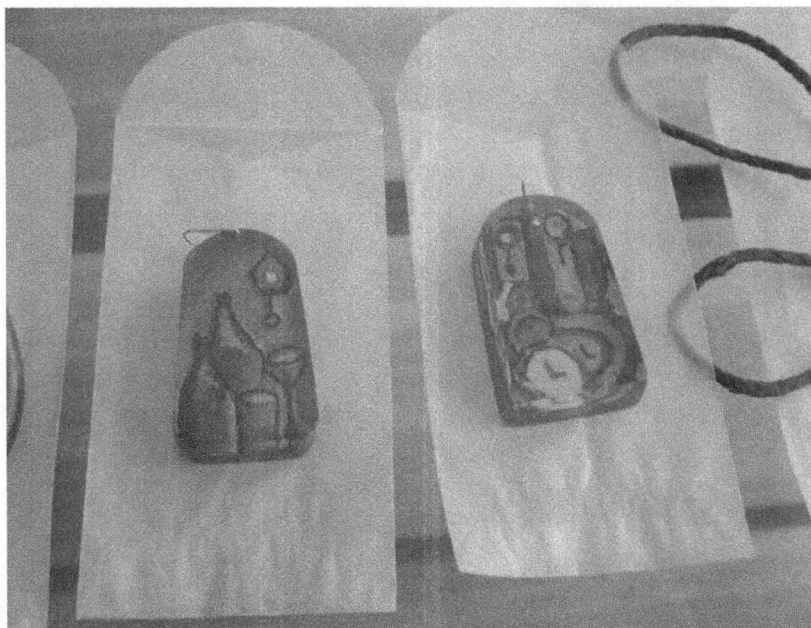

8. Pendants created in the political prisons on display at the Museum of Memory (MUME). Photograph by the author.

Communing with these objects of created sentience, then, is a communing with the inner voice of the prisoner, bypassing written language and opting for a material communication. These objects, though they cannot speak, are *suspect*; they were made by the hands of s/he who suffered. Pedro's, Roberto's, Marcelo's, María Elsa's, Eva's, Nubia's, and Stela's experiences are all very individual in nature, yet they remain representative of many lived experiences in the space of the prisons and camps. They reflect the process of turning to the imagination as a suture, a means of accessing that which is denied. Roberto refuses to succumb to the pain (both physical and psychic) inflicted on him by the prison. Instead, he turns to imagining, producing craftwork in the workshops, and in doing so he self-modifies that over which he previously had no control. He self-eliminates the helplessness of pain in the making-real of imagined objects, in the creation of 'limit' pieces,[54] of artifacts of resistance.

A catalogue from the Museum of Memory and Human Rights in Chile describes the communicative power of these objects, stating that in the Chilean prisons, creation was a way in which

La víctima construye las oportunidades para interactuar con el entorno y el medio social, recurriendo a primitivas formas de comunicación, creando espacios imaginarios y haciendo artefactos culturales con intención de comunicación en diferido (creación de dibujos y poemas). Las personas privadas de libertad construyen intencionadamente una cotidianidad y un espacio de pertenencia desde donde protegerse, resistir y superar la adversidad comunitariamente, con la promoción de un comportamiento ético coherente y la optimización de los recursos propios.[55]

(The victim constructs opportunities to interact with his environment and the social mediums in it, defaulting to primitive forms of communication, creating imagined spaces and making cultural artifacts with the intention of a deferred communication [the creation of drawings and poems]. People deprived of liberty intentionally construct a sense of normalcy and a space of belonging from which to protect themselves, to resist, and to overcome adversity communally, with the promotion of a coherent ethical behavior and the optimization of personal resources.)

The creation of a cohesive narrative relating the day-to-day struggle of survival in the prisons and the camps was not a possibility for most detainees. Instead, the objects that were created both in secret and in the workshops were imbued with information (both intentionally and unintentionally, by virtue of their process of creation) that documents truths and relays information from the interior space of detention to the exterior, both to families within the country and, as was their hope, to foreign populations that could perhaps advocate on behalf of the prisoners. Deferred communication (*comunicación en diferido*) occurred primarily through symbolism, but also through the documentary nature of the object, its durability through time, its ability to transgress the limits through which the prisoner was not permitted to pass. Stela Reyes explains the effort that went into the creation of these powerful symbols, even when the created object and its symbolism was to remain with the prisoners:

Hubo épocas en que tuvimos telares. Hubo épocas en las cuales no . . . sacaron los telares, en que no tuvimos telares. Pero yo te voy a mostrar que aun sin telar . . . esta manta que yo tengo fue hecha sin telar. Es una manta que tiene nubes y, para nosotros, la luna.[56]

(There were periods when we had weaving looms. There were periods in which. . . they took away the looms . . . in which we didn't have looms. But

9. Blanket woven in Punta de Rieles prison. Photograph by the author.

I'm going to show you that even without a loom . . . this blanket I have was made without a loom. It's a blanket that has clouds, and, for us, the moon.)

Stela explains that there was always a symbolism within the objects the prisoners created, the moon being a particularly significant one, since the female prison had all of the windows covered and they were not able to see the exterior and, thus, the only access they had to the moon was via the imagined image of it in the craftwork they created. Such a meaning goes beyond an expressive symbolism; the object has a documentary function. The significance of the image for the prisoners is present in the object, yet absent from the access of the ordinary viewer who is not privy to the object's story. The information is engrained [Image 9] (here, literally *woven*) in the object itself, yet the whole story remains inaccessible without the voice of the person. The object's meaning is at once present and absent. Stela describes the conditions in which this blanket was made:

Te quería explicar esta manta. Nosotras no teníamos telar, pero esta manta fue hecha igual, si vos la mirás, ésta es hecha en un telar. Nosotras lo que hacíamos era . . . y teníamos prohibido no hacerlo. Por eso nos sacaron los telares. Colgábamos la lana de la cucheta de arriba a la cucheta de abajo tirantes así, ¿no? Y era como si estuviéramos en un telar, ¿no? Y lo tejíamos pasando con una aguja no más. Este . . . llevaba . . . yo qué sé . . . esta manta creo que años, no sé. Y la teníamos que esconder. O sea, cuando venían, se abrían las rejas y nosotras poníamos debajo del colchón de la cucheta de arriba. Tratábamos rápidamente así, así, así, así, así, y la metíamos.[57]

(I wanted to explain to you this blanket. We didn't have a loom, but this blanket was made anyway. If you look at it, it looks like it was made on a loom. What we did was . . . and we weren't permitted to do it. That's why they took the looms away from us. We ran the yarn from the top bunk to the bottom bunk tightly like this. See? And it was as if they were on a loom, see? And we wove passing just with a hook. This . . . took . . . I don't know . . . this blanket I think took years, I'm not sure. And we had to hide it. That is, when they came, they opened the cell doors and we put it under the mattress of the upper bunk. We worked quickly, like this, this, this, and we put it away.)

The danger posed by the creative work of the prison craftwork is evident in the story of the blanket, as the guards tried desperately to avoid such production by taking away the looms from the prisoners. Yet, the women found a way to produce even in conditions where they lacked the tools to do so. And, as Stela pointed out to me, one would have a difficult time viewing the blanket and believing that the prisoners didn't have access to a loom when producing it. The determination to produce the blanket from within these conditions, the danger the prisoners ran every time the guards entered the cell as they scrambled to hide the blanket, shows the importance of such creative production. The turn to the material world, to the use of found objects to create new, imaginative pieces of craftwork, is, I argue, a result of the new valorization of the object produced by the very process of unmaking the world explored in the first chapter of my project. The subject who experiences torture lives a newly made reality in which s/he cannot help but notice the objects that surround him/her. The noticing of things produced by the limit experience of the camps consequently also creates a being in the world that denies presence-at-hand and reorders the material world with a constant state of readiness-at-hand. This readiness-at-hand resulted in the imaginative work of the *artesanías carcelarias* and the *manualidades*.

Conclusion: Extraordinary Object Witnesses?

If, as Idelber Avelar states, "maintaining experience — maintaining it as material that can be narrated, that is to say maintaining it as such — is the very condition of survival, its constitutive moment,"[58] then prison craftwork and its subsequent preservation by survivors, family members, and museums can be read as the ultimate testament of survival, as the maintaining of a material that can be narrated. While Avelar here most likely meant "material" not in terms of physical matter, but in terms of information, a literal reading of "material" in this context still rings true. For her part, Scarry sustains that

> Artifice is more modest and fragmentary than imagining, its objects have the immense advantage over imagined objects of being real, sharable; and because the objects are sharable, in the end artifice has a scale as large as that in imagining because its outcome is for the first time collective.[59]

The phenomenon of prison craftwork in the Uruguayan political prisons and the Chilean concentration camps is a small monument to important acts of resistance, to the making real of pain via imagining and work. Once created, each object is shareable, pointing to an important possibility of collective memory. For if the object was envisioned and made real in order to protect the prisoner from the pain s/he was suffering, then such material objects have important stories to tell. Throughout this chapter I have cited various examples of the *artesanías carcelarias* and the *manualidades* that to this point have gone largely undocumented and unstudied. In my interactions with Pedro and Stela, each told me their stories through a narration of the significance of the objects they, their friends, and their significant others made while in detention and prison. But, what happens when the person is not present to narrate the object's past? In the next chapter we will examine more closely if and how the object itself might give testimony and ask whether the object itself can be a witness.

Part Two

Toward a Testimonial

Theory of Objects

CHAPTER THREE

After Detention or Disappearance—Spectral Testimony in the Museum of Memory

❧

Contrariamente a la permanencia y la riqueza de la piedra o el metal precioso de otros calendarios que buscaron establecerse en su función y su belleza (baste pensar en el azteca o el maya), éste se embellece de su propia precariedad, de la fragilidad de sus pequeños papelitos, de las huellas de los trazos, de la vulnerabilidad de su existencia, de su trayectoria, de la marca personal y por encima de todo de su condición de verdad.[1]

(Contrary to the permanence and richness of the rock or precious metal of other calendars that sought to establish themselves for their function and beauty (one need only think of the Aztecs or the Maya), this one embellishes itself through its own precarity, through the fragility of its little papers, of the traces of the lines, of the vulnerability of its existence, of its trajectory, of the personal mark and above all else its condition as truth.)

"...todas las marcas, objetos y signos encontrados y documentados y los que siguen apareciendo por estas horas, hablan. Nos cuentan particularidades sobre las cuales hay que trabajar, recomponiendo tiempo y lugar, situando esos hallazgos con la mayor precisión posible, para poder acercarnos a lo que esas señales quieren decirnos"[2]

(...all the marks, objects, and signs found and documented and those that continue to appear through time, speak. They tell us particularities with which we must work, rebuilding time and place, situating these discoveries with the most precision possible, to be able to get ourselves close to what these signals want to tell us.)

UGUST OF 2013 MARKED the release of the book and reproductions of Jorge Tiscornia's *almanaque* (almanac), a series of small material papers upon which he recorded the day-to-day happenings of
the time he was held as a political prisoner in Uruguay. These reproductions
of the actual cards that helped Tiscornia track the ten years of his detention
in Uruguay are now sold accompanied by a book that explains their significance. The *almanaque* itself was recognized by UNESCO as a part of the
patrimony of the Registro Regional Memoria del Mundo (Regional Registry
of World Memory) in 2014.[3] In an article published previous to the book,
Tiscornia explains that his first *almanaque* was the wall of his *calabozo* (cell)
in the political prison Punta de Rieles:

> Traté de mirar hacia afuera sin éxito esta vez, pero me topé con un clavo y
> una Gilette, ambos herrumbrados [...] Al clavo doblado y herrumbrado
> lo tomé en mi mano todavía húmeda. Me conectó con la profesión, con
> mis gustos y hasta con aquello de no haber sido elegido, o haberse doblado
> en el trayecto. Lo rescataría de su triste destino, a mí sí me serviría. Con él
> rayaría el muro, sería mi lápiz de carpintero.[4]

> (I tried to look outside unsuccessfully this time, but I hit myself on a nail
> and a Gilette, both rusty [...] I took the bent and rusty nail in my still
> damp hand. It connected me to my profession, to my likes and even to
> that which had not been selected, or had been distorted in the trajectory. I
> would rescue it from its sad destiny. For me, it would serve a purpose. With
> it, I would scratch on the wall, it would be my carpenter's pencil.)

This first *almanaque*, carved into the wall of his cell with a discarded nail,
remains in the past of Punta de Rieles. Tiscornia's second attempt at his *almanaque*, this time on the more conventional material that he would also later
use for the ones that survived his detention—paper—was also lost during
his transfer from Punta de Rieles to the Penal de Libertad: "Este que hoy doy
comienzo quedó, con todas mis otras cosas, en una pila de objetos, ropa y li-
bros, en Punta de Rieles, el 17 de octubre de 1972"[5] (This, which today I begin, remained, with all my other things, in a pile of objects, clothes, and books
in Punta de Rieles, the 17th of October 1972). While it was the carvings on
the wall, and later the small folded papers that reminded Tiscornia of the
passing of time during his incarceration, in the context of the present from
which he is writing—reflecting on the importance of those items for him

during the past—, it is a photograph of a very specific object that provokes Tiscornia's memory: "Levanto la vista del teclado y miro una foto, sacada casi treinta y cinco años después, de dos clavos herrumbrados, que cuelga aquí en mi casa"[6] (I look up from the keyboard and I see a photo, taken almost thirty-five years later, of two rusty nails that hangs here in my home). For Tiscornia, these nails themselves also serve as a sort of calendar today, a way of remembering the first *almanaque* that he carved into the wall in the Punta de Rieles prison, the second that was lost in his transfer and its importance for the creation of the *almanaque* that helps his memory today: "El almanaque enterrado en Punta de Rieles florecería en *Libertad* y fueron estos los que utilicé para engancharme con el pasado"[7] (The calendar buried in Punta de Rieles would flourish in Libertad and it was those ones that I used to connect myself with the past).

In light of the changed relationship to the object world experienced by the prisoner that I explored in Chapter One, and the use of the artifact as an imagined extension of the self as I proposed in Chapter Two, I now shift temporalities to the period after violence to the memory projects in the post-dictatorship, which are taking up these material remainders of the past in order to create a memory politics that perpetuates and transmits the lessons learned, a labor that works in an exemplary manner to testify to the past in an effort to prevent future atrocities.[8] In this chapter, I turn to the objects that remain in the wake of violence and ask whether or not the object itself is capable of witnessing. While in Tiscornia's case (and in the case of other authors of written *testimonios*, or those that have testified in court) we have the survivor present to us, able to tell his story, in the case of many of the victims of the dictatorships we cannot engage with them in a direct dialogue. The disappeared or murdered victim cannot explain to us the significance of the object, its creation, its meaning. These voices of the past cannot be heard, yet even so, material traces of their past presence, their "personal marks" as Ana Tiscornia puts it above, remain vividly present in the wake of disappearance. The doubt that remains attached to material objects, their integral function in not only the dictatorship's project of control, but in the resistance by the detained, changes the prior context of the object, imbuing it with not only its own past, its own "condition as truth,"[9] but a phantasmal presence that remains residually attached to its materiality even after the disappearance of the person for whom it represents hope, resistance, rebuilt subjectivity, and even life.

The material object poses a unique possibility to memory scholarship at the same time that it presents us with new limits with which to grapple. The importance given to objects from the past in spaces of memory asks us for a reconsideration of their interpretative power.[10] The attempt to narrate the realities of genocide is an act that has received much critical attention, especially in relation to the Jewish Holocaust and the recent period of violence in Southern Cone Latin America. In terms of the former, Dori Laub argues that "what precisely made a Holocaust out of the event is the unique way in which, during its historical occurrence, *the event produced no witnesses.*"[11] In terms of Latin America, the same paradox motivates Idelber Avelar to argue that allegory constitutes the most adequate (and perhaps only) means for approximating a representation of the terrors of mass violence.[12] Both of these analyses focus largely on the means by which to facilitate the subject's testimonial capacity to speak. The question remains as to how we can access the stories of the past when the subjects who lived them are not present to relate their experiences to us? In the absence of a surviving *complete* witness,[13] in the silencing of the subject due to disappearance or death, can the material act as an "invaluable record—a testimonial object, a point of memory"[14] as Marianne Hirsch and Leo Spitzer posit?

In order to interrogate this potential for the object to serve as a witness, this chapter first examines some of the scholarship on Latin American *testimonio* in order to build the case for how the object can be viewed as a form of material testimony, especially in regard to the use of objects in current memory projects in the Southern Cone. It then illustrates this stance by considering examples of how such objects have been deployed as material witnesses in memorial museums, memory sites, and archival projects. Lastly, it argues that when we reconsider the everyday object—once present with the disappeared or at the scene of torture or detention and presently occupying the role of witness in the space of the museum—and reevaluate this material in light of testimonial and spectral theory, it becomes clear that material objects speak a truth about the past, giving what I term "spectral testimony" in lieu of the voices of their disappeared or not present owners—a type of testimony that continuously evokes the productive nature of simultaneous presence-and-absence and that promotes an ongoing questioning of the past in the temporality of the present.

Testimonio as Genre:
The Difficulty and Crisis of Bearing Witness

A cohesive definition of the genre of Latin American *testimonio* has long evaded scholars of the field. However, what nearly all of the early attempts at definition seem to agree on is that *testimonio* stems from an authentic narrative relayed through language, either written or oral, that is tied to some sort of conflict. George Yúdice emphasizes that *testimonio* is fundamentally an act;[15] for René Jara it is a form of struggle (*lucha*) born out of an urgency to narrate;[16] and for Ileana Rodríguez it is embedded in a given sociopolitical moment and responds to or contests enduring issues.[17] If we take all of these aspects of testimonio to be true, the question remains as to why the genre must hinge on language. As was explored in Chapter Two, prison craftwork was a deliberate and organized act, it was a form of resisting from within the space of detention, borne out of an urgency for survival, embedded in the sociopolitical moment of detention (if we consider that the material used was often encountered in the space of detention itself, this embedded nature is quite literal), and it responded to and challenged the repression of the moment. This means that prison craftwork especially is marked with a specific content that reveals how prisoners (citizens) navigated their place in the dictatorship (society). If all of these not yet "codified" criteria have been met, why not accept these objects as a form of testimony?

As was briefly explored in the introduction to this book, new scholarship on *testimonio* is working to expand the genre in ways that would ostensibly be open to including material objects as vessels of testimonial content. Similarly to such emerging scholarship, Javier Sanjinés has explored forms of performative testimony in the Bolivian context, specifically theatrics and dramaturgical actions that go "beyond testimonial discourse."[18] For Sanjinés the key element of testimony is that it is "an act of political participation"[19] that promotes a dialogue about the past. He argues that "without authentic dialogue, the efficacy of testimonial narratives seems to be left behind in the transitional moment of social change that marked the downfall of military authoritarianism."[20] In my consideration of the object in this chapter, rather than limiting the discussion to the way the material is often evoked as an element of forensic truth in the juridical context, I hope to show how the object can go beyond this capacity and offer up its past for an authentic dialogue (in the realm of the spectral, I argue) that is capable of facilitating change via the promotion of critical reflection in the present.

The focus on *testimonio* by the lettered world has subjected it to analysis that reveals the ambiguities of its limits, often hinging on the question of its veracity and the threshold of its capacity to relate such an atrocious truth. Yet, this very "porosidad"[21] (porosity) of the restrictions on telling posed by the text, ultimately points to a differently productive nature of the subaltern testimony, which doesn't necessarily depend on its measure of truth, but rather calls attention to pre-existing or pre-conditioned value notions attached to the definition of truth and truth-telling in the first place. Given the scrutiny the testimonial (and, most especially, the subaltern) voice has received, the material object's lack of access to a voice that can narrate its past and its importance truthfully within written language merits further examination and perhaps must be rejected as an element that prohibits the object from being seen as *testimonio*.

The lack of a definition of the genre of *testimonio*, along with its indiscernibility in terms of a discipline, has implications for the consideration of its aesthetics. Georg Gugelberger reflects on the difficulty of categorizing Rigoberta Menchú's subaltern *testimonio*, identifying its intersectional nature and locating it at the midpoint of a number of binaries ("oral v. literary; authored/authoritarian v. edited; literary v. anthropological; autobiography v. demography; masterpiece v. minority writing; postmodernism v. postcolonialism"[22]). For Gugelberger, this intersectional nature begs the question of not only where such a text belongs in the academy, but also challenges us to think about "what happens if we use such a text."[23] The preoccupation over the text's use points not only to the ethical implications of its employment, but also to the difficulty of pinpointing the methodology by which to analyze the piece based on its aesthetic qualities. As Nora Strejilevich notes: "hay siempre una confrontación entre ver, decir y escribir, y la creación juega siempre con estos contrastes. Lo que surge es una labor artística en la que ética y estética coinciden"[24] (There is always a confrontation among seeing, speaking, and writing, and creation always plays with these contrasts. What develops is an artistic labor in which ethics and aesthetics coincide). Objects from the past sit neatly in this in-between framework and even add to the binaries under consideration a material nexus between past versus present: said versus unsaid, legible versus illegible, accessible versus inaccessible. Objects also productively ask us to think about what happens *if we use them*, and, in their unfixability, continually evoke a play between seeing, telling, and (if not writing) interpreting. In the case of objects created in resistance by prisoners in the detention centers, ethics and aesthetics coincide and ask to be considered.

Testimonio endeavors to share the voices of a deleted past, relating an experience, most often traumatic in tone. For John Beverley, "el testimonio transforma una narrativa pre o para-literaria en un libro"[25] (testimonio transforms a pre- or para-literary narrative into a book.) Such a reliance on literature to put experience (and often traumatic events that evade representation in language) into words entails, for Marta Rojas, a necessary defense of language.[26] By proxy, this means a defense of the artifice of language, the aesthetic as a means of rendering a representation of reality capable of transmitting knowledge from one being to another. Seen in the light of postmodernist theory, and the difficulties it poses for those who would like to accept language as a transparent system capable of recording reality, it makes sense that Derrida would question the relationship between testimony and literature, suggesting that perhaps the two should remain distinct.[27] Derrida also observes that in working through language, in relying on the conversion of a para-literary experience into a narrative, *testimonio* necessarily needs to grapple with the opacity of language.[28] In relying on the artifice of language in order to communicate, to witness a previous event, the testimonial subject relies on a system that is a construction, inherently overlapping with the literary in its very employment, therefore, once again we might ask, why can't that opaque system be an object?

In considering the question of authenticity—George Yudice's identification of *testimonio* as an "authentic narrative"[29]—the object, in its unchanging and lasting materiality holds a forensic truth value unique from the malleability of language. The object *was there*, it *witnessed*. What happens if we use it now in an effort to uncover testimony to atrocity? Elzbieta Sklodowska affirms that *testimonio* uses the literary tradition as a tool for political emancipation.[30] She argues that testimony is "una nueva modalidad de novela"[31] (a new modality of novel). For Beverley, it is a form of narrative that is "fundamentally democratic and egalitarian"[32] because it "implies that *any* life so narrated can have a kind of representational value."[33] Gugelberger argues that *testimonio* helps "make ourselves visible to ourselves."[34] Beverley similarly contends that if this representation doesn't produce the real (i.e. truthful) past, "then certainly a sensation of *experiencing the real* and that this has determinate effects on the reader that are different from those produced by even the most 'realist' or 'documentary' fiction."[35] Thus, for both scholars, *testimonio* has the power to impact us in significant ways.

Michael Lazzara contends that "truth utterances are malleable, that they are crafted in the present based on a speaker's motivations and perceived outcomes."[36] He affirms, then, that post-authoritarian truth-telling is "the aggregate of discourses—official and unofficial, factual and fictional, written and performative—that have the capacity to transform society and help it imagine a better future, without forgetting its past,"[37] a view that once again gestures to Avelar's identification of a need for allegory in representing the atrocities of mass violence. The material object when considered in this debate presents a unique memory opportunity. It is not a narrative in the traditional form of a written text, but it does offer a narrative up to be read by the one who encounters it. The object holds a very specific truth value; one need only look to the use of material evidence in trials or to forensic teams that work to recover these fragments of the past to see this regime of truth at work.

For example, at the site of the former detention center, El Club Atlético, in the heart of San Telmo in Buenos Aires, excavation work has uncovered a number of items that range from pieces of the infrastructure of the building, to fragments of police uniforms, food packaging, clothing, dishes, and (as has become rather infamous about the site) ping pong balls from the table at which the guards played in between torture sessions. The excavation of the site began in April of 2002 after a call by a group of former detained-disappeared "en el marco de su lucha por la Memoria, la Verdad y la Justicia"[38] (within the frame of their fight for Memory, Truth, and Justice). A visit to this memory site is made up firstly of a walk through the excavations-in-progress on the site of the former detention center. A guide shows the various rooms, in different stages of recovery, and explains the confluence between the materials one observes around him/herself and the testimony that has been given by survivors who were detained there. After one has observed the infrastructure, s/he has the opportunity to visit the objects that were recovered, which are held in a separate building, so as to be monitored by a group of forensic archivists who care for the preservation of these fragments of history. The objects were used as evidence in some of the recent trials in Argentina, and as such they demonstrate the important perception that such forensic proofs "speak," as Eduardo Tavani, the director of the former Institute for Spaces of Memory, remarks in the quote at the outset of this chapter.

However, the object, at the same time possessing an unchanging forensic truth from the past, also represents an element of artifice that halts our ability to read the truth behind it. Just as Lazzara states about post-authoritarian truth-telling above, the object is the aggregate of discourses. While it is true that it was created and used in a specific context and remains constant through time, the one who encounters the object in the present and attempts to read its story brings with him/her an entirely new set of discourses. To illustrate how this process plays out via interactions with the material witness, I turn now to a consideration of objects in memory projects of the post-dictatorship in three venues: in the memorial museum, in the democratized online memorial archive *Vestigios*, and in the archival workshop inspired by a countermonumental mentality that seeks to construct memory "from below" (*desde abajo*), *Química de la Memoria*. In what follows, I will offer the concept of spectral testimony as a theoretical framework for discussing how the object creates a productive memory dialogue between the living generations of the present and the lost generations of the past.

Haunted Objects in the Memorial Museum

Many of the examples of prison craftwork discussed in the previous chapter were from private collections held by survivors in their own homes, especially in the case of the Uruguayan survivors. However, there are numerous examples of material remnants of the past (including prison craftwork) that make up the holdings and exhibits of the museums of memory in Chile and Uruguay. The Museum of Memory and Human Rights in Chile has more than 2,000 material objects in its collection that help transmit to the visiting public the memory of the recent history in Chile. Within the museum's archive, the objects are divided amongst six official classifications:[39] the *arpilleras* (quilt-work) collection, the personal object collection, the remnants collection—which consists of "restos de algún objeto o lugar de carácter histórico" (remainders of an object or place of historical value)—the prison craftwork collection, the general craftwork collection (notably "hechas en otros contextos, ejemplo talleres laborales," [made in other contexts, for example labor workshops]) and the historical objects collection—which are general objects "que dan cuenta de situaciones de violaciones y de defensa y protección de los DD.HH." (that give an account of situations of violations of, defense of, and protection of human rights).[40]

The displays of these objects within the permanent exhibits are accompanied by small, explanatory paragraphs drafted by the archivists and arranged to fit the narrative logic of the museum. The objects derive much of their power from the highlighting of their remarkable pasts in these paragraphs, but there is an entirely other element to their power that remains hidden underneath their surfaces. The confluence of that which the visitor to the museum can access and that which s/he cannot readily capture about each object places the individual object's ability to give testimony permanently in an in-between space of ambiguity; the visitor knows this object has a relevant past to transmit, that it was a witness to the history being recounted, yet the object itself cannot speak and the visitor is powerless to access it, save for the small explanatory paragraph created by the museum. The object's testimony remains to come, deferred, permanently haunted by the possibility of trans-mission. Yet, this possibility itself is productive as it mandates contemplation, reflection, pause. It requires the productive labors of memory upon its very encounter. It effects change in the viewer, thus creating the conditions for the destabilizing activism upon which testimonial practices are premised.

While not all of the objects on display at the Museum of Memory and Hu-man Rights are examples of prison craftwork, all hold a past that evidences in-teraction with the survivors, victims, or perpetrators of the political violence of the dictatorship in some facet. Jennifer Hansen-Glucklich, in her study of artifacts in memorial museums, specifically in Holocaust museums, argues that the role of such objects in museum exhibits is to promote a type of vi-sion she calls "witnessing vision,"[41] defined as "a way of seeing that responds to authentic artifacts within displays that are presented as witnesses to atroc-ities."[42] For Hansen-Glucklich, these objects have the capacity to transform visitors into "vicarious witnesses."[43] Such objects can "act as traces metaphys-ically embodying their former owners"[44] and thus allow visitors contact with places and times that are otherwise beyond reach. This power of the object for Hansen-Glucklich hinges on its authenticity, on the aura of the *thing* at-tached to it by virtue of its remarkable past. In analyzing the exhibit of a pile of shoes at the United States Holocaust Memorial Museum, she argues that the display's presentation of these items as witnesses encourages visitors to

> see the shoes as material witnesses bearing testimony to the suffering of the victims. Their aura of genuine presence and the traces they bear of their former owners, who wore them and touched them and held them in their hands, evokes empathy.[45]

This empathy is precisely the type of pedagogical function the Museum of Memory and Human Rights (and, really, memorial museums in general) seeks to perform. As noted by Amy Sodaro in her study of the museum, the mission of the site is "to reveal the truth about what happened and to allow dignity for victims and their families, stimulate reflection and debate and to promote respect and tolerance in order that these events never happen again."[46] The encounter with the authentic object-witness, the encounter with its deferred testimony, transforms the visitor into a vicarious witness, moving the visitor to a place where s/he must contemplate the object in order to recognize a truth about the past and reflect on the impact that past has on the present.

In a similar fashion to the objects on display at the Museum of Memory and Human Rights in Chile, the collection of *manualidades* on display at the Museum of Memory in Uruguay places the work, the material that was made as a resistance in the past, on display as a witness to the fight against the human rights violations of the dictatorship: "Allá en la ex Quinta de Santos, el Museo de la Memoria intenta reflejar los esfuerzos del pueblo uruguayo en su lucha contra el terrorismo de Estado"[47] (There in the former Santos Mansion, the Museum of Memory intends to reflect the efforts of the Uruguayan people in the fight against State terrorism). The director of the Uruguayan Museum of Memory (MUME), Elbio Ferrario, himself a former political prisoner, explains:

> Toda la acción del Museo de la Memoria estará orientada a combatir la mentalidad que dio lugar a la implantación de la dictadura en nuestro país en el pasado reciente, para que nunca más origine los hechos y realidades pavorosas que tuvimos que vivir, para que nuestros hijos y los hijos de nuestros hijos nunca más tengan que sufrir el terrorismo de Estado y la violación de los derechos humanos. El Museo de la Memoria promoverá los valores de la paz, la Democracia, la Justicia Social y los Derechos Humanos.[48]

> (All of the actions of the Museum of Memory will be oriented toward combatting the mentality that gave way to the implementation of the dictatorship in our country during the recent past, so that the events and horrific realities that we had to live never rise again, so that our children and our children's children never again have to suffer State terrorism and the violation of human rights. The Museum of Memory will promote the values of peace, Democracy, Social Justice, and Human Rights.)

There is a pedagogical function here (a continuation of the *lucha*) in the use of the objects of the past as a form of material testimony in the museum. Recently, Daniel Link argued that the contact *testimonio* has had with the community, outside of the realm of the judicial, has an outreach component — which he terms the "fuerza pedagógica"[49] (pedagogical force) — that is currently causing the main fracture in debates over *testimonio*'s ability to "tell" truths. Link argues:

> El testimonio no está del lado de la verdad, sino del lado de la experiencia. Y la experiencia no es previa al acto de discurso en el que se constituye (la narración), como tampoco puede ser previo el sujeto al proceso mismo de subjetivación y de desubjetivación (ascesis) del que paradójicamente depende. Por eso mismo, la fuerza pedagógica del testimonio no se resuelve en sede judicial, epistemológica o estética, sino en sede ética.[50]

> (Testimonio is not on the side of truth, but rather the side of experience. And experience is not prior to the discursive act in which it is constituted (narration), just as the subject can't exist prior to the very process of subjectification and desubjectification (ascesis) on which it paradoxically depends. For this very reason, the pedagogical force of testimonio does not determine itself within the judicial, epistemological or ethical sides of testimonio, but in the ethical side.)

This view echoes an early one articulated by Ariel Dorfman, that the majority of the initial testimonial efforts in Chile were "urgidos por la necesidad de denuncia política y de instruir a una opinión pública conmovida y asqueada"[51] (170) (urged by the necessity of political denunciation and of creating a moved and nauseated public opinion). In this same essay, Dorfman argues that there are three main functions to testimonial writing: "*acusar* a los verdugos, *recordar* los sufrimientos y epopeyas, *animar* a los otros combatientes en medio del repliegue"[52] (*to accuse* the executioners, *to remember* the suffering and heroic deeds, *to animate* the other combatants in the midst of retreat). The last of these functions, *to animate*, points to a pedagogically motivated function in which testimony is meant to spur to action others who are currently in the fight against repression, or in the case at hand, in the retreat from the struggle and at the precipice of the fight for the recuperation of the exemplary memory of the past.

The object in the museum, standing in for the survivors and victims, itself holds a prior knowledge, the marks of having-once-been. As discussed above, in the space of the museum the material witness has the capacity to effect change, to create empathy, to animate. These objects, as Francine Masiello urges that art must do in the post-dictatorship, "force us to think of interpretive strategies of resistance, interrogating the past and leading to a politics of cognition with which to move toward the future."[53] This is not a parallel agency to the human, nor is the object a stand-in for the past person. To say that it were would undermine the authority and power of movements that seek to find lost loved ones—who definitively remain in *limbo*— *disappeared*, not *dead*. Yet, the object does remain haunted by the past presence of the detained or the disappeared, even if that person is still alive, known, and can speak.

In their analysis of books carefully crafted by Holocaust victims in the concentration camps, Hirsch and Spitzer note that objects were "collectively made in the camp in communal acts of defiance and resistance, constituting unconventional collective memoirs marked by the bodily imprints of their authors."[54] As Hirsch and Spitzer note in their study, the meaning found in many of these objects for the prisoners themselves is lost to us, but the objects still constitute a species of "invaluable record—a testimonial object, a point of memory,"[55] which transmits information meant to be lost to oblivion, wiped away with the elimination of peoples and bodies. It gestures to the rebellion presented by the imbuing of memory in such objects and evidences the destabilizing presence these physical items continue to have. These objects—evidence which stays behind even after the extreme act of disappearing the detained was undertaken by dictatorship forces—show that the spectral presence of the disappeared cannot be erased or removed from society.

Haunted Objects in the Archive

In addition to incorporating material witnesses into memorial museums, memory projects in the Southern Cone also employ such strategies in archival-like exhibits that seek to provide an outlet for everyday citizens to contribute their memories of the past to the documentation of the dictatorship's violence. I turn now to a consideration of two of these projects, the online/virtual exposition *Vestigios* and the workshop and temporary exhibit *Química de la memoria* from 2007 at the Museum of Memory in Rosario, Argentina by Argentine artist Marga Steinwasser, and Argentine sociologist

María Antonia Sánchez. Together, these projects highlight how objects from the time period of the dictatorship carry with them the specters of the violence of the time, waiting for the moment in which that ghostly aura will be activated to bring the past into the present via a haunting that produces, as Avery Gordon terms it, "a something-to-be-done"[56] capable of creating movement and change.[57] In what follows, I will explore how this process is activated in each of these projects.

Vestigios, an ongoing memory project by the Argentine non-governmental organization Memoria Abierta (Open Memory), invites survivors and families in the post-dictatorship to submit photographs and written histories showing and explaining what they consider important objects of memory connected to the period of the last military dictatorship in Argentina. The project casts a wide net for participation in the creation of this archive, inviting "familiares y amigos de víctimas—u otras personas que hayan tenido participación política durante la última dictadura militar"[58] (family members and friends of victims—or other persons that had political participation during the last military dictatorship) to contribute objects that they've kept from the years of repression. The proposal of the exhibit looks to

> explorar la capacidad que tienen los objetos para establecer relaciones entre pasado y presente de manera que puedan ser utilizados como vehículos para la transmisión de la memoria y que, al mismo tiempo, promuevan el debate y la reflexión . . . creemos que de esta manera se accede a una dimensión distinta del periódo de terrorismo de Estado, una perspectiva personal habitualmente ausente en los relatos históricos y que contribuye a la construcción de una memoria colectiva.[59]

> (explore the capacity that objects have to establish relationships between the past and present such that they can be utilized as vehicles for the transmission of memory and, at the same time, promote debate and reflection . . . we believe that in this way one accesses a distinct dimension of the period of State terrorism, a personal perspective that is habitually absent from the historical accounts and that contributes to the construction of collective memory.)

In their proposal, one can observe the recognition of the testimony held in the object, as well as see the dedication to a type of democratization of the archive, including personal perspectives that official history often ignores—a premise shared by testimonio as a literary genre. Incorporating these absented views via the contribution of objects gestures toward Gordon's project of exploring the role of haunting in the sociological imagination by attempting to access that which has been pushed out or outright ignored in the desire to construct and maintain a status quo that conserves an orderly approach to the past.

In contrast to the encounter with the object in the Memory Museum, the visitor to *Vestigios* doesn't approach the physical object to contemplate it in person, however the photograph and short narrative that they encounter still transmits a knowledge about the object that can promote contemplation of the object's past. Julian Bleecker identifies an agency held by internet objects (what he calls "blogjects"[60]) in the virtual times in which we live, arguing that these blogjects hold an agency that, though not parallel to the human, is an agency nonetheless, capable of impacting our cultural behaviors. In *Vestigios* the photographed object holds this agency, more weighted than an object of mourning, or one that metonymically affects our neurological processes of memory. In her exploration of Domingo Gribaldi's effort to use photography as a contribution to the creation of collective memory in Peru following the report by the Peruvian Truth and Reconciliation Commission, Margarita Saona considers the memorial power of photographed objects, what she terms "plain things" and argues that such objects "consistently embody mnemonic mechanisms highlighted by current research on cognition."[61] Saona contends that plain things carry a "metonymic aspect in the way objects represent absence."[62] Exploring metonymy and space, she argues that plain things "produce in us 'memory-like' effects"[63] in that "we feel as if we 'remember,'"[64] a process that occurs even for those who have not experienced the traumatic event. While I do not disagree with Saona's assessment, I wish to push this process a bit further and examine the way the object does transmit a (spectral) form of knowing to the visitor, even s/he who has no personal memory of the event in question, and even if that transmission simultaneously communicates memory and calls attention to the impossibility of that same transmission of memory.

Vestigios, as a virtual space of memory, a work in progress, provides a space for the labors of memory to take place. The puzzle-like placement of the images of the objects on the website transmits to the visitor an understanding of this memory as recuperative work in progress, inviting participation into the struggle for completion. While the narratives submitted alongside the ob-

10. *Anillos de Elena Kalaidjian*. Colección Vestigios, Memoria Abierta.
Reproduced with permission from Memoria Abierta.

jects are compelling in and of themselves, the true impact of these renderings of the past come from the accompanying images of the objects themselves. We are not only being told about a ring that had been worn by a disappeared sister, which was discovered along with her bodily remains, we are shown an image of the recovered ring in its full material form [Image 10].

Although the examples of objects included in *Vestigios* are not all examples of collective labors, or even all handmade items such as the *manualidades* and the *artesanías carcelarias*, they can be read as a type of material memoir that carry the bodily imprints of their past owners via the visible manifestation of their individual personalities, tastes, and attempts at survival. Many of the objects included in *Vestigios* are things that have been preserved by family members of disappeared loved ones, or, as in the case of these rings, that have been recovered since the time of the family member's disappearance. The written story/explanation that accompanies these rings on the website explains that they were recovered by the Equipo Argentino de Antropología Forense (Argentine Forensic Anthropology Team [EAAF]) when they located the body of Elena in the cemetary of La Chacarita. The rings were returned to Elena's siblings upon informing them of the identification of the body. With the forensic anthropology team's information, Adriana relates that "los anillos supuestamente los tenía puestos el día que la fusilaron"[65] (the rings, she supposedly had them on the day that they shot her). While she recognizes the tortoiseshell ring, the other she does not, leading her to speculate that "alguien se lo dio en el campo clandestino donde estaba secuestrada o es algo que ella encontró"[66] (someone gave it to her in the clandestine camp where she was kidnapped or it's something that she found). The rings, encountered by the EAAF on the recovered body of Elena, are haunted objects of the past that carry with them a story to tell. Yet, they cannot narrate that story on their own; their ghostly aura requires activation from the present. This haunting of the object, this suspicion, produces "a something-to-be-done,"[67] which in the case of the forensic inquiry is an investigation into the object's history. In the space of the online archive the "something-to-be-done" produced by the object is a critical reflection on Elena's story, as related via the object, provoked in the viewer-turned-vicarious-witness to the past.

The 2007 exhibit *Química de la memoria* at the Museum of Memory in Rosario, Argentina operated from a similar stance as *Vestigios*, but instead of inviting submission of photographs of objects and their written stories to an online archive, it advertised an open call for participation in workshops to create the exhibition, during which participants "were asked to bring an object that would remind them 'biographically' of the time of the dictatorship; this object was to be attached to a small information card that would explain details about it or why it was selected."[68] The "chemistry" of the exhibit resulted from the way in which the objects came together in three separate displays over three tables [Image 11]. The first consisted of objects brought by those who were living during the dictatorship and were aware of its power. The second table was filled with objects brought by those who were living during the dictatorship, but unaware of its abuses. The third table consisted of objects submitted by those who were born after the dictatorship (after 1976).[69]

The exhibit departed from the stance that "todo objeto es porteador de una historia, y de manera visible o invisible, lleva inscripta la huella de sus poseedores"[70] (every object is a carrier of a history, and in a visible or invisible way, carries inscribed on it the trace of its possessors). Thus, the gathering together of these objects within the exhibit is not purely a compendium of inanimate *things*, but the gathering together of material witnesses haunted by their former possessors, placing on display the impact of the dictatorial past

11. *Química de la Memoria.* Reproduced with permission from Marga Steinwasser.

on a collective humanity and asking the objects to, as a collective, transmit a spectral testimony from the past. For historian Juan Felipe Hernández,

> the objects of *La Química* strive to acquire their own voice from the abyss of forgetfulness and instrumentalization, and in this vocalization they try to emit broken sounds that slowly weave the larger fabric of the project. *La Química* can effectively be located in the constellation of contemporary memory art as a smart attempt to open channels of dialogue and interrogation in face of the official narratives of closure and the culture of forgetfulness.[71]

Química de la memoria is an example of the way in which objects from the past are haunted by their prior contexts; of how an object can serve as a punctum to bring forth and transmit an aspect of the past; and of how encountering the object in the museum, or within a narrative framework that activates the ghostly specter of the authentic material witness, conjures within the present that which was meant to be left in the past, as Hernández pinpoints, in the culture of forgetfulness that characterizes much of the official narratives related to the dictatorships. *Química de la memoria*'s success at accomplishing this mission can be observed in its repetition at the Museum of Memory in Uruguay (2011) and at the Museum of Memory and Human Rights in Santiago (2013). Additionally, it is an example that shows how all three countries under consideration in this study share a valorization of the object's ability to relate the past to the present.

Spectral Testimony: Toward a Theory of the Truth-Telling Capacity of Objects

As I explored in the first half of this project, emerging theories of the philosophy of objects posit that, like humans, objects have an interior being of their own: "tool-being"[72] or "vibrant matter."[73] This being normally hides in plain view, in the ready-at-hand tools that we use in the day-to-day.[74] Yet, every once in a while, human *Dasein* encounters a broken tool,[75] the tool becomes present-at-hand, and we, if only fleetingly, become aware of a being held within the object, for "equipment is not effective 'because people use it'; on the contrary, it can only be used because it is *capable of an effect*, of inflicting some kind of blow on reality."[76] In the case of the detention center, it is not necessarily the *object* that is encountered as a broken tool, but the occupied world that undergoes this transformation. The entire reality in which the prisoner exists is altered, thus calling attention to the tool-being of not only specific objects, but of *all* the matter that occupies the space of mistreatment.

The result of this re-ordering is the production of a new meaning of the object for the disappeared person, but also for the rest of society. The doubt that remains attached to objects—their integral function in not only the dictatorship's project of control, but in the resistance by the detained—changes the prior context of the object, imbuing it with not only its own past, but a phantasmal presence that remains residually attached to its materiality even after the disappearance of the person for whom it represented hope, resistance, rebuilt subjectivity, and even life.

The objects that remain after disappearance are indelibly marked by the past presences of their owners. At the outset of *Specters of Marx: The State of the Debt, the Work of Mourning, and the New International*, Jacques Derrida states: "the name of the one who disappeared must have gotten inscribed somewhere else."[77] This "somewhere else" forms the basis of his study, in which he inquires into the continual spectral presence of Marx in society. In

12. *Relojes de Gregorio Sember*. Colección Vestigios, Memoria Abierta.
Reproduced with permission from Memoria Abierta

the case of the disappeared in the post-dictatorship, this "somewhere else" where their name has been inscribed is, in one instance, the object, their former possession. The object becomes an intermediary, permitting access to the ghost, creating a means by which to speak with the haunting presence of the disappeared.

Another example from *Vestigios* highlights this notion very clearly: the father of this watch's [Image 12] disappeared owner, Gregorio Marcelo "Guyo" Sember, explains the origin of this object:

> Cuando estaba siendo secuestrado de su hogar, Guyo se quitó el reloj y se lo dio a su padre. Éste se lo puso ese día y no volvió a quitárselo esperando el regreso de su hijo.[78]

> (When he was being kidnapped from his home, Guyo removed the watch and gave it to his father. He put it on that day and didn't remove it again, awaiting the return of his son.)

The spectrality of the object is highlighted in the second portion of this account:

En 1978, el padre de Guyo fue asaltado y los ladrones se llevaron el reloj. Preocupado por que su esposa no note su ausencia compró otro similar. Dos años después el reloj que estaba usando se detuvo y cuando lo
llevó al relojero descubrió que otro cliente que estaba allí antes que él tenía el reloj de Guyo. Logró recuperarlo y desde entonces conserva ambos
relojes.[79]

(In 1978, Guyo's father was assaulted and the thieves took his watch. Wor-
ried that his wife would note its absence, he bought another, similar one.
Two years later, the watch that he was using stopped and when he brought
it to the watchmaker, he discovered that another client that was there before him had Guyo's watch. He was able to recover it and from that point
on he keeps both watches.)

The return of the watch signals that which Derrida posits regarding the
phantom presence of Marx, of the eternal waiting for that-to-come. The imbuing of a material object with the presence of its owner marks that non-
decomposable object with a durability that outlasts the decay experienced by
the body. The case of this watch, in its sudden appearance, and the father's
recognition of it, points to a haunting presence that objects hold in society, a
destabilizing memory possibility.

In the documentary film *Nostalgia de la luz*, Patricio Guzmán turns to the
material world's ability to speak and explores the Chilean Atacama desert's
own memory possibilities, saying that:

Es una tierra castigada, impregnada de sal donde los restos humanos se
momifican y los objetos permanecen. El aire, transparente, delgado, nos
permite leer en este gran libro abierto de la memoria hoja por hoja.[80]

(It's a condemned land, permeated with salt, where human remains are
mummified and objects are frozen in time. The air, transparent, thin, permits us to read this great open book of memory, page by page.)

In the space of the desert, the presence of the past is palpable. The dust-
covered, abandoned possessions of those who died in the desert still have
movement: a jacket sways in the air, hanging spoons sing, inanimate objects
seem not so inanimate. The preservative qualities of the desert provoke astronomers to seek "los secretos del cielo"[81] (the secrets of the sky) that "se
fueron cayendo sobre nosotros uno a uno como una lluvia transparente"[82]

(fell on us, one by one, like a transparent rain). But they also give hope to those who lost loved ones in Pinochet's dictatorship, who take to the dry land in an obstinate search for bodily remains.

Vicky Saavedra recovers "un pie. Un pie que estaba dentro del zapato"[83] (a foot. A foot that was within a shoe). This foot, her brother's, along with other fragments of his skull, yield enough information to determine that Pepe was shot twice, demonstrating the evidentiary capacity of human remains. But this capacity, a testimonial function, goes beyond the simply evidentiary. Vicky describes her last encounter with her brother:

> Recordaba esa mirada cariñosa y todo estaba resumido en eso. En unos dientes, en unos pedazos de huesos. Y un pie. Un pie que aunque parezca increíble, el último encuentro de mi hermano fue con un pie que yo tuve en mi casa. Porque cuando se encontró la fosa, yo sabía que era el zapato de Pepé. Sabía que era el pie de Pepé. Y en la noche como a las tres de la mañana yo me levanté y me puse a cariñar a su pie. Y tenía un olor de descomposición. Estaba en su calcetín. Un calcetín color así concha vino. ¿Granada? No sé. Un rojo oscuro. Y lo saqué de la bolsa. Lo miraba. Después me senté en un sillón del living. Estuve como horas sentada pero en blanco. Totalmente en blanco. No tenía la capacidad de pensar en nada. Estaba impactada, choqueada por eso. Y al día siguiente mi marido se fue a trabajar y pasé toda la mañana con el pie de mi hermano. Estábamos reencontrándonos. Fue el gran reencuentro y quizás la gran desilusión también. Porque en ese momento yo recién tomé conciencia que mi hermano estaba muerto.[84]

(I remembered his tender expression and this was all that remained . . . a few teeth and bits of bones. And a foot. And, even if it appears incredible, our final moment together, was with a foot that I had at my house. Because when they found the mass grave, I knew it was Pepe's shoe. I knew that it was Pepe's foot. That night at around three o'clock in the morning I got up and went to stroke his foot. There was a smell of decay. It was still in his sock. A burgundy sock. A dark red? I don't know—a dark red. I took it out of the bag and looked at it. I remained sitting in the living room. I was seated there for some hours, but with my mind in blank. Totally in blank. I didn't have the capacity to think about anything. I was moved, totally shocked. The next day, my husband got up and went to work, and I spent the whole morning with my brother's foot. We were re-encountering each other. It was the great re-encounter. And perhaps the great disillusionment as well because in that moment, I suddenly became aware that my brother was dead.)

Vicky attempts to find the answers, the representability of the past, in her exchange with her brother's foot, sock, and shoe. But, it ultimately leads to the disillusioning realization that her brother is dead. No longer disappeared, but confirmed dead. However, this disillusionment may also refer to the incompleteness of the testimony she is able to perceive from the material remains of her brother. We remember Agamben's paradox: the *Muselmann* is a "complete witness,"[85] a remnant that functions as a telos between he who can speak (has subjectivity) and he who cannot (the desubjectified, non-human, or the dead): "the remnants of Auschwitz—the witnesses—are neither the dead nor the survivors, neither the drowned nor the saved. *They are what remains* between them."[86] The foot, the shoe, the sock remain between Pepe and Vicky. They are Agamben's most complete witness—they were *there* at the scene of violence. But they may also be incapable of transparently witnessing.

If the Muselmann as a "complete witness" is this remnant, in the function of a telos, joining the living being and the speaking being, the human and the inhuman,[87] can the same function be extended to the material remains of the dead? And, can we extend this function to the material objects that are now seen in exhibits such as *Vestigios, Química de la Memoria*, and the permanent displays of the Museums of Memory? Here, I turn to a consideration of the object's ability to testify, asking: can the remnant be an object? Or, can an object be the witness to a remnant, a remain? To the ghostly presence of the victim? And, if so, to where is the object joining us?

Agamben declares: "we will not understand what Auschwitz is if we do not first understand who or what the Muselmann is—*if we do not learn to gaze with him* ... "[88] Agamben calls on us to look differently at the testimony offered by the Muselmann. The same call is echoed in Derrida's *Specters of Marx* and his declaration that *we need to learn to live with ghosts*.[89] Hansen-Glucklich evokes the same call in asking the museum-goer to activate witnessing vision and become a vicarious witness. And Gordon asks haunting to produce in us a "something-to-be-done."[90] However, in all of these encounters, one must accept that the full knowledge of the truth about the disappeared does not exist in a realm in which we are able to openly dialogue with it. No complete witness exists to answer our questions. We rely on the incomplete memory, this zone of the "in between" in order to construct in the present a knowledge about the past. In the absence of this witness, the object—mass-produced, manmade, or even corporal—steps in to help us (even if incompletely) in our labors to fill the gaps. Derrida writes:

> The specter, as its name indicates, is the *frequency* of a certain visibility. But the visibility of the invisible. And visibility, by its essence, is not seen, which is why it remains beyond the phenomenon or beyond being. The specter is also, among other things, what one imagines, what one thinks one sees and which one projects—on an imaginary screen where there is nothing to see.[91]

If objects are haunted by the spectral presences of their previous inhabitants, this hauntology constitutes a repetitive act whose comings and goings cannot be controlled.[92] This haunting presence reveals the destabilizing nature of the object in the case of the disappeared. These objects are specters of possibility,[93] a way of accessing memory and destabilizing homogenizing attempts at forgetting in transitional governments.

The residual phantom presence that haunts the object and gives it a "specter of possibility" also imbues it with the power of what I am calling spectral testimony. It is a different form of deferred agency that lies in the realm of the just beyond. It is a concept I connect to Agamben's notion of the third state of the Muselmann, but also to Derrida's ruminations on the specter of Marx that continues to haunt our society, as well as Avery Gordon's identification of the political capital of haunting. Spectral testimony interpellates the viewer in the present with a deferred past and requires him/her to do the work of memory, to contemplate what the object offers.

Going back to Idelber Avelar, the unrepresentability of the atrocities, of what *really* happened, by issue of its incomprehensibility produces a reliance on allegory: all testimonial recountings of the past end up in the realm of the allegorical, a tethering from the present to the third realm of an unrepresentable past. The object, the material, the non-subject that touched the subjectivity that was once present, is the tether between the two. It was present, but it cannot place into our system of understanding the words that would make coherent to us their experiences in the past. Instead, it activates the pedagogical force (Link) of testimony, it animates the viewer (Dorfman), and promotes ongoing dialogue (Sanjinés) and human rights work in the present.

In *Nostalgia de la luz*, it is not only the material form that holds a truth-telling capacity, but it is light that is equated to beingness, the calcium of the

13. *Colgante realizado en la cárcel por Diana Cruces.* Colección Vestigios, Memoria Abierta. Reproduced with permission from Memoria Abierta

stars directly identified with the calcium that makes up human bones. If we consider the following image [Image 13], of a pendant carved out of bone by a prisoner using a coin, one can see continuity between the material and the cosmos. There is a temporal jump between the present and the past; we are viewing stars that died long ago, yet remain present to us, gesturing to an ongoing continuity of presences.

In Guzmán's film, this continuity of presences is palpable. The physical terrain of the Atacama Desert, particularly its lack of humidity, produces conditions ideal not only for the preservation of material remains, but for the clear connection between earth and the cosmos, for both boil down to a question of light.[94] Astronomer Gaspar Galaz remarks:

Todas las experiencias que uno tiene en la vida en realidad, [. . .] incluso esta conversación, ocurren en el pasado. Aunque sean millonésimas o milésimas de segundos. Pero, claro, o sea la cámara que yo estoy mirando ahora está a unos cuantos metros de distancia. Por lo tanto ya está unas millonésimas o algo así digamos de tiempo atrás, en el pasado respecto al tiempo que yo . . . que yo tengo en mi reloj. Porque la señal se demora en llegar. La luz de la cámara ... o la luz tuya ... reflejada, se demora en llegar a mí. Una fracción de segundos, una fracción muy pequeña de segundos porque la luz es muy, muy rápida ... Ésta es la trampa. El presente no existe.[95]

(In reality all of our life experiences, including this conversation, happen in the past. Even if it is a matter of millionths or thousandths of a second. The camera I am looking at now is a few meters away and is therefore already several millionths of a second in the past in relation to the time I have on my watch. Because the signal takes time to arrive. The light from the camera or the light reflected from you takes time to reach me. A fraction of a second, a very small fraction of a second, as the speed of light is very, very fast ... That's the trick. The present does not exist.)

This link, the "misterio de la ciencia"[96] (mystery of science), both spatial and temporal, as emphasized by the astronomers in the film, creates a nexus between the fleeting present and the seemingly unreachable distance of the origin of things (this material origin being the elements, especially the calcium, that was produced in the stars). The overlay of the specks of light (the stars) upon images of women searching for remains of their disappeared loved ones in the desert augments this connection and conjures forth onto the camera's plane the simultaneity of existence between past (the measurable light/calcium/matter from the stars) and present (the calcium in the bodies of those who search, but also in that present in the hidden remains of the desert), producing a haunting commingling that is not just imagined but measurably real, and speaks in its own way through the materials that are left behind, even those that remain to be found; for as archeologist Lautaro Nuñez predicts in the film, one day the remains will appear. And when they do, they will conjure forth that truth which was already present and giving a spectral, always-to-come, yet still productive testimony. If the material world was so integral to the detained subject in prison, it also remains integral for those who seek to reconstruct the past, to access the third realm of the unrepresentable, to commingle with ghosts in order to know that which happened in the past, but remains remarkably present in the ever-fleeting today.

CHAPTER FOUR

Bodily Incarnations—Forensic Memory and Hauntings in the Everyday

❧

The desaparecidos—those 'vanished' victims whose deaths have consistently been denied or covered up by the military—offer a particularly salient problem with regard to narrating the past precisely because their voices have been silenced forever . . . Because they are dead, they will never bear witness to the abominable horrors they suffered, nor will they tell of how their bodies were tortured, mutilated, disposed of in common graves or dropped from military planes into the sea. To be certain, they are the dictatorship's most obstinate legacy: they stand as a marked narrative void in the history of the regime.[1]

Body Talk: Disappearance and Disappearance with Life

One of the most impactful legacies in the wake of the violence of the Southern Cone dictatorships is that of the policy of enforced disappearance of persons, whereby the state, instead of officially arresting someone, simply vanished them, their whereabouts remaining unknown to their family members in many cases to this day. During the repression in Argentina it is estimated that 30,000 people disappeared. In Chile, that number stands at roughly 3,500[2] and in Uruguay, according to a 2007 report from the Argentine Forensic Anthropology Team, an estimated 150.[3] The Argentine *Nunca más* (*Never Again*) report concludes that there were multiple reasons for which disappearance became a strategy of the Military Junta's reaction to quelling the momentum of what they deemed "subversive" politics during the Dirty War, including a desire to "paralizar el reclamo público" (paralyze public outcry); "bloquear los caminos de investigación de los hechos concretos" (block recourses to investigation of the concrete facts); and "impedir por todos los medios que se manifestara la solidaridad de la población" (impede by all means possible the manifestation of solidarity among the people).[4] In addition to disappearing those who they deemed a political threat to the state, the dictatorship's forces also disappeared many of the children of these actors, especially when mothers were pregnant at the time of their detention and gave birth during their captivity. In some of the most perverse cases, the dictatorship intentionally kept the mothers alive until the birth of their children, in order to then "give" the children to an upstanding military family who would raise them as their own, under the "correct" political ideology. The children of the disappeared that were appropriated at birth, or shortly thereafter, and raised as the children of military families, are in some circles (namely within the main activist group that searches for them, the Grandmothers of the Plaza de Mayo) known as *desaparecidos con vida* (disappeared with life).[5] The collocation of this identity sets them both in relation to their parents (both groups being *desaparecidos*) and apart from them (the children carry the descriptive identifier *con vida* [with life] while neither the same modifier nor its antonym, *con muerte* [with death], can be attributed to their parents). Many of these children survived and now constitute a "second generation" of victims, living lives without access to the truth of their identities. Activist groups, especially the Grandmothers of the Plaza de Mayo (a group composed of grandmothers whose grandchildren were disappeared), continue to search for those who were "disappeared with life" to this day. At the time I am writing at the end of 2019, 130 of these estimated 450 children have been located and "restituted," meaning they have had their identities returned to them, most often through blood and DNA testing. This biological link between the two generations of "disappeared" and the way it is being used to reveal histories meant to be hidden, as well as how this process impacts the representation of the body's testimonial capability forms the basis of this chapter's analysis.[6]

As news of cases of missing people began to circulate during the first Military Junta, the Commander in Chief of the Army, Jorge Rafael Videla, defined the term *desaparecido* in response to repeated inquiries by mothers regarding the whereabouts of their children. He (now infamously) explained: "It is a mystery, a *desaparecido*, a nonentity, it is not here: they are neither dead nor alive, they disappeared."[7] In juridical terms, this explanation meant that someone who disappeared did not figure into any official registries, their detention was not recognized by the police or the state, and a writ of habeas corpus (if presented) could be completely denied. With the 1994 adoption of the Inter-American Convention on Forced Disappearance of Persons, and the December 2006 adoption of the Disappearances Convention by the United Nations Assembly,[8] disappearance gained a concrete juridical category. However, what I am interested in pursuing in this chapter is not the juridical meaning of disappearance, but an exploration of the cultural impact of the practice and how the lack of access to the bodies of the disappeared produced a new awareness of the important potential the physical (the material) holds to fill gaps of information when the subject is no longer present to speak his/her story. For, what the preoccupation with disappearance has at its core is a worry over what the body could reveal post-mortem, over what evidence might be left behind and how that information (even if unidentifiable or unreadable at the moment of the crime—for example, DNA analysis was developed long after these crimes took place) could be used in the future.

In the opening quote to this chapter, Michael Lazzara eloquently identifies the *narrative void* left to impact society in the wake of disappearance in Chile. Like most considerations of testimonial production, his comment is often interpreted based on a privileging of the voice, in this case necessarily silenced and inaccessible due to disappearance.[9] As I explored in the previous chapter, the voice, the ability or inability to speak and be heard, to transmit via language one's experience has long preoccupied scholars of *testimonio*. Such preoccupations resonate perhaps even more strongly in the wake of disappearance, where the testimonial voice cannot even make the attempt to speak and be heard. But, Lazzara's comments also beg us to examine the narrative void left by the absence of the body. Disappearance, in removing access to the body, has the byproduct of producing an awareness of just how much information the material of the body has to offer, and calling attention to the narrative void left in its absence. In so doing, it contributes to the growing development of the present perception of the material's ability to speak in lieu of the voice, specifically the ways in which the bodies of the children of the disappeared are now perceived as a link to the memory of their parents, emphasizing the ability of their second-generation bodies (especially their DNA) to hold memory and yield a testimony about the past.

Disappearance, in not only ripping the subject from his/her life but eliminating the possibility of encountering any telling physical/forensic trace of that subject, actively (and purposefully) created a gap in knowledge about the past. In her study of the experience of the families of the disappeared, Ludmila da Silva Catela affirms that the search for the bodies of the disappeared "más allá de la necesidad de recuperar los cuerpos, se trata de una intensa voluntad de búsqueda de rescatar la historia de ese individuo"[10] (beyond the necessity of recovering the bodies, encompasses an intense will for a search to rescue the history of the individual). Thus, the search goes beyond the need to recuperate the body itself and looks forward to the body's ability to render visible or readable the individual experiences of the person, the life, the voice that once animated the physical remains. In short, the search ultimately seeks to fill the information vacuum, the narrative void, left by disappearance in the Southern Cone. As Pilar Calveiro puts it:

> La desaparición no es un eufemismo sino una alusión literal: una persona que a partir de determinado momento *desaparece*, se esfuma, sin que quede constancia de su vida o de su muerte. *No hay cuerpo de la víctima ni del delito*. Puede haber testigos del secuestro y presuposición del posterior asesinato, pero no hay un cuerpo material que dé testimonio del hecho.[11]

> (Disappearance is not a euphemism, but a literal allusion: a person that from a certain point on *disappears*, vanishes, without leaving a trace of their life or their death. *There is no body of the victim nor of the crime*. There can be witnesses to the kidnapping and a presumed posterior murder, but there is no material body that can give testimony to the event.)

Without a body, there can be no reconstruction of the crime. Death cannot be confirmed and few details of what happened to the subject can be established. But, fundamentally, these comments reveal that the byproduct of disappearance is a new awareness of the ability of the material body to give testimony to the past, even when the subject that inhabited that body is no longer alive to speak.

In this chapter, I propose to re-examine the place of the body in reconstructing events related to disappearance and the effects this work had on shaping the cultural production related to the Generation of HIJOS. While it is undeniably true that disappearance indicates the complete absence of body/voice and evidence of the crime, categorically affirming that the absence of a material body removes the possibility of testimony about the crime closes off the consideration of how second-generation bodies may contribute to the reconstruction of this *narrative void* left over from the past, eliminating the necessity of access to the body of the disappeared in order to yield information about this past. As Alexis Howe urges in the case of Chile, "as a practice, disappearance invites us to rethink not only the dictatorship but also the persistence of disappearance, and its effects or new practices, in the present."[12] In this chapter, I seek to first highlight the way in which evolving practices in the approach to investigating the disappearance of the "first-generation" victims influenced the narrative of memory related to the search for the "second-generation" victims. In Argentina, one of the most iconic symbols of the effort to keep the memory of the disappeared present in activism is the use of their photographs, portraits, and silhouettes to demarcate their absence.[13] This practice of using photographs also carries over into the searches for the "second-generation" disappeared, in those cases where disappeared children were known to the families prior to their disappearance.[14] In the case of the first generation, without a body to mourn, the photograph or the silhouette in the form of a human body stands in to highlight absence and conjure forth a specter from the past. In the case of the second generation, the photograph highlights absence, and begs society to question the lasting presence of the violence and to re-examine the truth of the familial relationships formed during that time, sowing suspicion around perceived resemblance between photographs of parents and the living beings of those who could have been their children in the present. In one well-known example, retold in the Argentine documentary film *El último confín* (Pablo Ratto, 2004), Horacio Pietragalla discovers that his parents are not his birthparents—a testimony that comes from an analysis of his blood. However, his girlfriend, upon finding out the news, finds such a striking similarity between a photograph of a disappeared woman she finds online and Horacio that she ends up locating his mother for him. Horacio explains:

> Faltaba saber digamos de qué familia era. A todo esto, ya mi novia se había metido en internet y había encontrado una foto de la . . . de mi mamá. Y vio tan parecido el rostro que . . . en primero . . . que me dijo 'para mí es tu mamá.' Y era mi mamá.[15]

> (What family I was from remained to be determined, you could say. Given this, my girlfriend had already gotten on the internet and had found a photo of the . . . of my mother. And she saw the face so similar that . . . at first . . . that she said 'for me, she's your mom.' And it was my mom.)

While in this case Horacio and his girlfriend already knew that his "parents" were not his biological parents prior to discovering the family resemblance between him and the photograph of the disappeared woman, family resemblance (i.e. the genetic link between the bodies of parent and child) between the first-generation victims and the Generation of HIJOS evokes a specter of doubt that remains within post-dictatorship society, as evidenced by the suspicion about the woman in the photograph. The legacy of *testimonio* and the activism of groups that search for the disappeared with life is precisely this effort to activate the doubt, and through an exploration of the genetic link between the bodies of the two generations, relate or reveal the truth about the past that haunts the present.

As I emphasized in the previous chapter, writing testimony is an act of memory transmission through time, meant to reconstruct information (often in order to denounce a crime) and fill a void of knowledge. In the case of the disappeared, these gaps, due to absence, in many cases remain unfilled. But this does not mean that memory work in the post-dictatorship—especially that undertaken by groups such as H.I.J.O.S—is not actively trying to fill these voids. The efforts to do so most often manifest through a reevaluation or re-signifying of the material world, most often centered on highlighting the presence of the body's absence.[16]

In this simultaneous presence and absence, the figure of the *desaparecido* translates rather directly to the notion of the specter, an entity neither present (nonappearance constitutes the very core of being disappeared) nor absent (the figure of the *desaparecido* is now ubiquitous in discussions of the recent violent past). As I began to explore in my previous chapter, in *Specters of Marx*, Jacques Derrida locates the present in an in-between space and argues that Marxism's presence remains in this temporality, as a spectral figure, a spectral moment, a living on with which we must learn to reckon.[17] This premise recalls Giorgio Agamben's discussion of the figure of the Muselmann as a being located in a point between life and death, between the human and the non-human, between subjectivity and de-subjectivity. Similarly to the objects of the past, the disappeared (with this I refer to their actual material bodies) remain in this in-between temporality of an always delayed forever-to-come, as their deaths are not confirmed and the full history of what happened to them remains pending.[18] The absence of their bodies (and the history they offer) has a spectral effect that undoes the opposition between past present and future present; there is a continual doubt regarding the possibility of their experience, of the encounter with their remains. What's more, even after that encounter with the material of the found body, the frustration it produces in us as we attempt to read a whole truth from it recalls to us simultaneously the demand for and the limitations of knowing. Derrida argues that the disjuncture in Marx's writings comes from the demand (which can never be always present, it can only be possible in order to remain a demand), from the immanence of revolution. The power of the disappeared, their ongoing political power, stems from their absence coupled with the possibility of their return: "a funerary note already echoed there—crepuscular, spectral, and therefore resurrectional. Re-insurrectional."[19] This re-insurrectional aspect of the presence-to-come does not need to wait for the body's re-appearance, for the act of re-appearing would negate its insurrectional quality; it would negate its power. This is the political power of the disappeared body that threatens return, and this is why Derrida insists that we must learn to speak with ghosts.

The ghosts of the disappeared affect political power via their motivational quality.[20] For this reason, we see the Madres de la Plaza de Mayo drawing inspiration from the past political acts of their children and wearing scarves with the names of their missing children while they go about their efforts to create change in the present. The scarf, originally made from the cloth diapers the mothers used on their children, is a spectral object haunted by the disappeared person, whose ghostly presence in society conjures forth the always-to-come disappeared, speaking with their absence—the cloth contains the residues of the past, the "secret stains,"[21] impossible for the mothers to forget. In much the same way, the body of the child of disappeared parents is a spectral object haunted by this disappearance. The identification of his/her body as a present manifestation of this DNA of the past generation marks the child with the simultaneous absence of his/her parent as a living subject and the spectral presence of a part of that parent, in the continuation of the parental DNA within the child's DNA. The identification/restitution of the child conjures forth the knowledge of the past, yet the continuing absence of the parent creates an ongoing expectancy or doubt over that which is to come. In the cases of the children of the disappeared who were appropriated, reappearance through restitution of identity is only ever partial, as they will forever be "marked" by the experience, yet it speaks with the absence of the disappeared parents and attempts to decipher information about the past.

As Derrida notes, there is not a singular specter of Marx that haunts, but a multiplicity of his previous being. Deciphering equals a species of transformation. In the case of Marx, deciphering re-codes his words. Similarly, the interaction with the specter of the disappeared changes from person to person, from child to child. Each invocation of the disappeared's specter remains marked by not only that particular spectral memory but also the subjectivity of the invoking person. It will never be the same evocation as the original, but it will always retain a piece of the original.[22] This evocation reads in Derrida's terms as "conjuring": "For to conjure means also to exorcise: to attempt both to destroy and to disavow a malignant, demonized, diabolical force, most often an evil-doing spirit, a specter, a kind of ghost who comes back or who still risks coming back post-mortem."[23] This is the danger of the disappeared for efforts at transitional democracy that want to exorcise the demonizing memory of the past: "effective exorcism pretends to declare the death only in order to put to death."[24] The fact that "the dead can often be more powerful than the living"[25] is observed in the political activism of H.I.J.O.S and the Mothers and Grandmothers of the Plaza de Mayo, all of which formed as groups after, and as a direct result of, the disappearance of their parents, children, and grandchildren. The destabilizing or revolutionary efforts attempted by those who eventually disappeared now, after disappearance, after conversion into a spectral presence, reach their culmination, their lasting destabilizing effect: "La lucha que nos parió" (the fight that birthed us), as H.I.J.O.S. often proclaims.[26] Thus, while for Derrida "the enemy to be conjured away is Marxism,"[27] in the case of post-dictatorship Southern Cone Latin America, the enemy to be conjured forth (and away) is the memory of violence, of trauma, the impact of disappearance, and the legacy of a political fight stopped in its tracks. Yet, that process continues to be disquieted as material traces continue to emerge. For each emergence, each new identification of a disappeared child is a return of the ghost, a conjured moment of spectral testimony that works in the present to negate closure and to reactivate the fight for memory.

In lieu of ontology, Derrida argues for the practice of hauntology (a performative interpretation, an interpretation that transforms what it interprets). Thus, in the case of the post-dictatorship, the study of the disappeared via an approximation of "hauntology" transforms the object of the disappeared (the discussion of their absent bodies) into a discourse that challenges the dominant, hegemonic narrative of forgetting. Derrida asserts that we have to "assume the inheritance"[28] of Marxism. In the case of Argentina, the children of the disappeared quite literally assume the inheritance of their parents, genetically continuing the material of the bodies of the disappeared with their very *being* in this world. The practice of "hauntology," the transformation of the object into a discourse that challenges, is observed in the ongoing cultural production related to the Generation of HIJOS that highlights this link.

This chapter explores the impact disappearance had and continues to have on Southern Cone post-dictatorship society's view toward the capacity of the body to remember and to "speak" or "testify," especially the bodies of the children of the disappeared that are the living physical material remainder of their parents. This chapter will first explore the emergence of a forensics of memory in Argentina, examining the work of the Argentine Forensic Anthropology Team (EAAF) and the technique of osteobiography they developed for making human remains speak, a practice directly born out of the search for the disappeared. It will then connect such advances to the emergence of a "poetics of DNA" in the activism of the Grandmothers of the Plaza de Mayo, a narrative element that promotes the notion that the fullest truth of the past is found via an analysis of the body that speaks through its DNA. Finally, it concludes that the body of the child of disappeared parents is uniquely positioned to not only contribute forensic testimony, but in its very physical existence constitutes another type of artifact, a material that is haunted by the former activism of the child's parents and yields a spectral material testimony that continues to sow doubt and animate action in the present day.

Bodies that Speak: The Argentine Forensic Anthropology Team

When discussing the post-dictatorship, the ongoing effect of disappearance often means that activist efforts focus on signifying disappearance by highlighting the lack of the body and, via this lack, the absence of the person, attempting to make them "present" within the present time and thus highlighting the absenting of that person in the past. In Buenos Aires, family and friends of people who disappeared assemble to create and install handmade sidewalk stones (*baldosas*) to identify the places in the city where their loved ones were "disappeared," placing the stone permanently at the person's last known location before having been arrested/detained (or kidnapped, to use a more accurate term) and, ultimately, disappeared. Such interventions within the city attempt to signal the ongoing presence of these absented subjects within the present time of the city. The aforementioned silhouettes used as a strategy for highlighting the absence of the body are another example that seeks to accomplish the same task. Yet, in some cases, the bodies of those who disappeared do re-emerge, and the completeness of the dictatorship's project of disappearance is challenged. One of the most significant examples of this challenge to disappearance is the work of excavating mass graves, uncovering suspect material bodies that have been located and can be studied to, in part, counter the narrative void of disappearance.[29]

Once a body is located, that subject arguably ceases to be "disappeared," since a defining aspect of disappearance is precisely the absence of the body. For this reason, the exhumation of mass graves caused controversy with some groups, such as some sectors of the Mothers of the Plaza de Mayo, who argued that exhumations destroy the living collective legacy of their disappeared children by transforming it into a past story of individual deaths.[30] The initial stance of the Association of ex Detained-Disappeared also opposed exhumations, arguing that they would only serve to prove what was already known, that the dictatorship had murdered people.[31]

However, I argue that this conversion is slightly exaggerated in such fears, as the move away from disappearance to death is never entirely complete. The finding of the body is ultimately the locating of another material object capable of yielding testimony about the disappearance of the person, but disappearance remains a distinguishing feature in that subject's identity. This is due, in part to what Adam Rosenblatt describes as a discrepancy between the hopes of the families and friends of the disappeared and the limits on the abilities of groups that use forensic techniques to analyze recovered bodies: "Another dynamic that occurs across all of these stakeholders is the discrepancy, often quite large, between what they hope and expect from forensic investigations, on the one hand, and the results that forensic teams are able to produce, on the other."[32] Confirmed death can only give a certain degree of information to fill the narrative void of disappearance; it can only infallibly confirm the outcome of the journey of disappearance, not the details of the experience. These limits on knowing, combined with the fallible nature of forensic science—nothing about the information forensic science yields is a true one-hundred-percent guarantee, despite popular culture's promotion of such techniques, and, as I will explore later, specifically of DNA as the key to the absolute truth—mean that something of the narrative void surrounding disappearance will always remain, even after the body's reappearance. The specter of possibility of more information will also remain, as the completely infallible reading of it will always lie just beyond reach. For, as Rosenblatt writes in his study of the investigative work of digging for the disappeared, "the past that is under study can never be revisited or replayed."[33] Due to this impossibility, I argue that the recovered body of the disappeared can be read as another material object capable of providing spectral testimony. In the rest of this section, I examine this process and, specifically, the place of osteobiography as the technique developed for deciphering the recovered body, considering its productive possibility as well as the limits it poses for our understanding.

In an early attempt (1984) to move past the "narrative void" of disappearance, the Equipo Argentino de Antropología Forense (Argentine Forensic Anthropology Team [EAAF]) was formed with an initial charge to "investigate the cases of at least 9,000 disappeared people in Argentina under the military government that ruled from 1976–1983."[34] The group's creation took place at the request of both the truth commission that investigated the violence of the dictatorship shortly after the return to democracy—the Comisión Nacional sobre la Desaparición de Personas (CONADEP), or the National Commission on the Disappearance of Persons—and the Grandmothers of the Plaza de Mayo. The Grandmothers' initial request was for assistance from the Science and Human Rights Program at the American Association for the Advancement of Science (AAAS) for the search for children who disappeared with their parents. The AAAS sent a delegation to Argentina to help the two groups and upon arrival found mass exhumations already taking place under the supervision of non-experts. They called for an immediate halt to the exhumations until specially trained archaeologists, anthropologists, and physicians could be called in to help. Among those in the initial delegation was renowned forensic anthropologist Dr. Clyde Snow who helped train the original thirteen-member team of the EAAF.[35]

Even before the emergence of DNA testing, Snow developed a forensic technique for accessing the past held in human remains, namely identities of the remains and what their bones could reveal about their lives and how they died, that he termed "osteobiography": "a very informative way of putting together the life history of the individual from the evidence preserved in the skeleton."[36] Osteobiography was a way of using the markings found on the recovered body to create a fact-based narrative for what happened to the body, a "biography" for the person based on the evidence preserved in the skeletal remains:

> In a single human skeleton, you have roughly two hundred bones, as well as all the other evidence, including clothing, belt, buttons, and bullets. They all tell you something about that person, which will help determine who he or she was and also how he or she died and when.[37]

Snow's work in Argentina trained the original experts of the EAAF in this technique and his findings with the group were used as forensic testimony in the 1985 trial of the military juntas, thus signaling an early stamp of validity for forensic science's ability to render a truthful account of the violence meant to be left in the past. Regarding that experience, Snow observes: "to be effective as an expert witness, you have to learn that in a way you're translating the skeletons themselves. The bones are the ones telling the story. Bones make wonderful witnesses: they don't forget, they don't lie."[38] The work of the forensic expert in reading remains by developing an osteobiography, then, is the performative interpretation germane to *hauntology* as Derrida describes it. The work of the expert is to commune with the voices of the dead that remain embedded in the bones they left behind, conjuring their spectral testimony to the present. Forensic identification of bodies—in the cases of both the remains of the dead who have been located and, as will be explored later in this chapter, the bodies of children of the disappeared—is an act of material reading (performative interpretation) that deciphers hauntings of material entities. Moreover, though, it is a reading of information that was present all along. The forensic anthropologists do the work of revealing these present-but-hidden-bodies via excavation of mass grave sites, and the team of forensic experts that employ osteobiography simply acts as the translator that speaks with the ghost that haunts the remains, waiting to be heard. The EAAF explains their mission, stating that they are:

> Applying forensic anthropology and related sciences, and in close collaboration with victims and their relatives, EAAF aims to recover and identify remains, return them to families and provide evidence in court proceedings. Through this work, we seek to shed light on human rights violations, contributing to the search for truth, justice, reparation and prevention of violations.[39]

Put in other terms, their work conjures forth these ghostly traces of the past, deciphers their meanings and, in so doing, speaks in the present with the haunted remnants of the past, effecting political change in the search for justice. Carlos Somigliana of the EAAF explains how such deciphering sutures together past and present, yielding specific information about what happened to individuals:

> La identificación lo que hace es atar esa distancia como un jarrón que está roto, lo volvés a pegar, podés volver a establecer toda la historia. Permite

volver a ese hilo, reconstruir una realidad que es dolorosa, pero que termina de cerrar el círculo de esa vida en términos del conocimiento de lo que pasó. Cuál fue el final, con quiénes, de qué manera, en qué lugar, quién lo dispuso. Eso es lo mágico, abandonás generalidades en las que es muy difícil hacer pie y hablás de hechos concretos y específicos en términos individuales, pero también colectivos.[40]

(What identification does is link this distance like a jar that is broken. You glue it back together to return to establishing the whole story. It permits one to return to the thread, to reconstruct a painful reality, it ends up closing the circle of a life in terms of knowledge of what happened. What happened in the end, with whom, in what way, in what place, who arranged it. This is the magic of it, you abandon the generalizations through which it is very difficult to make sense and you speak of concrete acts and specifics in individual and collective terms.)

The work of the EAAF and of forensic anthropology is a direct example of the move away from a reliance on the voice and toward the potential of the material for narrating the past, in this case the body's potential to speak. As Joyce and Stover assert: "Though the dead may speak softly, only failure to listen and interpret the evidence can dishonor their final testament."[41] Yet, as a broken jar can never become fully what it was before having been broken, something of the fullness of the testimony about the past will remain beyond reach, continuing to haunt the present. For this reason, I insist that such testimony by material objects be considered spectral, as it will never be the "full" truth of the past; it can never reconstruct for us the completeness of the event.

It is important to recognize that such acts of interpretation tend toward the creation of a narrative that is of necessity incomplete. The osteobiography created by Snow does not render the whole picture pursued by families of the disappeared; it does not fulfill what is sought by the "intensa voluntad de búsqueda de rescatar la historia de ese individuo"[42] (intensely willed search to rescue the history of that individual), but rather creates a narrative limited to that material we have available with which to speak. Just as Pepe's foot revealed an incomplete truth about the past to Vicky in *Nostalgia de la luz*, the spectral testimony we read in the material of the body at once gives us information we seek, and at the same time calls attention to its own incomplete, and inaccessible nature. In the present, a similar phenomenon is ongoing in the identification of the appropriated children of the disappeared. Restitution of identity to children disappeared with life simultaneously reveals a truth about the past and opens up a plethora of de-stabilizing questions that conjure forth the violence of the past, that call attention to a hidden or inaccessible knowledge that the appropriated child to that point in his/her life was not even conscious of missing.

A "Poetics of DNA": The Grandmothers of the Plaza de Mayo

The work of the Argentine Forensic Anthropology Team and the testimonial potential of techniques like osteobiography solidified within Argentina an awareness of the capacity of the body to reveal information about the violence of the period of the dictatorship. But, a second group also contributed to this awareness of the body's truth-telling capacity. Since 1977, the Grandmothers of the Plaza de Mayo have tirelessly worked to identify those children (the grandmothers' grandchildren) who remain "disappeared with life," living victims who were kidnapped, deprived of knowing their own identities and raised by (mostly military) families as their own children. Their initial search efforts relied on pieces of information ("tips") that were given to them by witnesses who had observed irregularities in the conduct of families that, without evidence of a pregnancy, suddenly had children. Their tactics included sleuthing out the veracity of such clues by comparing them to any archival information they could find and relying on family resemblance and patchwork narratives to denounce individual cases of appropriations of children. Unsurprisingly, such methods were not always reliable and some of the early cases resulted in contentious battles for custody between the grandmothers laying claim to their grandchildren and the appropriators insisting that the child was their own biological spawn.

In the 1980s, the grandmothers began to work with experts to develop blood tests that could help further prove allegedly false family ties. The Grandmothers' website lists "blood group and Rh, Histocompatibility (HLA, A, B, C, DR), investigation of erythrocytic isoenzymes, and investigation of plasmatic proteins"[43] as the initial analyses they used to "translate" the unknown histories of their grandchildren's bodies. This method, which the Grandmothers developed in consultation with scientific organizations in the United States, predicted kinship with a 99.9% probability rate and was termed "The Grand-Parenting Index."[44] As the science of DNA developed, the Grandmothers, who had continued to travel the world asking scientists to help them utilize such techniques for cases where only grandparental DNA was available, incorporated this testing into their protocol. In 1987, Ley 23511 (Law 23511) was passed, creating a national DNA databank (El Banco Nacional de Datos Genéticos).[45] The DNA bank

> surgió como necesidad durante la recuperación democrática para la identificación genética de hijos/as de personas desaparecidas por el Terrorismo de Estado entre 1976 y 1983 y que fueron privados de su identidad y apropiados por represores de acuerdo a un plan sistemático diseñado e implementado desde las más altas jerarquías de la dictadura militar.[46]

> (emerged as a necessity during the democratic recovery for the genetic identification of children of persons disappeared during the state terrorism between 1976 and 1983 and that were deprived of their identity and appropriated by the repressors in accordance with a systematic plan designed and implemented from within the highest ranks of the military dictatorship.)

In provoking the creation of the DNA data bank specifically for helping identify the children of the disappeared, the emerging science once again called attention to the "narrative void" left by disappearance, to the absence of the bodies of the parents of these children, but it also highlighted the ability of the child's body to yield truth-telling information about that past, relying on the spectral testimony of the residues of their parents that remain in the blood of the living child.

Prior to the emergence of DNA testing as a method to confirm appropriation and restitute the child to his/her original identity, the Grandmothers of the Plaza de Mayo were already emphasizing the bodily tie between mother and child in an effort to create awareness about their missing grandchildren. An advertisement titled "Mamá, niños desaparecidos"[47] from 1977–1978, reads "mamá" across the top, evoking a familial narrative. The poster features a pastiche of photographs of children (many held in the arms of grandmothers identified as members of the organization by the white handkerchiefs they wear on their heads), an image of a visibly pregnant woman, a card made by a child dedicated "para vos mamita" ("for you, momma"), and a poem that asks "¿adónde están?"[48] ("where are they?"). The child in this advertisement, which predates blood and DNA testing, is linked to the figure of the mother, and motherhood and birth (and, thus, the biological and bodily connection between mother and child) are depicted as the foundation of the link in their identity.

Another poster from the 1980s shows a child seated on a street corner while two silhouettes, presumably those of his disappeared parents, walk down the sidewalk behind him. Specters from the past, always a step behind, they never fully arrive at the same place where the child sits. The advertisement reads,

> Estoy triste y espero . . . Y yo los voy a seguir buscando. Por vos papá, por vos mamá, por todos los papás desaparecidos, por los chicos secuestrados y la niñez que nos robaron. Te lo prometo papá habrá JUSTICIA.[49]

> (I am sad and waiting . . . And I will continue looking for them. For you, dad, for you, mom, for all of the disappeared parents, for the kidnapped children and the childhood that they robbed us of. I promise you, dad, there will be JUSTICE.)

This advertisement elaborates a view of the child as haunted not only by the disappearance of his parents, but by the violence of the past. The child is the one who will carry on the legacy of the outcome of his parents' revolutionary activities. The fight for justice is the child's inherited legacy, engrained into his very being, passed down to him within his body.

Such advertisements, created by the Abuelas de la Plaza de Mayo, produced a conditioned field in which those who discover they are children of disappeared parents enter into a world where an expectation for action awaits them. The image of the child haunted by the specters of his parents created at once a poetics of DNA, locating memory and a past truth in the body, and an expectation for action, based solely upon a genetic tie—"I promise you, dad, there will be JUSTICE." In more recent advertisements, the focus on DNA testing as a form of identifying crimes committed in the past places the body of the child disappeared with life in a privileged testimonial position. It is the body, its material, that holds the memory and evidence of what happened in the past. But, what's more, in many cases, the physical traits of the children of the disappeared bear resemblance to those of their parents. Although they have now surpassed the age of their disappeared parents, the continuities between the two generations stand out.[50] As anthropologist Marius Kwint argues, "human memory can be regarded as a mere elaboration of the basic ability of all organisms to 'read' the substances that surround and constitute them (beginning with their own DNA)."[51] The publicity campaigns of the Abuelas de la Plaza de Mayo highlight this bodily capacity to tell, to create memory, to testify to a truth from the past that lies hidden in the present. By so doing, they promote the notion that Argentine society's responsibility is to learn to read such truths. In cases where the child surpasses the parent in age, the tale of their longevity evokes a specter of possibility for what might have been: how would the parent they resemble have aged if they hadn't disappeared?

The work of the Grandmothers reveals a hope that centers on the capacity to make readable the biological link between the first-generation and second-generation victims. The nature of genetics demonstrates that there are some histories one cannot alter, in this case the DNA of the body. The truth of the past actions of kidnapping and appropriation of minors can be revealed via this reading of the body's testimony. Thus, the body once again unsettles the dictatorship's attempt to erase its own violent actions. This belief in the inalterability of the body is also demonstrated in the early advertising for their mission that the Grandmothers employed. An early poster created by the group featured an open hand with cloth and fabricated ink fingerprints covering its real fingerprints and the phrase "la identidad no se impone"[52] (identity is not imposed) above the image. The poster promoted identity as a fixed notion, largely contained in the body (in this case, in the underlying skin and fingerprints), and denounced the appropriations of children under the dictatorship, represented by the attempt to impose a new, false bodily identity via the cloth with "false" ink fingerprints, affixed around each finger with wire. But, what's more, the advertisement put forth the premise that the body itself contains the truth of the past, the memory that can't be altered by state terrorism. It promoted the notion of corporal memory as the truest form of memory.

As explored by Ari Gandsman, the Grandmothers' mission is fundamentally to promote a healthy skepticism about one's identity among the Generation of HIJOS in Argentina—not just among those who have ties to the repression, but among all Argentines contemporaneous to this group—a valorization of that identity through a desire for self-analysis and investigation.[53] As is seen in the cultural production of the Grandmothers over time, this mission has continually promoted the body as the key to unlocking that truth of identity. As DNA analysis developed, and the DNA data bank was created, the Grandmothers increasingly incorporated allusions to DNA into their advertisements, promoting the notion that DNA is the way to unlock

the secrets of the body's past. A Facebook post from the Córdoba branch organization of the Grandmothers of Plaza de Mayo at the end of 2015 visually
cited DNA as the identity-revealing process that brings Grandmother and
disappeared grandchild together. It featured a Grandmother (identified by
the iconic white kerchief worn by the Mothers of the Plaza de Mayo) and a
young woman, presumably the restituted granddaughter, embracing. They
are tied together by their scarves, which float in the wind, connected in a visual representation of the double-helix strands of DNA. The description be-
neath the image reads: "There's a mother in this world / that together with
other mothers / will not rest / until it's written in history / the just memory
/ of identity." In this image, the "just" (or true) memory of identity is hidden
in the body, revealed (or translated) by the reading of DNA.

This reading of DNA as the way of revealing identity is also seen in the
Grandmothers' advertisement for the activities commemorating International Human Rights Day in December of 2016. The images in the advertisement feature a grandmother (again identified by the headscarf) placing the
final puzzle piece to complete an image of the double-helix model for DNA.
The implied message is that DNA is the key to restituting the identity contained in the body (the plenary address advertised is about "art, identity, and
human rights," thus the double helix image should be understood as an illus-
tration of the human right to identity, which the Grandmothers are promoting as lying within DNA), and the work of the Grandmothers is to reveal that
identity via reconstructing the puzzle pieces of DNA [Image 14].

Other advertisement production by the Grandmothers, unrelated to the
direct task of restituting identities, also evokes a poetics of DNA. For instance, an advertisement by the group for a session (an "editatón") in which
they will edit Wikipedia articles related to the work of the group so that
they more accurately reflect the history of the Abuelas de Plaza de Mayo also
evokes a poetics of DNA. A double helix is woven through the image, surrounded by the information about the event [Image 15].

In this advertisement, it is no longer a true identity that is restituted by
DNA, but the accuracy of the online presence of the organization. North
American scholar Judith Roof, in analyzing the influence of forensic science
(specifically DNA testing) on U.S. cultural production, proposes the term
"poetics of DNA,"[54] to refer to the phenomenon in which science looks for
an accessible rhetoric with which to present its advances to the public, but

14. Abuelas de Plaza de Mayo, Sitio Oficial. Facebook, December 6, 2016. Reproduced with permission from Abuelas de Plaza de Mayo.

during which, simultaneously, that public rhetoric turns back to influence science. In the case of the Grandmothers, the "poetics of DNA" can be used to describe not only the way their understanding of a random news story about paternity led them to travel the world in search of a DNA specialist who would hear their plight and help them develop a test for grandpaternity, but also the way in which the search for an accessible rhetoric with which to present scientific advancement to the public ends up being adopted by activist groups and integrated into their own agendas. In the case of the Grandmothers, the evocation of DNA in their advertisements occurs most often via the image of the double helix strand that makes up DNA. In the advertisement for the editatón, the poetics of DNA in the double helix of this image evokes the notion that DNA, or bodily memory, is associated with truthful memory. The truth of the body—in the "accessible rhetoric" that presents DNA as the standard for one-hundred-percent accurate verification of iden-

¡EDITATÓN CON ABUELAS DE PLAZA DE MAYO!

Juntos podemos enriquecer los artículos de Wikipedia relacionados con las Abuelas de Plaza de Mayo.

Participá de nuestra jornada de edición el Sábado 21 de noviembre de 10 a 15 hs.

¡NO TE OLVIDES DE TRAER TU COMPUTADORA Y CREAR TU USUARIO EN WIKIPEDIA!

ABUELAS DE PLAZA DE MAYO   WIKIMEDIA ARGENTINA

15. Abuelas de Plaza de Mayo, Sitio Oficial. Facebook, November 16, 2015. Reproduced with permission from Abuelas de Plaza de Mayo.

tity (even when this is a falsehood)—is conjured forth in tandem with a call to make current representations of the history/memory of the Grandmothers more "truthful" through the process of editing.

In yet another example, a section of a mural, commissioned from the Argentine artist Pedro Fiori by the Network for Identity of San Martín de los Andes for the Grandmothers' campaign "*Murales con historias*" (Murals with Histories) in March of 2015, evokes a poetics of DNA in its representation of the interruption of family identity posed by disappearance [Image 16]. The use of a stump in the mural evokes a truncated family tree, highlighting the result of an action that cut off the future-oriented growth part of that tree, severing the family ties and identities that would develop from it. In the mural, next to the Grandmother's iconic tagline "Y vos ... ¿Sabés quién sos?" (And you, do you know who you are?), rather than showing normal tree roots

16. Mural by Pedro Fiori, San Martín de los Andes, Abuelas de Plaza de Mayo, Sitio Oficial. Facebook, April 7, 2015. Reproduced with permission from Abuelas de Plaza de Mayo.

coming from the stump, people appear holding hands, forming a curvy line, in what constitutes an abstract representation of the chain links of DNA. A poetics of DNA heralds the hidden information that contains the memory of the family genealogy, of identity, hidden under the earth, waiting to be accessed and translated for those above ground. The greenery that grows from the stump, next to the grandmother (again identified with the white headscarf), represents the future familial growth that can result from the uncovering of identity, from the reading of that DNA, and thus contextualizes the Grandmothers' intervention as crucial for rectifying the loss of the past.

The Espacio Memoria y Derechos Humanos (ex ESMA) Facebook page also has instances where it has incorporated a poetics of DNA into its representations of the Grandmothers and their restituted grandchildren. In the image that accompanies a Facebook post they used to announce a March 24, 2014 march in commemoration of the military coup, and also marking the tenth anniversary of the recovery of the ex ESMA as a space of memory, a Grandmother (again, marked by the iconic white headscarf) and (presumably) her granddaughter ride together on a bicycle, their scarves floating behind them in the wind, twisting together to form the double-helix structure of DNA. While this time the explanation of DNA as the most "just" truth is not articulated, the use of this image for this type of advertisement for two importantly symbolic anniversaries evidences the way a poetics of truth has been solidified in cultural production related to the work of the Grandmothers and in the denunciation of the legacy of the violence of the dictatorship more generally. In the post-dictatorship it is not only science, but the merging of science with the desire for collective memory that influences this poetics. In the next chapter, we will explore how the influence of this poetics of DNA also permeates the cultural production of the Generation of HIJOS.

Conclusion: Children of the Resistance / Children as Resistance—Spectral Testimony in the Body

In addition to being seen as the material continuation of the parents' bodies, children of the disappeared can also be seen as a different type of artifact, a material that is haunted by the former activism of the child's parents. While the body of the disappeared subject (whether parent or child) offers a forensic truth about the past, it is also the case that the child's bodily existence is in itself an example of a spectral testimony left through the actions of his/her parents. The child's body is the material proof of his/her parents having been, it is the telos between past and present, regardless of whether that true parentage is known. In the case of a number of children, their body is also the haunted material manifestation of an ideology of resistance, of a deliberate act of rebellion within circumstances of great oppression. Like the artifact that stands as an extension of the prisoner as I explored in Chapter Two, the child's body here is the made-material agency of the parents. The child is the direct result of decisions made by his/her parents entirely of their own volition in situations and a political atmosphere in which they possessed very little independence or control.

The documentary film *Encontrando a Víctor* (2004) relates the quest of the director, Natalia Bruschtein, to find more information about her past, specifically her disappeared father, Víctor. The film dramatizes her search, but also reveals a schism between the HIJOS and their parents' past political resistance. Bruschtein critically questions her parents' decision to conceive and give birth to her amidst their militancy. As Ros notes, "the sons and daughters of *desaparecidos* often struggle with the idea of not having been important enough for their parents to stay out of harm's way."[55] It is precisely this feeling that informs Natalia's challenge to her mother. Her mother responds by telling Natalia that for Víctor and herself, having a child was a continuation of their resistance, of bringing new life into a shared community of caring:

> Since there was such a deep affective bond among *compañeros* and we all thought, loved and felt so similarly, you knew that if something happened to you, a comrade would immediately replace your affection for your child,

it was going to be alright and protected; there wasn't a risk that he or she wouldn't develop well.[56]

Natalia's mother addresses Natalia's resentment toward their having exposed her to the possibility of such a loss as the disappearance of her father, saying:

> Yours is a *legitimate* feeling but, although we took much care of you, we never pondered whether in the future you will feel our absence or be angry because we exposed ourselves. Our priority was that you live in a fairer world. And this might sound like a *cliché* today, but it was also a *legitimate* feeling.[57]

What these comments reveal is that Natalia's very existence is the material result of a deliberate act on the part of her parents, a making material of their agency. As their child, she is the living proof of the actions of both her mother and her disappeared father. In this sense, her survival is an artefactual forensic testimony to the ideological fight of her parents. They were the ones that *decided* to have her, to give birth to her, to bring her into a community and a world they were fighting to make a reality. Like the *artesanías carcelarias* and the *manualidades*, Natalia's body is the ideological struggle of her parents made manifest, made material, made physical. It is the *remains* left as a lasting legacy for the future, a reminder from the past in the "fairer world" of the present that her parents dreamed of and struggled for.

In her study of the objects the dead leave behind in the wake of their passing, Margaret Gibson considers the body and its meaning postmortem. She argues "our bodies themselves are relics (and remainders) of the dead. Through processes of identification and mourning we encrypt within our own embodied selves the embodied selves of significant others."[58] Gibson's observations are arguably heard even more strongly in relation to children of disappeared parents, many of whom were never even able to meet their mothers and fathers, but whose own bodies constitute relics (and remainders) of the past.

For a concluding example of the body as a relic that contains remainders of the past capable of yielding a spectral testimony, I turn to the story of Mariana Eva Pérez, which forms part of the anthology *Re-encuentros: Por la identidad y la justicia. Contra el olvido y el silencio*. Mariana was twenty days old when she was taken from her parents. At the time of her disappearance, her grandfather had only seen her a few times. Mariana suspected her parents were not her biological parents and upon receiving the results of her DNA analysis, she finds herself being introduced to an old man (her biological grandfather) by a judge. The old man looks at her hands and declares "tiene las manos grandes como mi nieta"[59] (she has big hands, like my granddaughter). He repeats this observation, takes her hands into his and holds them "con el mismo cuidado y la misma seguridad con que se toca un pájaro asustado"[60] (with the same care and the same security with which one touches a scared bird). Then, her grandfather tells Mariana "mi nietita tiene un lunar en la cadera en forma de aceituna"[61] (my little granddaughter has a mole on her hip in the shape of an olive). Mariana to this point in her life has believed what her captor mother[61] had told her, that the birth mark that has so ashamed her during bathing suit season was the result of a pregnancy craving for black olives. After this remark, Mariana believes the old man is her grandfather. He explains to her that

> A mi papá le gustaba mucho mi lunar. Que cada vez que me cambiaba los pañales me daba un beso ahí. Mi papá pintaba. Y mi abuelo cuenta que mi papá decía que era una mancha de tinta china con la que él me había marcado para siempre. A mi mamá le daba un poco de pena pensar que tal vez nunca iba a querer ponerme bikini por culpa del lunar. Tenía razón. Pero mi papá decía que ese lunar era como su firma al pie del cuadro, de su cuadro más logrado, que era yo.[63]

> (My mole pleased my father very much. That every time he changed my diaper he gave me a kiss there. My father painted. And my grandfather tells that my father said that it was a stain of India ink with which he had marked me forever. It pained my mother to think that maybe I'd never want to wear a bikini because of the mole. She was right. But my father said that that mole was like his signature at the bottom of a painting, of his most accomplished painting, which was me.)

Learning to read the body's secrets means revealing how "esas marcas son el tesoro que los represores no lograron borrar ni arrasar: restos, trazos, para reconstruir en la historia singular la historia de todos. Memoria que escribe la identidad, identidad de un sujeto, de un pueblo, de una generación"[64] (these marks are the treasure that the repressors didn't manage to erase or destroy: remains, traces, to reconstruct in a singular history the history of everyone. Memory writes identity, the identity of a subject, of a people, of a generation). It is not just that, as Colin Davis eloquently states, "the dead inhabit the minds of the living,"[65] but that the specters of the past, specifically of disappeared parents, inhabit the bodies of their living children. The mole/ stain that so ashamed Pérez becomes (or was it always?) a physical mark that destabilizes the standard of forgetting that the dictatorship made such an effort to guarantee through programmatic disappearance. Pérez's body, reappeared with life, cannot be silenced. Even amidst the horrific legacy of disappearance, the body speaks, evidences, reveals a dynamic past that refuses to disappear completely. The work of H.I.J.O.S, "como red—afectan al poder que ordena olvidar"[66] (as a network—alters the power that orders to forget). They are, and in the case of Pérez quite literally so, "la mancha que declara con su presencia lo que no se puede borrar, porque son el retoño vivo de lo que se quiso arrasar"[67] (the stain that declares with its presence that which cannot be erased, because they are the living return of that which was desired to be destroyed).

CHAPTER FIVE

Reappearance—Learning to Live
and Speak with Ghosts

꙳

Much of the horror and fascination with death, as well as its comfort, stems from the knowledge that we will become solely material and meld with our surroundings, that the subject will return to the object.[1]

Están conmigo en cada momento de dolor y de alegría.[2]
(They are with me in every moment of pain and happiness.)

La gente que murió, básicamente, era gente que estaba viva . . . la gente viva . . . la gente . . . sobre de todo . . . Víctor o . . . o mis hermanos. Vidas muy vitales. Entonces, este parece injusto que el recuerdo de ellos se convierta en recuerdos de muerte solamente."[3]

(The people who died, basically, were people that were alive . . . the live people . . . the people . . . above all . . . Víctor or . . . or my brothers. Very vital lives. Therefore, it seems unjust that the memory of them is converted into the memory of death only.)

Vivenciar es volver a vivir, con el afecto que ello hace emerger, recobrar algo de lo perdido en el presente o vivir—incluso—aquello que no llegó a vivirse como tal.[4]

(To experience is to live again, with the affect that it brings out, to recover something of that which is lost in the present or to live—including—that which one didn't get to live as such.)

PILAR CALVEIRO DESCRIBES THE concentration camps in Argentina as "un sistema de *compartimentos* o *contenedores*, ya fueran de material o madera, para guardar y controlar cuerpos, no hombres, cuerpos"[5] (a system of compartments or containers, whether they were of material or wood, to keep and control bodies, not men, bodies). She reports:

> la desnudez, la capucha que escondía el rostro, las ataduras y mordazas, el dolor y la pérdida de toda pertenencia personal eran los signos de la *iniciación* en este mundo en donde todas las propiedades, normas, valores, lógicas del exterior parecen canceladas y en donde la propia humanidad entra en suspenso.[6]

> (the nakedness, the hood that hid the face, the restraints and gags, the pain and the loss of all personal belongings were the signs of the *initiation* into this world where all properties, norms, values, logics of the outside appear to be canceled and where humanity itself becomes suspended).

In this space of suspended humanity, however, as I have explored in previous chapters, small acts of resistance took place that defied the dehumanization that reigned over detention, acts often of a creative and artistic nature. In this chapter, I will explore how the material objects both created and left by prisoners and discovered in the wake of disappearance are being used to recreate and transmit memory by second-generation actors in the post-dictatorship. First, I will argue that projects such as the *Sala de la Memoria* in the space of the former detention center Villa Grimaldi in Chile and the project *Memorias de Vida y Militancia* undertaken by the groups that inhabit the ex ESMA in Argentina are using the former belongings of the disappeared in order to conjure forth their individual specters in an effort to rehumanize them and permit them to speak, thus resisting the emptying of their identities that lies at the core of disappearance as a systematic form of repression. Second, I will consider how the virtual art exposition *Proyecto Tesoros* took these projects further in an attempt to weave together the voices and materialities of the past and present generations in the creation of memory narratives that interrupt the impersonal and collective narrative of disappearance. Lastly, I will examine how the film *Cautiva* (Gastón Biraben, Argentina, 2005) and theatrical productions by Lola Arias further enmesh the material and the voice in an effort to dramatize the testimonial encounter with the objects of the past, depicting a scene of communion in which the present experiences the ghosts of the past through an affective commingling and conversation with material belongings.

Combatting Disappearance: Rebirthing Subjectivities

The children of the disappeared continue to suffer the absence of their parents, although, in many cases, they have surpassed the age their parents were at the moment of their disappearance. Disappearance is different from death in that it suspends closure, interrupting processes of mourning in creating a narrative void where information is simply not available. But, in the cases where the children of the disappeared were too young to have memories of their living parents, disappearance also interrupted the ability of these children to experience their parents as individuals, with personalities, interests, political perspectives, and hopes for the future. According to Elvira Martorell, the fact that children lost their parents to disappearance means that these now adult children must give birth to their parents once again:

> Si la desaparición apunta a la muerte subjetiva, podemos pensar que los hijos realizan la operación inversa: apuntan a hacer del desaparecido, de ese agujero en lo real, un sujeto, devolverlo a ese estatuto que se pretendió arrasar. Ahí, el padre es parido por el hijo vivo.[7]

> (If disappearance points to subjective death, we can think that the children perform an inverse operation: they point to a making out of the disappeared, from this hole within the real, of a subject, returning him/her to the status that was supposed to be destroyed. In that way, the living child gives birth to their parent.)

Today, this effort to return the disappeared's subjectivity to him/her is taking place frequently in the realm of the material, in the re-signifying of an absent subject through the display and narration of his/her material possessions. In putting together a pastiche of objects, or even selecting one particular object as evidential or emblematic of who the disappeared subject was as a dynamic being, the activism of subsequent generations in the present reconstructs the past, and counters processes of forgetting through a marked turn to the material object's power to narrate and witness the past.

The legacy of disappearance during the dictatorship produced other, secondary forms of disappearance in the post-dictatorship, including that of the singular identity within the collective. The Madres de la Plaza de Mayo are careful to balance the use of the individual identities of their children in their activism with their call to collectivize their suffering. Rather than bring attention to the individuality of disappearance, they opt to "socialize motherhood" and draw attention to the collective magnitude of the 30,000 disappeared. In his work, Emilio Crenzel argues that the trials of the military junta produced a *humanitarian narrative*, which de-politicized the past actions of those who disappeared, in another way disappearing who they were.[8] Gustavo Remedi reminds us of the need to remember, but also cautions us that this means "to remember the dead and the disappeared as they were when they were alive. We need to recover their lives, their struggles, their thoughts, their dreams, their plans. Their errors too."[9]

Those who ran the concentration camps and detention centers believed themselves to have ultimate control over life and death.[10] The exercise of this absolute power was used as a method of social control and discipline through fear.[11] Part of this exercise was the removal or erasure of individual identities, especially within the space of detention. Pilar Calveiro explains this erasure, comparing it to the methods of the Nazis during the Holocaust:

> Los números reemplazaban a nombres y apellidos, personas vivientes que ya habían *desaparecido* del mundo de los vivos y ahora *desaparecerían* desde dentro de sí mismos, en un proceso de 'vaciamiento' que pretendía no dejar la menor huella. Cuerpos sin identidad, muertos sin cadáver ni nombre: desaparecidos. Como en el sueño nazi, supresión de la identidad, hombres que se desvanecen en la noche y la niebla.[12]

> (Numbers replaced first and last names, living beings that had already *disappeared* from the land of the living and now *would disappear* from within themselves, in a process of 'emptying' that hoped to not leave the slightest trace. Bodies without identity, dead people without cadavers or names: the disappeared. Like in the Nazi dream, suppression of identity, men that vanished in the night and fog.)

However, as we can see from the resistance efforts explored in the previous chapters, identity was never completely suppressed—there were small acts that expressed an agency still held by the prisoners even within the confines of detention. Through creation, through craftwork, through the organizing of a workday and the efforts to provide, even if only in a small way, for a family outside of detention, prisoners expressed their *individuality*, left remainders of their personalities and their past presence in the prisons and camps. The *manualidades* on display in the Museum of Memory in Uruguay were not made by machines, but painstakingly crafted by individual hands aching to be heard. Each small piece of art is the antonym of the impersonal and massive manufacturing of modern-day goods; these are handmade items that retain the *aura* of their makers. These *auras* of the past operate as spectral remainders of the disappeared. They remain attached to the small object, tethered to the material that was worked for hours on end by hands hoping to retain some aspect of their humanity.

At the same time, the disappeared were not born in the moment of their detentions—they were whole and dynamic individuals with life histories who left an impact on the world, a material mark, in the years leading up to their detentions. While the individual people who disappeared are not here in the present to relate their stories, their belongings are. Such collections of personal belongings render an image of who each person was and give clues to their personalities, to their passions, to their beings. In the present, the material of the past is used to remember the disappeared not as the dead, but as "gente viva" (living people) who, as Natalia's uncle in *Encontrando a Víctor* reminds us, lived "vidas muy vitales" (very vital lives).

Reappearing Lost Loved Ones: Villa Grimaldi's Sala de la Memoria

In Villa Grimaldi: Corporación Parque por la Paz, the only structure that remains standing from the time when the Chilean property was used as a brutal clandestine detention center is a small building that was formerly a guard shack. In 2004, that building was converted into the *Sala de la Memoria* of the peace park, "con el fin de recordar la identidad y vida de las personas que murieron o desaparecieron en este centro de detención"[13] (with the goal of remembering the identity and life of the people who died or disappeared in this detention center). In the room, the public encounters sixteen small display cases, each devoted to representing and humanizing a victim that disappeared from the site, using former belongings to make real to present and future visitors those identities and lives that risk fading into the expansiveness of the terror that took place in the space of the park.

A series of compartments are used this time not to isolate, dehumanize and disappear, but to illuminate, rehumanize, and deliberately re-appear individual lost loved ones. In her analysis of the Argentine post-dictatorship, Martorell argues that the children who lost their parents during the repression are missing not only the memories (*los recuerdos*), but the experiences (*las viven-*

17. *Marta Lidia Ugarte Román*, *Sala de la Memoria*, Parque por la Paz:
Villa Grimaldi. Photograph by the author.

cias) of their parents.[14] The *Sala de la Memoria* creates the circumstances in which visitors—both relatives of the disappeared and strangers—can experience individual personalities, identities, and lives via an encounter with the objects that were important to the individuals they are arranged to represent.

The display cases, made by the families of the disappeared, use material objects to relate the essence of the lost subject, in an attempt to re-humanize the individual and display the experience of who s/he was before disappearance. Each case is devoted to celebrating the *life* of the person, not to agonizing over the horror of his/her death. This attempt to facilitate experience is done through the deliberate and careful staging of objects. The family of Marta Lidia Ugarte Román [Image 17] explains:

El significado que tiene este lugar, de sufrimientos y agonías, están impregnados en todos los lugares de lo que fue la VILLA GRIMALDI, ahora PARQUE DE LA PAZ. A pesar de todo trataremos de exponer con estos pequeños objetos, dar a conocer a una mujer que entregó su vida en tan trágicas circunstancias solo por tener ideales. Recordar lo que fue en vida MARTA, es como tejer una fina tela abrigadora, cálida, eterna que nos da pena sacar. Ver y tocar este CINTURÓN que era del abrigo con que desapareció el 9 de agosto de 1976, está ahora aquí como mudo testigo.[15]

(The significance that this place holds, one of suffering and agony, is imprinted in all of the corners of what was VILLA GRIMALDI, now the PARK FOR PEACE. Despite everything, we have tried to showcase through these small objects, to introduce people to a woman who gave her life in such tragic circumstances just for having her ideals. Remembering who in life was MARTA is like weaving a fine tapestry, warm, eternal, one that pains us to remove. Seeing and touching this BELT that was from the coat she had on when she disappeared the 9th of August of 1976, is now here as a silent witness.)

The experience of who Marta was as a unique individual is staged through the display of her former belongings. These are not just *representative* objects of who Marta was, but these are *the* objects that contributed to, and participated in, making her who she was in life. Our relationships with each other, with the world, occur only in part through the voice. Other aspects are, of necessity, mediated by objects. Our impact on each other occurs through communication on paper, through the creation of gifts, through a helping hand that produces work, through a making external of an interior state of sentience. Here, the object is made manifest to us, and although the belt is present only as a "mudo testigo" that cannot speak to us directly, its presence evokes the specter of Marta. Its past conjures forth into the present a past truth about who Marta was. Marta's family explains:

En la tela de este cinturón están entrelazados recuerdos que son el testimonio de la personalidad de Marta, mujer, generosa, sensible, luchadora que también se preocupaba de darle a su arreglo personal un toque de armonía y delicadeza. Aquí está este pequeño collar que tiene una larga historia de aromas, viajes, tareas políticas, penas y alegrías que siempre compartía con su familia.[16]

(Within the fabric of this belt are interlaced the memories that are testimony to the personality of Marta, a woman, generous, sensible, a fighter who also preoccupied herself with giving her personal appearance a touch of delicate harmony. Here is this small necklace that holds a long history of aromas, travels, political work, pain, happiness, all of which she shared with her family.)

The belt that was worn by Marta carries her experiences—it was *there*, it was *present*, and therefore it can offer a form of testimony (I argue, spectral testimony) to who Marta was in life, and, what's more, "here it is" ("aquí está") in the present. It is *here*, it was chosen by her, worn by her, it experienced life with her, and now *we* are able to experience *it*. While we have the words written by her family to explain the belt's significance to us, the spectral testimony it yields continuously brings present to us the deferred nature of any information we may gain from it. The residue (here, attached to the object) as Nelly Richard reminds us, is a remainder from the past that bursts forth to interrupt the discourse of consensus.[17] We want to know the *whole* truth about who Marta was and the belt simultaneous conjures forth that truth and reminds us of its inaccessible nature—we remain in an indeterminate and intermediary gray space.

In her study of objects and mourning, Margaret Gibson argues "we knew the deceased only as the embodied being that they were."[18] For Gibson, the inseparability of spirit and matter grounds the spiritual in the material, gesturing toward what she calls the "other life"[19] of objects. Evidencing this other life of the object (what I argue constitutes the inaccessible but continuously present spectral side of the object), the display explains: "Entre las curiosidades que Marta guardaba está este BOTÓN que era de su gamulán y que supo de sus preocupaciones, de sus largos viajes en que conoció otros países, idiomas, personas y por supuesto todas las bellezas de nuestro país"[20] (Among the curiosities that Marta held onto was this BUTTON that was from her sheepskin jacket and that knew of her worries, of her long travels in which she got to know other countries, languages, people, and of course all of the beauty of our own country). *We* will never be privy to Marta's worries, to her travels, her experiences, but *the button was* and its "other side" continues to be privy to Marta's past even from the display case in the present. The button guards a secret, inexpressable to us, but undeniably there and creating change in the present space of the museum. This object by virtue of its testifying presence creates a punctum in the display. For Roland Barthes, photographs consist primarily of a studium (the context/the conceptualization of the image created by the photographer as artist) and a punctum, a point or object that stands out within the photograph, that commands our attention.[21] In the display, the object, which we know to have pertained to Marta, serves as a punctum that interrupts our consideration of who Marta was, humanizing her by conjuring forth her worries. It asks us to question what these worries may have been. However, it also casts doubt on our encounters with other objects we may find from the past.

Marianne Hirsch and Leo Spitzer have also studied this exemplary power of the object as a witness. Hirsch's canonical text, *Family Frames: Photography, Narrative and Postmemory* (1997) shed light on the nature of photography as an object with the power to call attention to the absence of the photographed subject, the life that is no longer, as well as its ability to mediate memory transmission from one generation to the next, contributing to the creation of what she terms postmemories in the second generation of Holocaust victims.[22] Since writing that text, Hirsch's scholarship has moved from an analysis of the photograph itself to a consideration of other material objects, focusing on the way in which the object might function as a link from past to present, much like the image presented by the photograph. Together with Leo Spitzer, Hirsch argues that the object presents an alternative testimonial form, functioning as a point of memory that creates an intersection between past and present while calling attention to the work of remembering. Hirsch and Spitzer assert that "In relation to memoir and testimony, and to historical accounts and scholarly discussions, as within new artistic texts, archival images function as supplements, both confirming and unsettling the stories that are explored and transmitted."[23]

Hirsh and Spitzer's article, "What's Wrong With This Picture? Archival Photographs in Contemporary Narratives," builds on the discussion they began in an earlier essay ("Testimonial Objects: Memory, Gender, and Transmission"), and explores the supplementary nature of both the photograph and object as a point—much like Barthes' photographic punctum—of memory (both spatial and temporal); a function that can "produce insights that pierce and traverse temporal, spatial and experiential divides. As points multiply, they can convey the overlay of different temporalities and interpretive frames, mitigating straightforward readings or any lure of authenticity."[24] For Hirsch and Spitzer, this function differs from Pierre Nora's concept of the "lieux de mémoire"[25] because it contains a personal (and, I would emphasis, individual) value, rather than a national, collective one. Hirsch and Spitzer argue that the elusiveness of the photographic image (and, later, they include the object) shows us a fleeting and evolving truth, one that is its own and that can teach us about the past:

> It seems to us that this may be the clearest articulation of what we fantasize and expect of archival photographs: that they have a memory of their own that they bring to us from the past; that that memory tells us something about ourselves, about what/how we and those who preceded us once were; that they carry not only information about the past, but enable us to reach an emotional register. That they require a particular kind of visual literacy, one that can decode the foreign language that they speak.[26]

In "Testimonial Objects," Hirsch and Spitzer consider a book of recipes and a miniature artists' book, both found in Nazi concentration camps. This movement, from the photograph to the book-as-object, maintains a focus that asserts that both the photographic image and the material object work in similar manners, as memory punctures that interpellate the living with the memory of the dead.

Another display in the *Sala de la Memoria*, devoted to Jacqueline Paulette Drouilly Yurich [Image 18], briefly and succinctly explains the horrific fate of a young woman: "Detenida Desaparecida, a los 24 años, junto a su marido, Marcelo Salinas Eytel, el 30 de octubre de 1974. Fue vista por numerosos testigos de este lugar"[27] (Detained Disappeared, at 24 years old, together with her husband, Marcelo Salinas Eytel, the 30th of October of 1974. She was seen by numerous witnesses of this place). A very short description, the introduction to the display avoids dwelling on the unchangeable fate of the collective past. Instead, it shifts focus to the present, individual level and continues: "Los objetos contenidos en la vitrina son originales y le pertenecieron. El color y la textura del papel de fondo evocan el chaleco tejido por ella, que se puso al ser llevada a un destino desconocido"[28] (The objects contained in this display case are original and belonged to her. The color and texture of the paper in the background evoke the vest she wove herself and put on as she was taken to an unknown destination). By emphasizing that the objects are *original* and *belonged to* Jacqueline, the compartment emphasizes for the viewer that s/he is not encountering any ordinary representation of a life, but is commingling with, experiencing an aspect of *this* lost life. These objects are *orginal, authentic, proof.* They *belonged* to Jacqueline, meaning she, with all the complex facets of a human personality, selected these objects as hers, as the way in which she would interact with her world, with her friends, with her family.

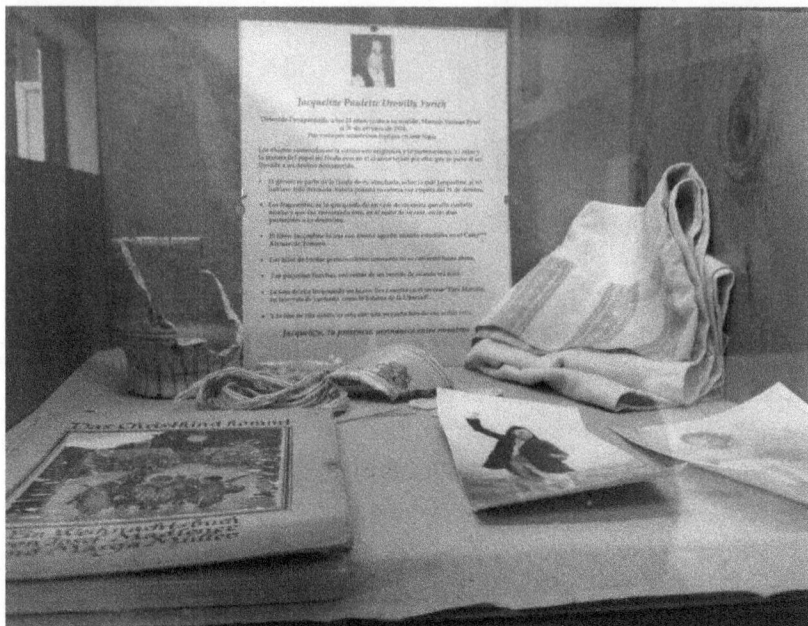

18. *Jacqueline Paulette Drouilly Yurich, Sala de la Memoria*, Parque por la Paz:
Villa Grimaldi. Photograph by the author.

The witness quality of the object is evoked to testify to, to prove, the violent nature of Jacqueline's disappearance: "Los fragmentos, es lo que queda de un vaso de cerámica que ella cuidaba mucho y que fue encontrado roto, en el suelo de su casa, en los días posteriores a su detención"[29] (The fragments are what remain of a ceramic vase that she took great care of and that was found broken, on the floor of her home, in the days after her detention). The other objects evoke the ghostly quality of absence: "El género es parte de la funda de su almohada, sobre la cual Jacqueline, si no hubiese sido detenida, habría posado su cabeza esa víspera del 31 de octubre"[30] (The fabric is part of the case for her pillow, upon which Jacqueline, if she hadn't been detained, would have rested her head on the evening of the 31st of October) [Image 19]; "Los hilos de bordar permanecieron intocados en su costurero hasta ahora"[31] (The embroidery threads remained untouched in her sewing basket until now). Why emphasize that the thread has remained *untouched* since Jacqueline's disappearance? By doing so, the display deliberately conjures forth the past presence of Jacqueline. These threads were last touched by the disappeared

19. Detail (pillowcase) of the display dedicated to *Jacqueline Paulette Drouilly Yurich, Sala de la Memoria*, Parque por la Paz: Villa Grimaldi. Photograph by the author.

young woman. Their materiality is the lasting remnant of her hand's presence. The last inscription in the display also evokes the permanence of this presence. It affirms: "Jacqueline, tu presencia permanece entre nosotros"[32] (Jacqueline, your presence remains among us).

The use of the object to conjure forth a disappeared life is also palpable in the depiction of Miguel Ángel Boitano, one of the disappeared individuals represented in the series *Memorias de Vida y Militancia*, a project by the Espacio Memoria y Derechos Humanos (ex ESMA) in Argentina. The premise of the project "busca recuperar las identidades individuales y colectivas de las personas desaparecidas y/o asesinadas en el centro clandestino que funcionó en la ESMA durante la última dictadura"[33] (looks to recover the individual and collective identities of disappeared and/or assasinated persons in the clandestine detention center that operated in the ESMA during the last dictatorship). The project consisted of the creation of postcards—montages that encapsulate a part of the essence of who the disappeared individual was during his/her lifetime. Additionally, within the project, some of the postcards are expanded upon in short videoclips that enhance what is depicted on paper. Boitano's postcard includes an image of a small plane that he constructed as a child. The back of the card explains that the object is an: "Avión de madera realizado por Miguel Ángel Boitano"[34] (Wooden airplance made by Miguel Ángel Boitano). Just as in the *Sala de la memoria* in Chile, the past presence of Boitano's hands is emphasized to the audience. The object's *authenticity* is underlined and asked to speak.

While Boitano also appears in the photograph, the object featured on the card conjures forth in an acute fashion his personhood. In July of 2013 I spoke with Miguel Ángel's mother, Ángela Catalina Paolin de Boitano (Lita, for short), who explained to me that when she first saw the postcard's design it was around the time she gave her testimony in the third Megacausa ESMA (trials that are currently still underway in Argentina). She was taken aback by the presence of the plane, which she immediately interpreted as an allusion to the death flights that ended the lives of so many of those who disappeared from the ESMA.[35] It wasn't until one of the people who had created the project explained to her that it was the plane that Miguel had made when he was young that she made the connection to her son's childhood. Through the object we see the fruits of a small child's creative labor. The object brings the mother—and ultimately the viewer—back to her son's individual personality, acting as a memory punctum, it rehumanizes him in the face of the monumentous atrocity of the death flights. Miguel Ángel's hands carefully constructed the plane, and his mark on this world via its crafting cannot be denied.

In the videoclip that expands upon the postcard project, Lita describes who her son was as an individual.[36] Like a proud mother, she mentions his accomplishments in school, the fact that he was rewarded with a trip to Italy, and that he had "pasta de líder" (natural leadership talent), demonstrated through his actions with the Juventud Peronista in the architecture school of the Universidad de Buenos Aires. The videoclip presents a montage of still images of Miguel Ángel, juxtaposed with letters from his friends (also shown in the postcard design). One of the significant features of the videoclip is that the only animated movement (aside from an intermittent shot of Lita speaking to the interviewer) is the small handcrafted plane that happily flies through the scenes, looping in carefree circles as if driven by a stunt pilot, bursting with life. The plane acts as a memory punctum in both the postcard and the videoclip, breaking the paralysis of the still photographs, conjuring forth the work of Miguel Ángel's hands and calling his individuality to the viewer's attention. Observing the plane juxtaposes the viewer in the present with the individual being of the past. It creates a moment in which to experience a part of the personality of Miguel Ángel, it stops the viewer in his/her tracks and begs him/her to think about Boitano's humanity, not just his tragic end.[37] The plane opens a space for a new experience with the past, for the creation of a ghostly *vivencia*.

This use of objects is repeated in many of the postcards that make up the project. In the postcard related to Carlos Alberto Chiappolini, the background is made up of his chessboard and in the lower right-hand corner appears an image of "una réplica del arma en madera que talló para obsequiarle a su suegra"[38] (a replica of the wooden gun that he made to give to his mother-in-law); The background of Franca Jarach's postcard is a painting she made while in France. The background of Hugo José Agosti's is a "cortinado familiar"[39] (family curtain). The background of Jorge Simón Adjiman and Estela María Gache's postcard is "el diseño de un jarrón pintado por Estela Gache"[40] (the design of a vase painted by Estela Gache). The background of José Antonio Cacabelos and Cecilia Inés Cacabelos's is "un entramado realizado por Cecilia en su cuaderno-diario"[41] (a lattice made by Cecilia in her daily notebook). The background of Jaime Eduardo Said and Alberto Ezequiel Said's postcard is a "libreta de recuerdos escolares de Alberto"[42] (notebook of Alberto's school memories). Within the repeated incorporation of specific objects in the backgrounds of these images, as well as in the use of personal objects in the displays in the *Sala de la Memoria* in Villa Grimaldi, there exists a specific relationship to the object in the wake of disappearance, especially with regards to personal objects—whether they were made by the hands of those who disappeared, or were mass-produced objects that were for some reason or another special to the disappeared person. This specific relationship has produced a reliance on objects to help give testimony where voices are lost, to evoke how such objects help create an individual in the past. Such projects demonstrate how after death or disappearance, we hold a new relationship to this object world.

In her study of how people deal with the objects or personal belongings left behind when people die, cultural sociologist Margaret Gibson observes: "As signs of the interface between personal and social, objects reveal the social construction of identity"[43] and affirms that "objects matter . . . because they are a part of us—we imprint objects and they imprint us materially, emotionally and memorially."[44] For Gibson, such objects are "memory traces"[45] that connect the living with the absence of the dead. The object thus acts as a suture, linking temporalities and memories, as well as individuals. However, Gibson observes that not all objects hold this power equally. Photography and clothing triggered stronger feelings of attachment than did mass-produced items, such as refrigerators or televisions. Yet, Gibson observes "the material legacies of death are often quite ordinary—a vase, a tea set, a pipe, a toy, a blanket, a chair, rings, books, clothing, photos; any number of personal and household objects."[46] Objects become imbued with these material legacies as they are imprinted with a trace of their former owner, such that they are transposed "into quasi-subjects, moving into that now vacated bereft place."[47]

Gibson's study considers the role of objects in the process of mourning in present-day Australia, unmarred by the jarring political context of the countries in the Southern Cone. In the case of the post-dictatorship context, I argue this imbuement of a quasi-subjectivity of the object is strengthened. Due to the disappearance of the body in these cases, the absence of confirmation of death, the lack of a body to mourn, the negation of a final place of rest at which to visit the deceased, and for many, the abruptly negated possibility of forming experiences with the dead combine to enhance the material object's importance as a stand-in for the disappeared person. Like a photograph, the former possession becomes the only material remainder of the disappeared body, the only residual presence of their past existence. Once imbued with metaphorical meaning by a third party, witness to the once present tie between the object and the disappeared subject, the object/artifact testifies to the continued presence of the disappeared ghost that is always to come, continually haunting the present material memories of the past.

By using objects in current activist projects, new generations are performing the conjuring required to speak with the ghostly remnants that remain attached to the objects of the past, to the belongings of the disappeared from the period before their detention. The Argentine virtual memory project, *Proyecto Tesoros* (an initiative of the group Colectivo de Hijos), is yet another example of how this haunted relationship with the objects of the past is being activated in the post-dictatorship in order to create encounters—experiences/ *vivencias*—with those who disappeared. The project's webpage explains that the initiative's "principal objetivo es la creación de un archivo que contenga los registros de aquellos objetos y documentos que pertenecían a nuestros padres, detenidos-desaparecidos y asesinados por el último genocidio en nuestro país"[48] (principle objective is the creation of an archive that will contain the record of those objects and documents that belonged to our parents, detained-disappeared and murdered by the last genocide in our country). In *Proyecto Tesoros*, ownership of the objects is again emphasized, tying the authenticity of the objects to the disappeared relatives. Yet, this project differs in an important way from the ones explored thus far in this chapter: rather than found objects of the past, the ones in this project are pieces that have stood throughout time in place of the parent. As Colectivo de Hijos explains, many of these "objetos y documentos nos acompañaron a lo largo de nuestra vida, otros los hemos descubierto con el tiempo. Todos dan cuenta de nuestra experiencia, que es particular pero también compartida con muchos otros"[49] (objects and documents accompanied us throughout our life, others we have discovered over time. All of them showcase our experience, which is particular, but also shared with many others). In place of the parent, the affective relationship built throughout the child's life ("nos acompañaron a lo largo de nuestra vida"[50] [they accompanied us throughout our life]) is with the object; the experience is with the material, not the person.

In *Proyecto Tesoros*, the evocation of the parent's story —of his/her personality—is not direct, but rather occurs mediated by a contemplation of the object. In place of the parent, the companionship normally felt between child and mother or father is with the object; the experience is with the *material*, not with the *person*. This, of course, is out of necessity. As Martorell notes, these *vivencias* with their parents are precisely what the children of the disappeared lack. While the family members that created the *Sala de la memoria* and contributed to *Memorias de Vida y Militancia* had experienced their loved ones prior to their disappearance, mobilizing those memories for others *to experience* their disappeared children/family members via the memory projects, in *Proyecto Tesoros* many of the participants never met their disappeared parents or were too young to create true experiential memories of them. Thus their experiences are with the objects left in the wake of disappearance; that relationship of affect that Martorell identifies as crucial to the creation of experiences occurs in an encounter with the objects their parents once held. The use of the object in *Proyecto Tesoros* truly relies on its spectral testimonial nature and creates the circumstances for a new set of ghostly *vivencias* to occur. Colectivo de Hijos affirms that it is "a través de estos fragmentos que podemos hoy hablar de nuestra propia condición, la de ser huérfanos producidos por el genocidio. El Proyecto intenta dar visibilidad a estas experiencias, y es por eso que elegimos una herramienta virtual para extender lazos hasta donde nos sea posible"[51] (through these fragments that we can talk today of our own condition, that of being orphans produced by the genocide. The Project attempts to give visibility to these experiences, and this is why we've selected a virtual tool in order to extend ties to wherever it is possible to reach). Thus, the project seeks simultaneously to showcase an experience with the disappeared individual, communicating something of him/her, but also to highlight the effect of that disappearance on the child. The object's testimony is thus a dual testimony, relating a truth about the past while simultaneously highlighting an effect on the present. *Proyecto Tesoros* created a series of videos, each of which presents an object while the child of the disappeared person explains what the object is and what his/her relationship is to it. The site explains:

> Además de fotografiar los objetos y documentos, registramos el relato de quien los atesora y les da un sentido, centrándonos en la relación de esos objetos con la propia historia. También realizamos tareas de restauración y conservación, con recomendaciones para guardarlos de la mejor manera posible para que no se deterioren.[52]

> (In addition to photographing the objects and documents, we record the story of he/she who treasures them and gives them meaning, centering ourselves on the relationship of these objects with the history itself. Additionally, we conduct restauration and conservation work, with recommendations on how to best store them so that they do not deteriorate.)

In *Proyecto Tesoros*, it is not "irrelevant" whether the biographical authors (the disappeared) of these objects are alive or dead, because the project is founded to create awareness of precisely this aspect. The point is that these objects *remain to be read*, or perhaps better stated, *remain to be engaged*. The projects explored in this chapter all engage these "dead" texts, appealing to the object world's durability to activate some possibility of dialogue with the dead. While the object can't answer in a language we speak, we can listen to the object and contemplate this lack of voice. Indeed, in the *Sala de la Memoria* we are asked to do precisely this—we are asked to reflect upon not a mass of disappeared bodies, but on the individual lives of young people who were never heard from again. We are asked to create an experience with these people via their personal belongings.

With *Proyecto Tesoros*, the children of the disappeared re-create the circumstances by which they were able to come to know a part of their parents. The visitor to the project's site experiences the same process that the child now narrates. As the visiting public, we look to the object, know it has a specific past, know it knew the disappeared person during his/her lifetime. We desire to know the truth, to dialogue with the ghost, yet we can never achieve that transparent dialogue which we seek. The specter it conjures forth remains a mute witness and leaves us suspended in our own desire. But, that same desire is also powerful. In placing us in the position of desiring to know more, but not being able to find out more, the object acts as a tether between our own place and that of the child of disappeared parents. While their experience of desiring to know their parents is beyond comparison, the frustration of our own inability to engage the object's voice can bring us to a realm of shared sentience with their experience, can help facilitate empathy by placing us partially in their shoes. Such an encounter both affirms the horror of the past and animates us in the present. In truncating our desire to know, in frustrating us, it elides the construction of a smooth historical narrative. As Colin Davis affirms:

> Hauntology is a part of an endeavor to keep raising the stakes of literary study, to make it a place where we can interrogate our relation to the dead, examine the elusive identities of the living, and explore the boundaries between the thought and the unthought. The ghost becomes a focus for competing epistemological and ethical positions.[53]

The ghost, in *Proyecto Tesoros* made manifest via the conjuring of the object, creates disruptions, it raises the stakes, it causes actions and promotes the ongoing contemplation germane to the fight for the protection of human rights, thus contributing not only to the reconstruction of the narrative void left from disappearance, but also honoring the legacy of the past in working to affirm that such atrocities never again occur in the future.

Ghostly Vivencias: Reappearance and Personal Belongings in Cautiva

Anthropologist Daniel Miller argues that "possessions often remain profound and usually the closer our relationships are with objects, the closer our relationships are with people."[54] Miller calls for us to listen to things in order to gain "access to an authentic other voice"[55] and, in so doing, echoes the issue that lies at the core of many of the considerations of *testimonio* explored in Chapter Three. Miller's stance is that the material belongings of people create a very individual aesthetic, one which we can engage in our search for information about the person.[56] For Miller, this aesthetic stems from the individual and is not random, but rather "above all [is] a configuration of human values, feelings and experiences."[57] The difference between Miller's study and the project at hand is that Miller is consistently able to visit the homes of the people who appear as subjects in his anthropological "portraits" of their possessions and speak with them at the same time that he views their living quarters.[58] He remarks in one case study: "To see the bridge between concern for objects and concern for people in Mr. Clarke requires listening carefully and putting together different stories."[59] Miller's subject is alive and well and he is able to answer questions and clarify points of contention. What happens when this same close-listening (reading?) is applied to the analysis of the former possessions of a person with whom a one-on-one dialogue is no longer possible? It is at that point in which the individual aesthetic combines with the ghostly aura attached to the object-as-witness and produces a spectral testimony.

To see this combination at work, I turn to Gastón Biraben's film *Cautiva*, in which a young woman discovers that she is the child of disappeared parents through an act of investigative analysis by a judge after she has surgery on her appendix.[60] Once again engaging a poetics of DNA (as was explored in Chapter Four), Cristina's blood speaks a truth from the past unbeknownst to her, revealing that her parents are really her appropriators and that her real birth occurred a year earlier than she has been told, on the day Argentina won the 1978 World Cup. Born to two young architects who disappeared, but whose family has been searching for her for years, a resistant Cristina is restituted her birth identity, Sofia. Sofia's re-encounter with the disappeared parents she never knew in person occurs first only through old photographs; then, gradually—with the help a friend who also has a disappeared father—her investigation yields more and more information. She is able to ascertain where her parents were held captive and her friend is able to locate one of the nurses that was present when Sofia's mother gave birth to her. Aside from these scant details, Sofia's encounter with her mother occurs through the discovery of the objects that belonged to her before she disappeared. The mother's childhood room, left intact by Sofia's grandmother, is a treasure trove of objects, each of which contributes to the creation of a material portrait, an aesthetic of who her mother was during her lifetime.

The film ends just after Cristina confronts her appropriators and accepts her "new" (true) identity as Sofia. After this volatile confrontation, she flees to the home her birth mother designed (she was an architect) and in which her birth mother's sister now lives with her family. Sofia is then shown crying over the photographs of her disappeared parents, then, in the next scene, we see her in the midst of a conversation with her maternal grandmother. Her last line of the film is "Nana, lo de la desaparición de ellos, es eterno?"[61] ("Nana, this thing with the disappearance of them, is it forever?") This comment marks Sofia's transition from her initial reluctance and refusal of a relationship with her blood grandmother to her acceptance and use of the family's affective term "Nana" to refer to her (up to this point she has refused to call her Nana). The camera then slowly pans over the objects that populate the bedroom used by Sofia's mother prior to her disappearance. In a long shot that gradually moves away from the bedroom and the house to eventually become an aerial shot of the city, Sofia is seen standing on the balcony of the house, gazing out into the night. This last line, asking if disappearance is eternal, immediately followed by a visual inventory of the belongings of her disappeared mother, highlights the new valorization of things left in the wake of disappearance. While Sofia's parents may be gone forever, these material proofs of their personalities remain behind, waiting for an encounter.

At the same time, another, more explicit, narrative of hauntology also marks the film. The grandmother's house is "haunted," according to Sofia's young cousin. As he enthusiastically tells Sofia, he even saw a ghost there once! Sofia herself experiences the ghost in a dream the first night she stays with her grandmother. At the end of the film, as she stands in the balcony of what was to be her childhood home, gazing out on the city, a breeze blows through the curtains that hang in the doorway behind her, another cinematic gesture toward the ghostly state of the places and the things of her newly restituted past. The re-encounter with the mother's room uses an aesthetic of the individual who disappeared to reveal the network of relationships she had, not only with people (presumably those family and friends who restituted Sofia's identity) but with the material world: her possessions. The image created in this scene is an aesthetic which produces a life narrative; the individual emerges out of the collective, the personality of the living person from the past is evoked, and the conditions for an experience with her are created. In the film this aesthetic runs parallel to what the vitrinas in the Sala de la Memoria were designed to do: individualize and humanize the often faceless and gargantuan violence of the past.

Merging Voice and Object: Spectral Testimony in the Work of Lola Arias

By way of conclusion, I would like to examine one last instance of the activation of the spectral testimonial capacity of the object in order to reconstruct and transmit knowledge about the past. The theatrical productions *Mi vida después* (2009) and *El año en que nací* (2012), conceptualized, written, and directed by Lola Arias, take the still-life initiative of projects such as the *Sala de la Memoria* and *Proyecto Tesoros* one step further by not only presenting objects and their stories, but creating a theatrical experience in which voices and objects combine to communicate to audiences—not only Argentine, Chilean, or Uruguayan, but international[62]—the memory of the recent past. Arias (originally from Argentina herself) explains the creation of her work, *El año en que nací*, a play that enmeshes the voice and the object to recount the multiple and often conflicting experiences of living during the Chilean dictatorship:

> In 2009, I did a play called *Mi vida después* in which a group of young people born during the Argentinean dictatorship (1976–1983) reconstruct the life of their parents with the help of photos, documents, [and] family films. I was invited with this piece to Santiago de Chile and in parallel to that, I did a workshop with the same concept of the Argentinean piece but with Chilean stories. I was looking for people whose stories reflects [sic] the 17 years of dictatorship in Chile. I wanted to have people with different backgrounds: people whose parents were in the guerrilla or in the military or went into exile or were indifferent to politics.[63]

Arias's work has been identified by Anna White-Nockleby as *teatro documental*, plays that "entienden, investigan y construyen este *antes* de la conciencia a través de *fragmentos*—de objetos, reproducciones y rumores que parecen haber sido sacados de la vida real de los actores"[64] (understand, investigate, and construct this *before* of the conscience through *fragments*—of objects, reproductions and rumors that seem to have been taken right from the real life of the actors). White-Nockleby explains that *Mi vida después* was written

A partir de entrevistas con los actores en las que ellos le contaron sobre las vidas de sus padres y le mostraron las pertenencias —fotos, ropa, cartas, grabaciones en cinta— de sus vidas reales. Desde allí, Arias escribió la obra. Así los espectadores sienten de manera visceral la relación entre las historias de los personajes y la vida de los actores que existe fuera del escenario.[65]

(Based on interviews with the actors in which they told her about the lives of their parents and they showed her the belongings —photos, clothes, cards, tape recordings— from their real lives. From there, Arias wrote the play. In this way the spectators feel in a visceral way the relationship between the histories of the characters and the life of the actors that exists outside the scene.)

Both *Mi vida después* and *El año en que nací*'s use of the objects of the past, of "photos, letters, tapes, used clothes"[66] infuses the very personal stories enacted by the actors with a spectral testimonial quality. While it is true that these items are being primarily utilized as props to accompany the actor's voice and actions, it is important to remember that these items, invoked within the scene, are also used to demonstrate and convey the memories (often in conflict even as they are presented on stage) that the second generation affected by the repression has from the generation of their parents. Some memories remain incomplete, and the actors are forthcoming about this. The play is, after, all a work in progress: "The piece is re-written because life is re-written all the time. Whenever something new happens in the life of the performers, it becomes part of the piece. The piece is like a living creature that is growing with the years."[67] Ultimately, in the same way that the animation of Miguel Ángel's plane in the videoclip of *Memorias de Vida y Militancia* creates a memory punctum that interpellates the present-day viewer with the past and facilitates a ghostly *vivencia* with the disappeared, the combination of the voices of the actors (who communicate their personal histories on stage) with the objects from the past in these plays enmeshes the material and the voice in an effort to dramatize the testimonial encounter with the objects of the past, depicting a scene of communion in which the present experiences the ghosts of the past through an affective commingling and conversation with material belongings.

In her examination of the mountain of shoes on display at the United States Holocaust Memorial Museum, Liliane Weissberg contends that "human beings give testimony. Testimony is also given by objects."[68] She continues to argue, "homogenized as one group, these shoes speak as a mass and exemplify mass murder."[69] The objects that make up the *Sala de la memoria*, *Proyecto Tesoros*, and are used in Lola Arias's plays perform the exact opposite task; while the piles of objects from the Holocaust testify to the incomprehensible scale of the violence, the use of objects in projects such as those explored in this chapter work to re-individualize the disappeared, to put unique profiles and personalities to those lost in the collective of disappearance, all the while calling attention to the incomplete nature of this commingling.

All of the projects explored in this chapter demonstrate that the postdictatorship generations have identified a productive power held in the (haunted) objects of the violent past and are turning to that potential in an effort to dialogue with the lost voices of the dictatorship (to speak with the ghosts) via the material and, at the same time, to facilitate that same conversation for others. Throughout this project I have limited my discussion of the ghost to Derrida's notion of the productive specter, turning away from thinkers such as Abraham and Torok who posit that the phantom is a psychic manifestation meant to protect the individual by carefully guarding a potentially traumatizing secret, thus repressing rather than revealing information about the past. I have done this, primarily, because the archival and artistic projects I found in my research all seem to hold a common, hopeful, outlook toward the objects of the past, a desire to turn to them in an effort to fill gaps in memory. Using *things*, such projects work to produce a material narrative capable of re-appearing the lost voices of the past, and they attempt to teach us to speak with the specters that lie on the "other" side of objects.

The Testimonial Splendor of Objects

꙰

She awoke when Adriana, iron in hand, roused her with a surprising gentleness, made her get up, and took her to the bathroom where she locked them both in without a sound, and, using a knife as a screwdriver, took the iron apart. It was the first time Sara had seen the inside of an iron. She marveled at how Adriana, with the fingers of a surgeon, extracted tiny pieces of paper that had been folded several times, handing them to her. At how she then put the iron back together and left the bathroom, closing the door behind her.[1]

At the concentration camp kitchen they made a list of her belongings [. . .] 'A wedding ring, a watch . . . dress color . . . bra . . . she doesn't wear one . . . shoes . . . she doesn't have any?' [. . .] When she thought the interrogation session was about to begin, they took her to a room. She walked down a tiled corridor, then an old wooden floor. After arriving at the wretched bed assigned to her, she discovered a ragged blanket.
She used it to cover her feet and did not feel so helpless.[2]

Con la almohada probaría, pues la relación con ella provenía desde mi niñez, había pasado por mi adolescencia, y por mi casamiento, donde no le permití a mi suegra más que hacerle una funda, sobre la que ya tenía. La había pedido cuando estuve en el cuartel, y había llegado pese a ser de lana y poder ser portadora de cualquier cosa adentro; había ido conmigo a Punta de Rieles y vuelto al cuartel.[3]

(With the pillow I would try, since the relationship with it came from my childhood, had passed through my adolescence, and through my wedding, where I didn't permit my mother-in-law more than to make it a pillowcase, which I still had on it. I had asked for it when I was in the military headquarters, and it had arrived to me even despite being made of wool and potentially hiding anything inside of it; it had gone with me to Punta de Rieles and returned to the military headquarters.)

THIS PROJECT BEGAN WITH my own frustration with not being able to make-up or make-real in my mind an image of the scenes I was reading in the testimonial accounts of the dictatorships that I encountered during my research. My privilege of growing up in the safety of a small city in the upper Midwestern United States where to this day some of my relatives leave their homes unlocked when they leave, coupled with my never having known violence outside of the movies, meant that I had very little, if anything, in common with the survivors whose accounts I read. I could not fathom their pain, could not visualize the magnitude of their mistreatment, even with pages and pages of description of sounds, of places, of smells. Even amidst such a wealth of sensorial detail, I found very little with which I could identify in order to visualize the scenes that the authors attempted to describe. I could empathize with the weight of their words, but I could not "see" this past—except for the objects (or so I thought). Alicia Kozameh described an iron and I could create its image, imagine its weight in my hand. A drawing of a tin cup appeared in her text and I could feel the tin cups my grandfather favored in the summertime on my lips, could taste the commingling of cold water with metal. Alicia Partnoy described a ragged blanket and I saw the comfort of the (now ragged) blankee from my childhood. Jorge Tiscornia described a pillow and I looked to the pillow on my sofa. It was through objects that I found a small element of common ground with these voices and it made me stop and deliberate as to why these everyday things helped me get to a space in which I could begin to visualize this past.

Objects mark our experience with the world. In any given day I sit where others have sat—on the bus stop bench, on the bus seat, in an office chair, in a classroom desk or a lecture hall seat, in a restaurant booth, even on a public toilet. I move through the same object world as those around me, occupying the places that others have experienced before me. At the same time, I also touch particular, less public, objects. I favor one pen over another when I sit down to write, choose one shirt over another in the morning when I dress, have a "favorite" and "most comfortable" pair of shoes, wear a jacket and carry a bag by which my friends recognize me from afar when we happen to pass each other at a distance. My desk is differentiated from others in our identical office spaces by small pieces that communicate my personality. Yet, most of the time, I myself notice none of these things. Until the pen runs out of ink, my shirt rips, my shoes begin to pinch, or the strap on my bag gives out. As Heidegger points out to us, the broken tool no longer hides from view.[4] We notice the *thing*, the work it was doing all along, its (as Harman puts it) *tool-being*.[5] When these things happen, I *notice* the things around me. I *notice* the *tool-being* of objects: that my working pen made an impression on my paper, thus facilitating my writing, that my shirt kept me warm, that my shoes made it comfortable to walk long distances, and that my bag extended and amplified the carrying power of my arms, of my body.

Yet, even this seemingly common ground I found with objects is deceiving. As I further examined the narratives I explore in Chapter One, I realized that in the concentration camp or the detention center, the order of *things* is different. One is stripped of all personal belongings, stripped down to, as Marcelo Estefanell puts it, "un hombre numerado"[6] (a numbered man), without individualizing identity. Objects meant to alleviate pain become producers of pain; everything has the potential to be a weapon. But, at the same time, the subject, broken down by the process of unmaking his/her world, undergoes a change. The subject can no longer help but notice the objects around him/her. It is not the tool that breaks here, revealing its tool-being, but the subject that breaks and in that very process acquires a new relationship to the world in which s/he cannot help but notice the *tool-being* of things. Seemingly useless objects (a water faucet, a matchbox) become the most crucial of allies. In Chapter Two, one sees how this new relationship to objects produced a material testimonial legacy in the *artesanías carcelarias* and the *manualidades*. The most unassuming of items were turned to in order to make real and exterior the seemingly inexpressible. The most common of items became crucial for survival, stepping in to fill the void of that which could not be accessed, to suture oneself to a semblance of individual agency and action. What we see left over from this process are bread crumbs that became beautiful and intricate floral sculptures and crayons as the basis of masterpiece works of art.

Testimonial narratives reveal this different relationship to objects, to the potential for survival they offer to the subject with their *tool-being*. In the camp or detention center, *things* like the iron never break, their purpose is simply modified. The change undergone by the subject produced an entirely new order of extraordinary things, a new utility of objects largely unconnected to their understood use. At the outset of this project, I was wrong to believe that my visualization of the object from my experience as a reader could approximate a common ground with these voices, because, as Alicia Kozameh puts it, I "don't know what a jacket is."[7] Thus, the iron described by Kozameh and the ragged blanket described by Partnoy may be imaginable in my mind, but their true meaning for the detained subject remains inaccessible to me. These objects, haunted by their pasts, bring me, the outside reader, to a place of shared sentience, but at the same time the difference between my subjectivity and that of the survivors' keeps my relationship to the object separate and different. That is the meaning of spectral testimony in this project. These objects, many made by the hands of those who are no longer here to speak, others emblematic of who these individuals were before disappearance, are at once the lasting, durable remainder we have of the past and a conscious reminder of the inaccessibility of the "truth" of the violence of that moment. In that sense, the spectral testimony yielded by objects is both frustrating and extremely productive.

As I delved further into my research, it became clear that this simultaneously frustrating and productive nature of the testimony of objects is being engaged with growing frequency in the post-dictatorship. Perhaps emerging out of the circumstances of the limitations of life, as many of the individuals who still hold live, vivid memories of the disappeared age and pass away, taking with them the firsthand knowledge of those individuals, more memory projects are turning to the material as a lasting way to access the past. Perhaps revealing that in the wake of the violence of the dictatorships, in the aftermath of the collective loss of 30,000 disappeared, even society-at-large undergoes a transformation in its experience with the material world, producing a new *noticing* of the memory capacity of things. Projects such as the exhibits in the museums of memory in Chile, Argentina, and Uruguay, the *Sala de la Memoria* in the Parque por la Paz: Villa Grimaldi, *Química de la Memoria, Proyecto Tesoros, Proyecto Vestigios*, and *Memorias de Vida y Militancia* all recognize that while a lifespan (and thus, a narrating voice) may be limited by nature, the material object remains with seeming permanence. *Things*, material witnesses, remain to tell us their stories, but they simultaneously call to our attention the impossibility of narrating the past, the magnitude of the violence that cannot be put into words. Object witnesses, with their silent and non-communicative *tool-being*, continually bring us back to the very frustration with which I began this project, but in that process they force us to undergo a journey that confronts this frustration, that experiences the labors of memory and along the way realizes an aspect of the past and animates us to work toward assuring that such abuse never again occurs in the future.

With this project, I sought to articulate an initial approach to theorizing the testimony yielded by objects. However, I recognize that this is only a first step. In the interest of placing parameters around this initial discussion, I did not fully engage one of the limitations of using objects to transmit this history, nor how that limitation impacts the object's transmission of its history. Many of the examples I explored in this project, especially in the period of the post-dictatorship, ultimately document or communicate the object to the viewer via a photographic register (be it still-image or video). While one could dismiss this register as simply a medium through which to disseminate accessibility to the object for the viewer, in terms of its impact on how the object gives testimony it merits further consideration. Walter Benjamin's lament of the loss of the auratic character of art[8] is largely tied to photography and film. His observation that the "changes it [the work of art] may have suffered in physical condition over the years … can be revealed only through chemical or physical analyses which it is impossible to perform on a reproduction"[9] is apt for the discussion of the objects this project has explored. Benjamin posits that "the authenticity of a thing is the essence of all that is transmissible from its beginning, ranging from its substantive duration to its testimony to the history which it has experienced."[10] Unlike the photograph, the object (what I have compared to Agamben's "complete witness") retains the aura of the past subject, the living "firsthand" witness, and in this way becomes the firsthand object witness. In a discussion of used clothing, Nelly Richard has posited that "the fabric of used clothing is a repository of odors and secret stains"[11] and that such a residue "introduces doubt, it posits uncertainty, it casts a suspicion that infects the sterilized vision of the world."[12] This aura, this secret stain on the object, this ghost, not only introduces doubt, put provides the productive possibility for memory to those who seek to dialogue with such hidden phantoms of the past. The question remains as to how the photograph or video alter this possibility.

Additionally, due to such an auratic memory possibility, the objects such as those in Uruguay's Museum of Memory remain protected under glass, revered for their authenticity, carefully preserved by archivists—while at the same time, I am free to purchase reproductions of such carefully crafted and relied-upon items (Pardal's deck of cards, Tiscornia's *almanaque*) and toss them in my backpack to take home with me from the museum. These reproductions are not haunted objects, for they lack the auratic charater of the originals. They do not ask me to learn to speak with their ghosts because those ghosts, those residues, simply do not exist. But does that completely negate their testimonial quality?

Conversely, the delicate flower sculptures Stela Reyes made in Punta de Rieles and allowed me to carefully hold when I visited her collection, are an object that is haunted—they are not copies but the originals, their material derived from the scant food (in this case, bread) that the prisoners were given to eat during their detention. Feeling the tiny, fragile, flowers in my hand, I *know* I'm holding a piece of history. As I carefully turn them to examine the material of which they are made, I ask myself, who else touched this material? Whose hands were involved that did not survive as Stela did? What secret stains lay enmeshed in the fragile material that forms the delicate petals? In the delicate dye coloring the prisoners leeched out of their sweaters? From that authentic character derives the object's role as witness. Feeling the weight of these flowers in my hand makes me keenly aware of the historical signifi- cance I am holding. What I hope to have shown in this project is that, much as Claudia Bernardi explains, "skeletons in a mass grave give me a profound tenderness . . . I am touching history with my hands,"[13] there is a testimonial power held in the object.

With this project, I aimed to explore the simultaneous existence of the hu- man and the material, untangling some of the nuances that occur within this relationship when it is altered by extreme acts of violence. Approaching from the reverse of Baudrillard's claim that "we have always lived off the splendor of the subject and the poverty of the object,"[14] I sought to position the object in the role of witness, as an ally in the prisoner's struggle for survival, and as a made-material testimony of that person's resistance. In introducing the con- cept of "spectral testimony," I offer an initial means of theorizing the object- as-witness in the temporality after violence, examining how the *thing*'s past is used in the present in an effort to create memory about the past, filling the narrative void left by disappearance in order to rehumanize those who lost their lives in a confluence of present voices, phantom subjects, and past ma- terial truths. However, I also contend that this work is incomplete and that this project, in establishing the testimonial importance of objects, ultimately serves as a call to our field for further study of the material objects from not just this period, but all contexts of genocide, mass atrocity, and dictatorship.

Introduction

1. Claudia Bernardi, "An Angel Passes By: Silence and Memories at the Massacre of El Mozote," in *Inhabiting Memory: Essays on Memory and Human Rights in the Americas*, ed. Marjorie Agosín (Texas: Wings Press, 2011), 36.

2. Ibid., 43.

3. Jean Baudrillard, *Fatal Strategies* (London: Pluto, 1990), 111.

4. Bernardi, "An Angel," 29.

5. Marjorie Agosín, *Inhabiting Memory: Essays on Memory and Human Rights in the Americas* (Texas: Wings Press, 2011), xvi.

6. Francine Masiello, *The Art of Transition: Latin American Culture and Neoliberal Crisis* (Durham: Duke University Press, 2001), 13.

7. See Pierre Nora, *Realms of Memory: Rethinking the French Past* (New York: Columbia University Press, 1996); Andreas Huyssen, *Present Pasts: Urban Palimpsests and the Politics of Memory* (California: Stanford University Press, 2003); Silvia Tandeciarz, "Citizens of Memory: Refiguring the Past in Postdictatorship Argentina," *PMLA* 122 no. 1 (2007); Elizabeth Jelin, *State Repression and the Labors of Memory*, trans. Judy Rein and Marcial Godoy-Anativia (Minneapolis: University of Minnesota Press, 2003); James Young, *The Texture of Memory: Holocaust Memorials and Meaning* (New Haven: Yale University Press, 1993).

8. Margarita Saona, "Plain Things and Space: Metonymy and Aura in Memorials of Social Trauma," in *Layers of Memory and the Discourse of Human Rights: Artistic and Testimonial Practices in Latin America and Iberia*, ed. Ana Forcinito, *Hispanic Issues On Line* 14 (2014).

9. See Ruth Vusckovic Cespedes and Sylvia Ríos Montero, *Libres en prisión: La otra artesanía. Artefactos creados en dictadura / Chile 1973-1990* (Santiago: Editorial USACH, 2015).

10. Jelin, *State Repression*.

11. Paul Sondrol, "1984 Revisited? A Re-examination of Uruguay's Military Dictatorship," *Bulletin of Latin American Research* 11 no. 2 (1992): 190.

12. Ibid., 190.

13. Emilio Crenzel, *Memory of the Argentine Disappearances: The Political History of Nunca Más*, trans. Laura Pérez Carrara (New York: Routledge, 2012), 16.

14. "ESMA: Entregaron fotos de desaparecidos arrojados al mar," *Todo Noticias*, 15 December 2011, https://tn.com.ar/policiales/vuelos-de-la-muerte-la-cidh -entrego-fotos-de-desaparecidos-arrojados-al-mar_076200.

15. *Encontrando a Víctor*, directed by Natalia Bruschtein (2004; Mexico: Centro de Capacitación Cinematográfica (CCC), La Lavandería Producciones, 2004), DVD.

16. See Mauricio Cohen Salama, *Tumbas anónimas: Informe sobre la identificación de restos de víctimas de la represión ilegal* (Buenos Aires: Catalogos Editoria, 1992).

17. See Roxana Seguel, et al., "Londres 38: Prospección exploratoria. Búsqueda, recuperación y análisis de evidencia biológica y cultural en un centro de detención y tortura" (Santiago: Dirección de Bibliotecas Archivos y Museos, Londres 38, Centro Nacional de Conservación y Restauración, 2012), https://www.londres38 .cl/1934/w3-article-93321.html.

18. Graham Harman, *Tool Being: Heidegger and the Metaphysics of Objects* (Chicago: Open Court, 2002).

19. Kimberly Nance, *Can Literature Promote Justice? Trauma Narrative and Social Action in Latin American Testimonio* (Nashville: Vanderbilt University Press, 2006), 5.

20. David Stoll, *Rigoberta Menchú and the Story of All Poor Guatemalans* (Boulder: Westview Press, 2008).

21. Georg Gugelberger, *The Real Thing: Testimonial Discourse and Latin America* (Durham: Duke University Press, 1996).

22. Arturo Arias, *The Rigoberta Menchú Controversy* (Minneapolis: University of Minnesota Press, 2001).

23. Louis Detwiler and Janis Breckenridge. *Pushing the Boundaries of Latin American Testimony: Meta-morphoses and Migrations* (New York: Palgrave Macmillan, 2012), 2.

24. Linda S. Maier and Isabel Dulfano, *Woman as Witness: Essays on Testimonial Literature by Latin American Women* (New York: Peter Lang, 2004).

25. Joanna Bartrow, *Subject to Change: The Lessons of Latin American Women's Testimonio for Truth, Fiction, and Theory* (Chapel Hill: University of North Carolina Press, 2005).

26. Detwiler and Breckenridge, *Pushing the Boundaries*, 2.

27. Nance, *Can Literature*, 158.

28. Detwiler and Breckenridge, *Pushing the Boundaries*, 3.

29. Ibid., 3-4.

30. Ibid., 4.

31. Ibid., 4.

32. Ibid., 5

33. Ibid., 5

34. Emilio Crenzel, *Memory of the Argentine Disappearances.*

35. Hugo Vezzetti, "El testimonio en la formación de la memoria social," in *Crítica del testimonio: Ensayos sobre las relaciones entre memoria y relato*, ed. Cecilia Vallina (Rosario: Beatriz Viterbo Editora, 2008), 27.

36. The concept of the "narrative void" left by disappearance has been articulated by Michael Lazzara in *Chile in Transition: The Poetics and Politics of Memory* (Gainesville: University of Florida Press, 2006) as well as by Gabriel Gatti in *Surviving Forced Disappearance in Argentina and Uruguay: Identity and Meaning* (New York: Palgrave Macmillan, 2014).

37. Hugo Vezzetti, "El testimonio," 29.

38. See Katherine Hite, *The Art of Commemoration: Memorials to Struggle in Latin America and Spain* (London: Routledge, 2012) and Jill Bennett, *Empathic Vision: Affect, Trauma, and Contemporary Art* (Stanford: Stanford University Press, 2005).

39. Jacques Derrida, *Specters of Marx: The State of the Debt, the Work of Mourning, and the New International* (New York: Routledge, 1994).

40. Dori Laub, "Bearing Witness or the Vicissitudes of Listening," in *Testimony: Crises of Witnessing in Literature, Psychoanalysis, and History*, eds. Shoshana Felman and Dori Laub (New York: Routledge, 1992), 58.

41. Ana Forcinito, *Los umbrales del testimonio: Entre las narraciones de los sobrevivientes y las señas de la posdictadura* (Madrid: Iberoamericana, 2012), 12-13.

42. Nance, *Can Literature*, 158.

43. Harman, *Tool Being.*

44. Elaine Scarry, *The Body in Pain: The Making and Unmaking of the World* (New York: Oxford University Press, 1985).

45. Giorgio Agamben, *Remnants of Auschwitz: The Witness and the Archive* (New York: Zone, 1999).

46. Judith Roof, *The Poetics of DNA* (Minneapolis: University of Minnesota Press, 2007).

Chapter One

1. Elizabeth Grosz, "Darwin and Feminism: Preliminary Investigations for a Possible Alliance," in *Material Feminisms,* eds. Stacy Alaimo and Susan Hekman (Bloomington: Indiana University Press, 2008), 64.

2. Elaine Scarry, *The Body in Pain: The Making and Unmaking of the World* (New York: Oxford University Press, 1985), 161.

3. Alicia Partnoy, *The Little School: Tales of Disappearance and Survival*, trans. Alicia Partnoy and Lois Athey and Sandra Braunstein (San Francisco: Cleis Press, 1998), 26.

4. Scarry, *The Body*, 39.

5. Partnoy, *The Little School*, 25.

6. Ibid., 26

7. Ibid., 26

8. Ibid., 26

9. Ibid., 27

10. " . . . that one-flowered slipper amid the dirt and fear, the screams and the torture, that flower so plastic, so unbelievable, so ridiculous, was like a stage prop, almost obscene, absurd, a joke." Partnoy, *The Little School*, 28.

11. Partnoy, *The Little School*, 28.

12. Ibid., 28.

13. Harman, *Tool Being*.

14. Jane Bennett, *Vibrant Matter: A Political Ecology of Things* (London: Duke University Press, 2010).

15. "The more efficiently a tool performs its function, the more it tends to recede from view" (Harman, *Tool-Being*, 21).

16. Martin Heidegger, "The Thing," in *The Object Reader*, eds. Fiona Candlin and Raiford Guins (New York: Routledge, 2009), 113-123.

17. Harman, *Tool-Being*, 20, emphasis in original.

18. Harman is very emphatic in his theoretical development of Heidegger's tool analysis that the tool is a category that does not limit itself to *equipment*, but envelops all material beings (including human *Dasein*): "No entity lies outside of tool-being; equally, no object has a privileged status with respect to it, whether it be *Dasein* or well-known devices such as lanterns" (*Tool-Being* 42). Harman's contribution to Heideggerian thought further develops the tool analysis and argues that the tool being of objects is observable in the way in which objects interact with each other, even without the presence of human *Dasein*. He gives the example of the earth's plates and their shifting, their interaction with each other, an agential movement that then causes the distinct consequence of earthquakes.

19. This chapter will limit itself to a consideration of found objects and the expression of possession over objects already present in the space of detention. Chapter Two will then continue this discussion in a consideration of objects created by detainees from the space of the detention center.

20. As John Beverley writes of the fear tactics of more recent employs of torture:

"Torture or practices approximating torture . . . are not primarily about information that may be useful in fighting terrorism. They have become themselves a form of terrorism, exercised by or with the complicity of the State, intended to reinforce or re-impose relations of power and inequality in situations where these have been challenged or come into question" ("Torture and Human Rights," 99).

21. Inge Genefke and Peter Vesti, "Diagnosis of Governmental Torture," in *Caring for Victims of Torture*, eds. James M. Jaranson and Michael K. Popkin (Washington D.C.: American Psychiatric Press, 1998), 47.

22. Hernán Vidal, *Chile: Poética de la tortura política* (Santiago: Mosquito Comunicaciones, 2001), 12.

23. Mario Benedetti's *Pedro y el capitán: Pieza en cuatro partes* (Mexico: Editorial Nueva Imagen, 1979) derives its power specifically from a revision of this scene—the prisoner being tortured actively asserts his individuality to provoke his torturer, asking him questions with the goal of humanizing not only himself but also his torturer, and thereby implicating the torturer personally in the mistreatment of a specific individual, rather than a numbered, unfeeling, body object.

24. Janice T. Gibson and Mika Haritos-Fatouros note hints of this phenomenon in "The Education of a Torturer," *Psychology Today* 20 (1986): 50-58, and Scarry's *The Body in Pain* also underlines this element in the design and implementation of torture as a political weapon.

25. CONADEP, *Nunca Más: A Report by Argentina's National Commission on Disappeared People* (London: Faber and Faber, 1986), 19.

26. See M. Edurne Portela, *Displaced Memories: The Poetics of Trauma in Argentine Women's Writing* (Lewisburg: Bucknell University Press, 2009); Mary Jane Treacy, "Double Binds: Latin American Women's Prison Memories," *Hypathia* 11 no. 4 (1996): 130-145; and Alicia Partnoy, "Cuando vienen matando: On Prepositional Shifts and the Struggle of Testimonial Subjects for Agency," *PMLA* 121 no. 5 (2006): 1665-1669.

27. In *Vibrant Matter: A Political Ecology of Things*, Jane Bennett theorizes a "vitality intrinsic to things as such" (xiii) that recognizes the impersonal political affect of *things* as a type of material/nonhuman agency. In using the term "vibrancy" here, I am gesturing toward Bennett's political theory of the agency of the material.

28. Sofía Pi, et. al. *Historias debidas. 11 entrevistas a ex presos políticos* (Montevideo: Ediciones del CIEJ, 2013), 28.

29. Partnoy, *The Little School*, 46.

30. Ibid., 30. Partnoy's perspective also resonates outside of the Argentine case. When asked whether there had been "gestos de humanidad" (gestures of humanity) in her experience in La Paloma (one of the detention centers in Uruguay), Martha Valentini remarked: "Para uno de mis cumpleaños, que casualmente fue un día de

paquete, varios compañeros de los que estaban en aquel patio sacrificaron la man-
zana que les había tocado ese día, para enviármela como regalo; quedé con cuatro
o cinco manzanas en la falda: vendada, atada, pero con manzanas de cariño y com-
pañerismo. Es un recuerdo entrañable" (Pi, *Historias*, 31) (For one of my birthdays,
which by coincidence was a day the family care packages arrived, various comrades
who were on that cellblock sacrificed the apple they had received that day to send
it to me as a gift; I was left with four or five apples in my skirt: blindfolded, tied-up,
but with apples of kindness and comradery. It's a moving memory.)

31. Partnoy, *The Little School*, 9, my emphasis.

32. Ibid., 84.

33. Ibid., 84.

34. Ibid., 84.

35. Ibid., 84.

36. Objects as acts of creation (making one's own world) will be further explored
in Chapter Two.

37. Partnoy, *The Little School*, 88.

38. Ibid., 90.

39. Alicia Kozameh, *Steps Under Water*, trans. David E. Davis (Berkeley: University of California Press, 1996), 75.

40. Ibid., 75.

41. Ibid., 72.

42. Ibid., 76.

43. Ibid., 76.

44. Ibid., 78.

45. Ibid., 79.

46. It is worth noting that the jacket is not made of cloth, but leather, a materiality that is consistently emphasized by Kozameh in her text. All leather, which is
treated cowhide, at some point in its existence was the skin of a living animal. Thus,
the jacket holds a materiality whose production has additional resonance in the
discussion of the realm of the living and the non-living. In this context, the identification of Hugo with the jacket, and now as a second-skin for the military officer, is
even more jarring.

47. Adriana Calvo, "Campos," in *Ni el flaco perdón de Dios: HIJOS de desaparecidos*, eds. Juan Gelman and Mara La Madrid (Buenos Aires: Editorial Planeta Argentina, 1997), III.

48. Jorge Tiscornia, "La llegada," *Cuadernos de la historia reciente 1968 Uruguay
1985: Testimonios, entrevistas, documentos e imágenes inéditas del Uruguay autoritario* vol. 3 (2006) Ediciones de la Banda Oriental: 66.

49. Tiscornia's original *almanaque* was reproduced for distribution in Novem-

ber of 2012, accompanied by a collection of texts that reflect on the creation of the *almanaque* and its importance within the context of the dictatorship. See José Pedro Charlo and Jorge Tiscornia, *El almanaque de Jorge Tiscornia* (Montevideo: Yaugurú, 2012). Further analysis of Tiscornia's *almanaque* will appear in Chapter Three.

50. For the longer collection of essays, see Jorge Tiscornia, *Nunca en domingo: Penal de Libertad, 1972-1985* (Montevideo: Ediciones de la Banda Oriental, 2014). For the film, see *El Almanaque*, directed by José Pedro Charlo (2012; Uruguay, Spain, and Argentina: Guazú Media, Media 3.14, Memoria y Sociedad, Morocha Films, and Chellomulticanal, 2012), DVD.

51. Tiscornia, "La llegada," 67.

52. Ibid., 67.

53. Ibid., 67.

54. Ibid., 74.

55. Ibid., 80.

56. Ibid., 80.

57. Ibid., 80.

58. Ibid., 80.

59. Ibid., 80.

60. Scarry, *The Body in Pain*, 145.

61. Harman, *Heidegger Explained: From Phenomenon to Thing* (Chicago: Open Court, 2007), 175.

62. I evoke Graham Harman's reading of Heidegger throughout this analysis because Harman is responsible for extending Heidegger's tool analysis and out of it developing the "Object Oriented Philosophy" that informs my discussion of *things* throughout this project. In order to remain consistent, I defer to Harman's reading in many instances throughout this analysis.

63. Scarry, *The Body in Pain*, 5.

64. Harman, *Heidegger*, 27.

65. Ibid., 3.

66. Marcelo Estefanell, *Un hombre numerado* (Montevideo: Ediciones Santillana, 2007), 27.

67. Harman, *Tool-Being*, 169.

68. Estefanell was a political prisoner in the Uruguayan prison Penal de Libertad for thirteen years, from 1972 to 1985.

69. Estefanell, *Un hombre*, 19.

70. Ibid., 19

71. Ibid., 19

72. Ibid., 19

73. Ibid., 20.

74. Harman, *Heidegger*, 29.

75. Estefanell, *Un hombre*, 20.

76. Ibid., 21.

77. Ibid., 19.

78. Ibid., 28.

79. Ibid., 38.

80. The full citation (clearly revealing a different relationship to things pre- to post-detention, this time focused on the tool/broken tool distinction) is: "En la vida normal, urbana y libre, la electricidad se convierte en un elemento cotidiano, casi tan natural como el aire o como el agua. Sin embargo, en aquel sitio de re-clusión, donde ni siquiera teníamos la posibilidad de encender o apagar la luz por encontrarse la llave y el portalámparas del lado de afuera de la celda, ser poseedor de una fuente de energía eléctrica parecía una incongruencia mayúscula, máxime cuando carecíamos de todo como consecuencia de una larga lista de prohibiciones casi draconianas y cuando no, simplemente estúpidas. En pocas palabras: no tenía-mos para enchufar; los electrodomésticos nos estaban vedados: radios, televisores, planchas, licuadoras, ventiladores y heladeras eran objetos que pertenecían al reino de los recuerdos" (Estefanell, *Un hombre*, 38) (In normal life, urban and free, elec-tricity becomes a quotidian element, almost as natural as air or water. Nevertheless, in that site of reclusion, where we didn't even have the possibility to turn on or off a light due to finding the switch and lamp holder on the outer side of the cell, to be a possessor of a source of electric energy seemed to be a tremendous incongruence, especially when we lacked everything as a consequence of a long list of almost dra-conian, if not simply stupid, prohibitions. In few words: we didn't have the means to plug things in; electrical appliances were prohibited for us: radios, televisions, irons, blenders, fans, refrigerators were all objects that pertained to the kingdom of memories).

81. Estefanell, *Un hombre*, 27.

82. Ibid., 39.

83. Ibid., 40.

84. Harman, *Tool-Being*, 20.

85. Mauricio Rosencof, *Conversaciones con la alpargata* (Montevideo: Ediciones de la Banda Oriental, 2004).

86. Rosencof, *Conversaciones*, 11.

87. Ibid., 11

88. Ibid., 11

89. I have chosen to translate this to "his" instead of "its" to purposefully high-light the subject the poems recognize within the shoe, rather than relegating it to an object that speaks.

90. Rosencof, *Conversaciones*, 20.

91. Ibid., 20.

92. Ibid., 20.

93. Ibid., 15.

94. Ibid., 15.

95. Ibid., 46.

96. Ibid., 48.

97. Ibid., 53.

98. Ibid., 54.

99. Ibid., 73.

100. Mario Benedetti, "Prólogo," in *Conversaciones con la alpargata* by Mauricio Rosencof (Montevideo: Ediciones de la Banda Oriental, 2004), 5.

101. Dori Laub, "An Event Without a Witness: Truth, Testimony and Survival," in *Testimony: Crises of Witnessing in Literature, Psychoanalysis, and History*, eds. Shoshana Felman and Dori Laub (New York: Routledge, 1992), 87.

102. DGO. "Entrevista con una llave de agua," in *Diario de Chacabuco 73, December 23, 1973* (Santiago: Museum of Memory and Human Rights Archive), 32.

103. Ibid., 32.

104. In the days following the September 11, 1973 coup d'état in Chile, the National Stadium was used to round up and hold hostage various sympathizers of the Allende regime, marked as "subversives" by Pinochet's governmental forces. The stadium was the site of widespread suffering, including torture and executions. Those who survived were transferred to various concentration camps throughout Chile, including Chacabuco.

105. DGO, "Entrevista," 33.

106. Ibid., 33.

107. Ibid., 33.

108. Ibid., 33.

109. Ibid., 34.

110. "Tomar caldo de cabeza" or "to drink head soup" was a euphemism for losing one's wits or going crazy within the confinement of the political prisons. In Chacabuco, due to the desert heat, this was of special concern.

111. DGO, "Entrevista," 34.

112. Michael Lazzara, *Chile in Transition*, 72.

113. P. De Silva quoted in Genefke and Vesti, "Diagnosis," 49.

114. Harman, *Heidegger*, 1.

Chapter Two

1. Martha Valentini quoted in Sofía Pi, *Historias debidas: 11 entrevistas a ex presos políticos* (Montevideo: Ediciones del CIEJ, 2013), 25.

2. Elaine Scarry, *The Body in Pain: The Making and Unmaking of the World* (New York: Oxford University Press, 1985), 162.

3. Mercedes Sosa, "Cuando estoy triste," *A que florezca mi pueblo*, Universal Import, 1975.

4. Ibid.

5. Ibid.

6. Pedro's box was donated to the Museum of Memory (MUME) in Uruguay for preservation.

7. Pi, *Historias debidas*, 19.

8. Rodrigo de Arteagabeitia, *Vicaría de la Solidaridad (1976-1992): Abierta a todos* (Santiago: Gráfica Nueva, 1992), n.p.

9. Ibid.

10. Scarry, *The Body in Pain*, 11.

11. Ibid., 11.

12. Ibid., 17

13. Pilar Calveiro, *Poder y desaparición: Los campos de concentració*n en Argentina (Buenos Aires: Ediciones Colihue, 1998), 24.

14. "Intento de totalización no es más que una de las pretensiones del poder. 'Siempre hay una hoja que se escapa y vuela bajo el sol.' Las líneas de fuga, los hoyos negros del poder son innumerables, en toda sociedad y circunstancia, aun en los totalitarismos más uniformemente establecidos" (Calveiro, *Poder*, 24). (Intent of totality is nothing more than one of the pretensions of power. 'There is always a leaf that escapes and flies under the sun.' The lines of escape, the black holes of power are innumerable, in every society and circumstance, even in the most uniformly established totalitarianisms.)

15. "Lo que excluye y a lo que se le escapa, a aquello que se fuga de su complejo sistema, a la vez central y fragmentario" (Calveiro, *Poder*, 25). (What it excludes and what escapes from it, to that which escapes from its complex system, at the same time central and fragmentary.)

16. Calveiro, *Poder*, 31 (emphasis in original).

17. Ruth Cespedes Vuskovic and Sylvia Ríos Montero, *Libres en prisión: La otra artesanía. Artefactos creados en dictadura / Chile 1973-1990* (Santiago: Editorial USACH, 2015).

18. Marcelo Estefanell, *Un hombre numerado* (Montevideo: Ediciones Santiallana, 2007), 17.

19. Ibid., 18.

20. Replicas of the cards are now sold at the Museum of Memory (MUME) in Uruguay. This quote and the following citation come from the explanation that accompanies the reproductions: Pardal, *Naipes "La Gayola"*, Centro Cultural y Museo de la Memoria (MUME). Montevideo, Uruguay.

21. Ibid.

22. Gabriela Castillo et al. "Mano a mano: un lenguaje para resistir," *Cuadernos de la historia reciente 1968 Uruguay 1985: Testimonios, entrevistas, documentos e imágenes inéditas del Uruguay autoritario* vol. 1 (2006), Ediciones de la Banda Oriental: 11-22, 14.

23. These comments were reported in interviews conducted by students of the Universidad de la República's Facultad de Psicología in Montevideo, Uruguay. Their investigation is based on interviews they conducted with a group of female former political prisoners: Susana Carli, Adriana Castera, Cristina Fynn, Paula Laborde, Nybia López, and María de los Ángeles Michelena. The citations included from their interviews do not carry individual names.

24. Gabriela Castillo et al., "Mano a mano," 14.

25. Ibid., 15.

26. Personal Interview, Stela Reyes.

27. Raquel Barratta, "La noche de la tijera," *Cuadernos de la historia reciente 1968 Uruguay 1985: Testimonios, entrevistas, documentos e imágenes inéditas del Uruguay autoritario* vol. 2 (2006), Ediciones de la Banda Oriental: 39-41, 41.

28. Sofía Pi, *Historias debidas*, 19.

29. Fundación Solidaridad, *Dignidad hecha a mano 30 años: Handmade Dignity 30 Years: 1975-2005* (Santiago, Fundación Andes Banco Estado, 2005).

30. Ibid., 9.

31. An article written upon the announcement of the impending closure of the Fundación Solidaridad explains the history of the arrangement between the prisoners and the Vicaría:

"La historia de esta heredera de la Vicaría de la Solidaridad . . . se remonta a 1975, cuando el equipo del Comité de Cooperación para la Paz recibió peticiones de trabajo de parte de los presos políticos. Sin saber muy bien, en un principio, cómo ayudar a los encarcelados, pronto fueron los mismos familiares los que indicaron cómo hacerlo" (Francisca Jiménez, "Los 36 años de la Fundación Solidaridad" 27 August-3 September 2011, http://www.masdeco.cl/los-36-anos-de-la-fundacion-solidaridad/). (The story of this inheritance of the Vicariate of Solidarity . . . dates back to 1975, when the team of the Peace Corporation Committee received job petitions from the political prisoners. Without knowing very well, at first, how to help the incarcerated, soon it was the families themselves that indicated to them how to do it.)

32. A similar use of material creation as a means of providing for family outside of the Argentine detention center is documented in the film *El Buen Pastor: Una fuga de mujeres*. In the documentary, a former prisoner explains: "Hagamos actividades. Gimnasia, estudio, y otras actividades del trabajo también. Así que nos organizamos más con tejidos, costura . . . sobre todo tejido, verdad. Mucho crochet y las agujas. Bueno, así hicimos cosas hermosas y todo se vendía afuera. Todo se vendía" (*El Buen Pastor: Una fuga de mujeres,* directed by Matías Herrera Córdoba and Lucía Torres, Córdoba: Cine El Calefón, 2010. DVD). (We do activities. Gymnastics, studies, and other types of work activities as well. This way we organize ourselves more with textiles, sewing . . . above all textiles, to be truthful. A lot of crocheting and knitting. Well, that's how we made beautiful things and everything was sold on the outside. Everything was sold.)

33. Vuskovic and Ríos affirm their dedication to this "sujeto creador colectivo anónimo" (anonymous collective creator subject) in their study (*Libres en prisión*, 37).

34. Personal correspondence with Marcela Andrades Álfaro.

35. Vuskovic and Ríos, *Libres en prisión*, 87.

36. Marcela Andrades Álfaro, whose mother made *soporopos* during her time in detention, uses this term to discuss the meaning of the *soporopos* (Taller de Soporopo Facebook Page).

37. Laura Villaflor, quoted in the ex ESMA exhibit.

38. See Claudia Feld, "El 'adentro' y el 'afuera' durante el cautiverio en la ESMA. Apuntes para repensar la desaparición forzada de personas," *Sociohistórica* 44 (2019) Universidad Nacional de La Plata: 1-18.

39. Norma Cristina Cozzi, quoted in the ex ESMA exhibit.

40. Vuskovic and Ríos, *Libres en prisión*, 99.

41. Personal correspondence with Marcela Andrades Álfaro.

42. Vuskovic and Ríos, *Libres en prisión*, 99.

43. Scarry, *The Body in Pain*, 162.

44. Ibid., 162.

45. Ibid., 166.

46. Ibid., 166-167. Perhaps serving as evidence to support Scarry's analysis, in the Chilean concentration camp Tres Álamos the female prisoners used pictures of food (often photographs they clipped from newspapers or magazines) to simulate or imagine that they were "tomando onces," eating the traditional Chilean snack meal. Where the women did not have real, material access to food, they relied on a different type of material to imagine that they were eating. Similarly, in the documentary film *La Venda*, one of the former detainees recalls: "Ya me acuerdo de cuando nos celebramos los cumpleaños, pescábamos la Variedad que era la única revista que podíamos leer y la parte ésa de las recetas y nos servíamos. . . . La revista

nos servíamos para cumpleaños" (*La Venda*, directed by Gloria Camiruaga, Santiago: ADOC, 2000, DVD). (I remember when we celebrated birthdays, we went fishing in Variety, which was the only magazine that we were permitted to read, and the part of it that had recipes and we served it. . . We served ourselves the magazine for birthdays.)

47. Nubia Becker Eguiluz, *Una mujer en Villa Grimaldi* (Santiago: Puhuén Editores, 2011), 95.

48. Scarry, *The Body in Pain*, 166.

49. Ibid., 167 (my emphasis).

50. Pedro Giudice, personal interview

51. Estefanell, *Un hombre*, 11.

52. Museum of Memory and Human Rights, Santiago, Chile, permanent exhibit.

53. Scarry, *The Body in Pain*, 164.

54. By the term "limit" pieces, I am referring to Scarry's assertion that imagining takes place as a last resort, when objects and language are not available to properly articulate experience beyond the ordinary, in the realm of the "extraordinary."

55. Museo de la Memoria y los Derechos Humanos, *Interfaz: Prisión Política y Recintos Carcelarios en Chile 1973/1990* (Santiago: Ograma, 2012), n.p.

56. Stela Reyes, personal interview.

57. Ibid.

58. Idelber Avelar, "Five Theses on Torture," *Journal of Latin American Cultural Studies* 10 no. 3 (2001): 253-271, 257.

59. Scarry, *The Body in Pain*, 171.

Chapter Three

1. Ana Tiscornia, "Una memoria, un documento histórico, una obra" in *El almanaque de Jorge Tiscornia*, eds. José Pedro Charlo and Jorge Tiscornia (Montevideo: Yaugurú, 2012), 73.

2. Eduardo Tavani, "Las marcas de la memoria," in *Las marcas de la memoria: 30.000 detenidos-desaparecidos ¡Presentes!*, ed. Eduardo Tavani (Buenos Aires: Instituto Espacio para la Memoria, 2012), 9.

3. "Almanaque de ex preso uruguayo declarado patrimonio por Unesco," *Uruguay Natural*, 11 December 2014. http://marcapaisuruguay.gub.uy/almanaque-de-ex-preso-uruguayo-declarado-patrimonio-por-unesco/.

4. Jorge Tiscornia, "Los almanaques," *Cuadernos de la historia reciente 1968 Uruguay 1985: Testimonios, entrevistas, documentos e imágenes inéditas del Uruguay autoritario* vol. 2 (2006) Ediciones de la Banda Oriental: 3-21, 12.

5. Ibid., 20.

6. Ibid., 17.

7. Ibid., 21

8. Here, I employ "exemplary" following the work of Tzvetan Todorov, *Les abus de la mémorie,* (Paris: Arléa, 1995), as a form of memory capable of effecting change, of serving to prevent a future repetition of the same past through the fostering of a critical reflection on the legacy and meaning of the traumatic past event.

9. Ana Tiscornia, "Una memoria," 73.

10. The second opening quote of this chapter comes from the executive director of the (at the time) Instituto Espacio Para la Memoria in Argentina, Eduardo Tavani. His words appear in the prologue of one of the Institute's publications, a book titled *Las marcas de la memoria,* which documents physical evidence (especially objects) that have been recovered from the various spaces of memory that form the institute's patrimony.

11. Dori Laub, "An Event Without a Witness: Truth, Testimony and Survival," in *Testimony: Crises of Witnessing in Literature, Psychoanalysis, and History,* eds. Shoshana Felman and Dori Laub (New York: Routledge, 1992), 80.

12. Avelar observes: "Allegorization takes place when that which is most familiar reveals itself as (an)other, when the most customary is interpreted as a ruin, and the pile of past catastrophes hitherto concealed under that storm called "progress" at last begins to be unearthed. The most familiar cultural documents become allegorical once they are referred back to the barbarism that lies at their origin" (Idelber Avelar, *The Untimely Present: Postdictatorial Latin American Fiction and the Task of Mourning* (Durham:, Duke University Press, 1999), 233).

13. Giorgio Agamben, *Remnants of Auschwitz: The Witness and the Archive* (New York: Zone, 1999).

14. Marianne Hirsch and Leo Spitzer, "Testimonial Objects: Memory, Gender, and Transmission," *Poetics Today* 27 no. 2 (2006): 353-383, 367.

15. George Yúdice, "Testimonio and Postmodernism," in *The Real Thing: Testimonial Discourse and Latin America*, ed. Georg Gugelberger (Durham: Duke University Press, 1996): 42-57.

16. René Jara, "Prólogo," in *Testimonio y Literatura*, eds. René Jara and Hernán Vidal (Minneapolis: Institute for the Study of Ideologies and Literatures, 1986), 1-6.

17. Ileana Rodríguez, *Liberalism at its Limits: Crime and Terror in the Latin American Cultural Text* (Pittsburgh: University of Pittsburgh Press, 2009).

18. Javier C. Sanjinés, "Beyond Testimonial Discourse: New Popular Trends in Bolivia," in *The Real Things: Testimonial Discourse and Latin America,* ed. Georg Gugelberger (Durham: Duke University Press, 1996), 254-265, 254.

19. Ibid., 254.

20. Ibid., 264.

21. Hugo Achugar, "Historias paralelas/ejemplares. La historia y la voz del otro," in *La voz del otro. Testimonio, subalternidad y verdad narrativa,* eds. John Beverley and Hugo Achugar (Ciudad de Guatemala: Universidad Rafael Landívar, 2002):, 61-84, 63.

22. Georg Gugelberger, "Introduction: Institutionalization of Transgression: Testimonial Discourse and Beyond," in *The Real Thing: Testimonial Discourse and Latin America,* ed. Georg Gugelberger (Durham: Duke University Press, 1996), 1-22, 11.

23. Ibid., 11

24. Nora Strejilevich, *El arte de no olvidar. Literatura testimonial en Chile, Argentina y Uruguay entre los 80 y los 90* (Buenos Aires: Catálogos, 2006), 20.

25. John Beverley, "Prólogo a la segunda edición," in *La voz del otro. Testimonio, subalternidad y verdad narrativa,* eds. John Beverley and Hugo Achugar (Ciudad de Guatemala: Universidad Rafael Landívar, 2002), 9-16, 10.

26. Marta Rojas identified this reliance on language in her contribution to Jara and Vidal's volume *Testimonio y literatura*: "El uso de lenguaje es básico para el testimonio y obviamente para toda la literatura porque la herramienta principal del escritor es su lenguaje. Se narra con el lenguaje, se construyen los diálogos con el lenguaje; se da una intención con el lenguaje, directo o figurado. La emoción, la fuerza, la ternura le llega al lector mediante el lenguaje. Ningún tema por grandioso que sea, por dramático, humano o espectacular que sea podríamos llevarlo fielmente al lector si no usamos un lenguaje adecuado. La defensa del testimonio está en la defensa del lenguaje; en la imaginación y talento de quienes lo escriben, además del hecho mismo: del protagonista, individual y colectivo" (Rojas 322–23). (The use of language is fundamental for testimonio and obviously for all literature because the principle tool of the writer is their language. One narrates with language, dialogues are built with language; an intention is given with language, directly or figuratively. Emotion, strength, tenderness arrive to the reader through language. No topic, no matter how grandiose, dramatic, human or spectacular it is, could we carry faithfully to the reader if we don't use the adequate language. The defense of testimony is in the defense of language; in the imagination and talent of those who write it, in addition to the fact itself: of the protagonist, individual and collective.)

27. "In our European juridical tradition, testimony should remain unrelated to literature and especially, in literature, to what presents itself as fiction, simulation, or simulacra, which is not all literature" (Derrida, *Demeure* 29).

28. "Yet, if the testimonial is by law irreducible to the fictional, there is no testimony that does not structurally imply in itself the possibility of fiction, simulacra,

dissimulation, lie, and perjury—that is to say, the possibility of literature" (Derrida, *Demeure* 29).

29. Yudice, "Testimonio and Postmodernism," 44.

30. "A contrapelo de la negación posmoderna de todo tipo de metadiscursos, el testimonio continúa la tradición comprometida de la literatura latinoamericana en el sentido de confiar en la eficacia de la palabra como herramienta de emancipación política" (Elzbieta Sklodowska, *Testimonio hispanoamericano. Historia, teoría, poética* [New York: Peter Lang, 1992], 100.) (Going against the grain of the postmodern negation of all types of metadiscourse, testimonio continues the committed tradition of Latin American literature in the sense that it has faith in the effectiveness of the word as an emancipatory political tool).

31. Ibid., 99.

32. John Beverley, "The Margin at the Center," in *The Real Thing: Testimonial Discourse and Latin America*, ed. Georg Gugelberger (Durham: Duke University Press, 1996), 23-41, 28.

33. Ibid., 28.

34. Gugelberger, "Introduction," 3.

35. Beverley, "The Margin," 34.

36. Michael Lazzara, *Chile in Transition*, 155.

37. Ibid., 155.

38. Club Atlético Site, visitor's pamphlet.

39. These categories were identified by the archivists of the museum in an effort to catalogue and better preserve the items on display.

40. Internal document, Museo de la Memoria y los Derechos Humanos, Santiago, Chile.

41. Jennifer Hansen-Glucklich, *Holocaust Memory Reframed: Museums and the Challenges of Representation* (New Jersey: Rutgers University Press, 2014), 120.

42. Ibid., 120.

43. Ibid., 121.

44. Ibid., 127.

45. Ibid., 131-132.

46. Amy Sodaro, *Exhibiting Atrocity: Memorial Museums and the Politics of Past Violence* (New Brunswick: Rutgers University Press, 2018), 111.

47. Yuyo Rasmussen and María Noel Domínquez, "Todo está guardado en la memoria," in *Cuadernos de la historia reciente 1968 Uruguay 1985: Testimonios, entrevistas, documentos e imágenes inéditas del Uruguay autoritario* vol. 4 (2006) Ediciones de la Banda Oriental: 61-66, 61.

48. Ibid., 62.

49. Daniel Link, "Qué sé yo. Testimonio, experiencia y subjetividad," in *Crítica*

del testimonio. Ensayos sobre las relaciones entre memoria y relato, ed. Cecilia Vallina (Rosario: Beatriz Viterbo Editora, 2009), 126.

50. Ibid., 126.

51. Ariel Dorfman, "Código político y código literario. El género testimonio en Chile hoy," in *Testimonio y literatura*, eds. René Jara and Hernán Vidal (Minneapolis: Institute for the Study of Ideologies and Literatures, 1986), 170-234, 170.

52. Ibid., 177.

53. Francine Masiello, *The Art of Transition: Latin American Culture and Neoliberal Crisis* (Durham: Duke University Press, 2001), 13.

54. Hirsch and Spitzer, "Testimonial Objects," 366.

55. Ibid., 367.

56. Avery Gordon, *Ghostly Matters: Haunting and the Sociological Imagination* (Minneapolis: University of Minnesota Press, 2008), xvi.

57. Ibid., xvii.

58. "Proyecto," Memoria Abierta, http://memoriaabierta.org.ar/vestigios /proyecto.html.

59. Ibid.

60. Julian Bleecker, "Why Things Matter: A Manifesto for Networked Objects—Cohabiting with Pigeons, Arphids, and AIBOS in the Internet of Things," in *The Object Reader*, eds.Fiona Candlin and Raiford Guins (London: Routledge, 2009), 165-174.

61. Margarita Saona, "Plain Things and Space: Metonymy and Aura in Memorials of Social Trauma," in *Layers of Memory and the Discourse of Human Rights: Artistic and Testimonial Practices in Latin America and Iberia*, ed. Ana Forcinito, *Hispanic Issues On Line* 14 (2014): 73-90, 73.

62. Ibid., 73.

63. Ibid., 74.

64. Ibid., 74.

65. *Vestigios: Un ensayo de transmisión a través de los objetos*, Memoria Abierta, http://memoriaabierta.org.ar/vestigios/index-2.html.

66. Ibid.

67. Gordon, *Haunting*, xvi.

68. Juan Felipe Hernandez, "La Química de la Memoria: A Benjaminean Approach," *Journal of Latin American Cultural Studies*, 22 no. 3 (2013): 259-270, 263.

69. Ibid., 263-264.

70. Marga Steinwasser and María Antonia Sánchez, "Química de la Memoria: Una experiencia de la desaparición," Museo de la Memoria, 1 April 2007. https:// www.museodelamemoria.gob.ar/page/muestras/id/20/title/Qu%C3%ADmica -de-la-memoria.

71. Hernández, "La Química," 264.

72. Harman, *Tool-Being*.

73. Bennett, *Vibrant Matter*.

74. "The more efficiently a tool performs its function, the more it tends to recede from view" (Harman, *Tool-Being*, 21).

75. Heidegger, "The Thing."

76. Harman, *Tool-Being*, 20, emphasis in the original.

77. Derrida, *Specters of Marx*, 5.

78. *Vestigios*.

79. Ibid.

80. *Nostalgia de la luz*, directed by Patricio Guzmán (Chile: Atacama Productions, Blinker Filmproduktion, Westdeutscher Rundfunk WDR, 2010), DVD.

81. Ibid.

82. Ibid.

83. Ibid.

84. Ibid.

85. Agamben, *Remnants*.

86. Agamben, *Remnants*, 164. The Muselmann, for Agamben, is the state at which a full reduction of the subject to a species of object has occurred. The living being here is reduced to pure corporality, pure objectivity, desubjectified, "non-human." Once one reaches the state of the Muselmann, one is at a point of no-return, which is why the Muselmann presents a crisis for witnessing. Agamben states: "At times a medical figure or an ethical category, at times a political limit or an anthropological concept, the Muselmann is an indefinite being in whom not only humanity and non-humanity, but also vegetative existence and relation, physiology and ethics, medicine and politics, and life and death continuously pass through each other. This is why the Muselmann's 'third realm' is the perfect cipher of the camp, the non-place in which all disciplinary barriers are destroyed and all embankments flooded" (*Remnants*, 48).

87. Agamben, *Remnants*, 158-159.

88. Ibid., 52 (my emphasis).

89. Derrida, *Specters of Marx*, xvii and xix. The way in which present generations are learning to live with the ghosts that haunt the objects of focus here will be explored in the fifth and final chapter of this project.

90. Gordon, *Haunting*, xvi.

91. Derrida, *Specters of Marx*, 100-101. In reference to Guzmán's employ of light in his title, it is noteworthy that frequencies form the basis of light in physics.

92. Ibid., 10.

93. Ibid., 12.

94. One must note that within physics all light boils down to a matter of fre-

quencies, thus emphasizing the fundamentally material nature of Derrida's claim that the specter "is the frequency of a certain visibility" (*Specters of Marx*, 100).

95. *Nostalgia de la luz.*

96. Ibid.

Chapter Four

1. Michael Lazzara, *Chile in Transition*, 101.

2. The Chilean Truth and Reconciliation Commission's final report documented 3,428 cases of disappearance (see Alexis Howe, "Rethinking Disappearance in Chilean Post-Coup Narratives," 2011, 5).

3. While the report estimates that 150 Uruguayans were disappeared, it also points out that 127 of them are believed to have disappeared in Argentina, a result of Operation Condor. The report also emphasizes that a larger number of people were imprisoned indefinitely in Uruguay as opposed to being disappeared.

4. desaparecidos.org, "Proyecto Desaparecidos: Por la memoria, la verdad y la justicia." http://desaparecidos.org/main.html.

5. This is the terminology the Grandmothers of Plaza de Mayo use to refer to their disappeared grandchildren during their search to recover them. It is also the term Ana Ros uses in her study to refer to the children who were appropriated during the dictatorship.

6. In this chapter, I refer to this second generation as the "Generation of HIJOS." I use HIJOS to evoke the organization H.I.J.O.S. (Hijos por la Identidad, la Justicia, y contra el Olvido y el Silencio [Children for Identity, Justice, and Against Forgetting and Silence], the activist organization/network formed by the children of the disappeared), even as I'm referring most directly to cases of restituted identity, not just to cases of children who are members of the organization more generally. For an extensive compilation of voices from this generation, see Juan Gelman and Mara La Madrid, *Ni el flaco perdón de Dios. HIJOS de desaparecidos* (Buenos Aires: Editorial Planeta Argentina, 1997).

7. Jorge Rafael Videla quoted in Ana Ros, *The Post-Dictatorship Generation in Argentina, Chile, and Uruguay: Collective Memory and Cultural Production* (New York: Palgrave Macmillan, 2012). The quote follows in context, in Spanish: "es una incógnita el desaparecido, si el hombre apareciera, bueno, tendrá un tratamiento X, y si la desaparición se convirtiera en certeza de su fallecimiento, tiene un tratamiento Z, pero mientras sea un desaparecido no puede tener ningún tratamiento especial, es incógnita, es un desaparecido, no tiene entidad, no está, ni muerto ni vivo, está desaparecido" (Jorge Jinkis, "Ni muerto ni vivo," *Página 12*, 3 August 2006, https://www.pagina12.com.ar/diario/psicologia/9-70866-2006

-08-03.html.) (the disappeared is an unknown, if the man appears, well, it will have X treatment, and if the disappearance becomes a certainty of death, it has Z treatment, but while he be disappeared he cannot have any special treatment, he is an unknown, a disappeared, he doesn't have an entity, he doesn't exist, neither dead nor alive, he's disappeared).

8. Alexis Howe, "Rethinking Disappearance," 5.

9. Gabriel Gatti uses a similar term, "narratives of the void" (*Surviving Forced Disappearance*, 5), to refer to the construction of identity in the world of the detained-disappeared. In his use of the term, he examined the sociological effects of the phenomenon of disappearance, especially on the Generation of HIJOS.

10. Ludmila da Silva Catela, *No habrá flores en la tumba del pasado. La experiencia de reconstrucción del mundo de los familiares de desaparecidos* (La Plata: Ediciones al Margen, 2001), 126.

11. Calveiro, *Poder y desaparición*, 26 (emphasis in original).

12. Howe, "Rethinking Disappearance," 3.

13. "En 1983, con el retorno de la democracia, una variante de las fotos [de desaparecidos] impactó durante algunos años y obligaba a acercarse a mirarlas: contornos de siluetas diseñadas sobre papel blanco aparecían pegadas en las paredes de muchas ciudades del país. En aquellos años las siluetas predominaban en las manifestaciones públicas. Montadas sobre papel, inscribían en su interior el nombre del desaparecido y la fecha de secuestro. El tamaño 'natural' tenía como objetivo central 'hacer sentir a los desaparecidos en la calle', poder ampliar el público que necesariamente pasaba a preguntase sobre el objetivo de estos dibujos" (Ludmila da Silva Catela, *No habrá flores*, 134) (In 1983, with the return of democracy, a variation of the photos [of the disappeared] had an impact during some years and obligated one to approach and view them: outlines of silhouettes designed on white paper appeared, stuck to the walls of many cities within the country. In those years the silhouettes dominated the public protests. Mounted on paper, they inscribed in their interior the name of the disappeared and the date of their kidnapping. The "natural" size had as its central objective 'to make felt the disappeared in the street', to be able to widen the public that out of necessity passed by to ask about the objective of the drawings). For an extended analysis of the strategy of using photographs and silhouettes to represent the disappeared, see Ana Longoni, "Fotos y siluetas. Dos estrategias contrastantes en la representación de los desaparecidos," in *Los desaparecidos en la Argentina. Memorias, representaciones e ideas (1983-2008)*, ed. Emilio Crenzel (Buenos Aires: Editorial Biblos, 2010), 43-63. The "siluetazo" interventions are not a strategy of the past, but continue to be utilized by activist groups in Argentina. One of the most iconic uses of the photograph to search for and locate a child "disappeared with life" was the use of a portrait of Mariana Zaffaroni—see *Por esos ojos*, directed by Virgina Martínez and Gonzalo Arijón, Uruguay/France: 1997.

14. It is important to note this distinction because not all of the children were known to their families prior to their disappearance. For those born in captivity, families have no photographs to use in this way.

15. *El último confín,* directed by Pablo Ratto, 2004, DVD.

16. One need only look to Lucila Quieto's photographic project, *Arqueología de la ausencia,* and its recycling of the photographs of the disappeared in its creation of a new family portrait—of a new narrative—in which daughter and parents finally emerge in the same scene, to see the power of the use of the body of the child of disappeared parents to highlight, humanize, and narrate the crimes of the past.

17. Derrida, *Specters of Marx,* XX.

18. This recalls Michael Lazzara's assertion that "the disappeared persist in a kind of limbo between life and death—like specters haunting the living, wanting to be heard, acknowledged and remembered" (*Chile in Transition,* 102).

19. Derrida, *Specters of Marx,* 36.

20. See Gordon, *Haunting.*

21. Nelly Richard, *Cultural Residues: Chile in Transition,* trans. Alan West, Theodore Quester, and Jean Franco (Minneapolis: University of Minnesota Press, 2004), 79.

22. The notion of the copy versus the original (and the evocation's variability) is important to consider in connection to the Generation of HIJOS and the way in which the material body speaks through DNA. Victor Penchaszadeh, one of the members of the team that developed the DNA testing for grandpaternity that is used to identify children of disappeared parents when parental DNA is not available, explains: "An essential peculiarity of the genome is its variability. That is, any particular pair of genes for a given characteristic may differ within an individual and among individuals... Individuals vary in their genetic endowment and this variability is inherited . . . using a large number of markers it is possible to exclude paternity in almost 100% of cases in which the putative father is not the real father. Conversely, the very fact of failing to exclude a putative father as the real father, assigns a high probability that the man is indeed the biological father. This is called the probability of inclusion" ("Abduction of Children of Political Dissidents in Argentina and the Role of Human Genetics in their Restitution," *Journal of Public Health Policy* 13 no. 3 [1992]: 295–97). While Derrida's comments refer to the individual who speaks with the ghost and the way in which each of these conversations brings with it a different background that nuances the encounter, the reading of the child's body is a conversation that does not change in this way. DNA results can be replicated, are invariable, and for this reason constitute a very concrete form of conjuring, of accessing the past.

23. Derrida, *Specters of Marx,* 48.

24. Ibid., 48.

25. Ibid., 48.

26. The notion that the fight gave birth to these groups is evoked not only by the children of the disappeared, but also by some of the Mothers of the Plaza de Mayo, who claim that upon their children's disappearance, they were reborn as political mothers.

27. Derrida, *Specters of Marx*, 50.

28. Ibid., 54.

29. For a consideration of the EAAF's work on the mass grave of the San Vicente cemetery in Córdoba, Argentina, see Olmo and Salado Puerto. For a complete view of the EAAF's work see their annual reports at eaaf.typepad.com/cr_argentina/.

30. Juan Gelman and Mara La Madrid, *Ni el flaco perdón de Dios: HIJOS de desaparecidos* (Buenos Aires: Editorial Planeta Argentina, 1997), 74-75.

31. Adriana Calvo, of the Association, explained: "exhumar restos era ofrecer pruebas a alguien que tiraba todas las pruebas a la basura" (Gelman and La Madrid, *Ni el flaco perdón*, 306) (to exhume remains was to offer proof to someone that threw all the proof in the trash).

32. Adam Rosenblatt, *Digging for the Disappeared: Forensic Science After Atrocity* (Stanford: Stanford University Press, 2015), 43.

33. Ibid., 21-22.

34. EAAF, "History of EAAF," eaaf.org.

35. See Christopher Joyce and Eric Stover, *Witnessing from the Grave: The Stories Bones Tell* (Boston: Little, Brown and Company, 1991).

36. Snow quoted in Eyal Weizman, "Osteobiography: An Interview with Clyde Snow," *Cabinet* 43 (2011): 68.

37. Ibid., 69.

38. Ibid., 72.

39. EAAF, "History of EAAF," eaaf.org.

40. Alejandra Dandan, "Son de campos que no hacían traslados aéreos," *Página 12*, 21 January 2013. https://www.pagina12.com.ar/diario/elpais/1-212298-2013-01-21.html.

41. Joyce and Stover, *Witnesses*, 241.

42. da Silva Catela, 126.

43. Abuelas de Plaza de Mayo, "Genetic Aspect—The Identity," *abuelas.org.ar/idiomas/english/genetic.htm*.

44. Ibid. It is important to note that this is not a complete 100% probability rate and that these blood tests, as happened in at least one case, can yield incorrect results. In the case of the false blood test, identity was later correctly shown via a DNA test. See "Capítulo 3: Laura" in Analía Argento, *De vuelta a casa. Historias de hijos y nietos restituidos* (Buenos Aires: Marea Editorial, 2009).

45. An article published by *El País* in June of 2017 reports that an average of 1,200 people a year go to the bank suspecting they may be children of disappeared parents (Mar Centenera, "El ADN, 30 años al lado de Abuelas para encontrar a los nietos robados por la dictadura," *El País*, 18 June 2017, https://elpais.com /internacional/2017/06/14/america/1497472745_062450.html).

46. Ministerio de Ciencia, "Banco Nacional de Datos Genéticos," *Argentina .gob.ar* https://www.argentina.gob.ar/ciencia/informacion-al-ciudadano /datosgeneticos.

47. Presidencia de la Nación Argentina, *76:11 afiches: Momentos que hicieron historia* (Buenos Aires: Jefatura de Gabinete de Ministros de la Nación Secretaría de Comunicación Pública, 2011), 17.

48. Ibid., 17.

49. Ibid., 23.

50. The example of Horacio Pietragalla from earlier in this chapter highlights this aspect. Pietragalla's encounter with his mother takes place first through the perception of similar physical features; his own body an echo of, an encounter with, the specter of his mother.

51. Marius Kwint, "Introduction: The Physical Past," in *Material Memories*, eds. Marius Kwint, Christopher Breward and Jeremy Aynsley (Oxford: Berg, 1999), 2.

52. Presidencia de la Nación Argentina, *76:11 afiches*, 47.

53. Ari Gandsman, "'Do You Know Who You Are?' Radical Existential Doubt and Scientific Certainty in the Search for the Kidnapped Children of the Disappeared in Argentina," *ETHOS* 37 no. 4 (2009): 441–465.

54. Judith Roof, *The Poetics of DNA* (Minneapolis: University of Minnesota Press, 2007).

55. Ros, 81.

56. Bruschtein, *Encontrando a Víctor*, quoted in Ros, 69.

57. Bruschtein, *Encontrando a Víctor*, quoted in Ros, 70.

58. Margaret Gibson, *Objects of the Dead: Mourning and Memory in Everyday Life* (Carlton: Melbourne University Press, 2008), 95.

59. Mariana Eva Perez, "Manos grandes," in *Re-encuentros. Por la identidad y la justicia. Contra el olvido y el silencio* (Buenos Aires: Fundación Contamíname, 2007), 35.

60. Ibid., 35.

61. Ibid., 35.

62. I use the term captor mother to highlight the fact that this was an appropriation, not a legal adoption.

63. Perez, "Manos grandes," 36.

64. Elvira Martorell, "Recuerdos del presente: memoria e identidad. Una re-

flexión en torno a HIJOS," in *Memorias en presente. Identidad y transmisión en la Argentina posgenocidio*, ed. Sergio J. Guelerman (Buenos Aires: Grupo Editorial Norma, 2001), 166.

65. Colin Davis, *Haunted Subjects: Deconstruction, Psychoanalysis and the Return of the Dead* (New York: Palgrave Macmillan, 2007), 15.

66. Martorell, "Recuerdos," 169.

67. Martorell, "Recuerdos," 167.

Chapter Five

1. Kwint, "Introduction," 9.

2. Ines Ulanovsky, *Fotos tuyas*, http://vi.zonezero.com/exposiciones/fotografos /ulanovsky/inicial.html.

3. Natalia's Uncle Luis, quoted in *Encontrando a Víctor*, directed by Natalia Bruschtein, 2004.

4. Martorell, "Recuerdos," 146.

5. Calveiro, *Poder y desaparición*, 47 (my emphasis).

6. Ibid., 62.

7. Martorell, "Recuerdos," 158.

8. Crenzel, *Memory of the Argentine Disappearances*.

9. Gustavo Remedi, "Tell Me How It Happened: Unbinding the Discourse on Memory, the Political Crimes of the Recent Past, and Human Rights" in *Layers of Memory and the Discourse of Human Rights: Artistic and Testimonial Practices in Latin America and Iberia*, ed. Ana Forcinito, *Hispanic Issues On Line* 14 (2014): 215.

10. Calveiro, *Poder y desaparición,* 57.

11. "Como forma de diseminación social del terror para disciplinar, controlar y regular una sociedad cuya diversidad y alto nivel de conflicto impedían su establecimiento hegemónico" (Calveiro, *Poder y desaparició*n, 59) (as a form of socially disseminating terror in order to discipline, control, and regulate a society whose diversity and high level of conflict impeded their hegemonic establishment).

12. Calveiro, *Poder y desaparición*, 47.

13. "Sala de la Memoria," *Villa Grimaldi*, http://villagrimaldi.cl/parque-por -la-paz/sala-de-la-memoria/.

14. "La vivencia está constituida por la representación más el monto del afecto; no es sólo intelectual o racional. Hallamos, entonces, aquello que no pueden recordar porque eran niños—marcas inconscientes que funcionan como un saber-no-sabido, pero también una carencia—lo que no vivieron" (Martorell, "Recuerdos," 145) (Experience is constituted by representation plus the sum of affect; it is not

only intellectual or rational. We discover, then, that which they cannot remember because they were children—subconscious marks that function as an unknown knowledge, but also a lack—what they didn't live).

15. *Sala de la Memoria,* Parque por la Paz, Villa Grimaldi.

16. Ibid.

17. See Richard, *Cultural Residues.*

18. Gibson, *Objects of the Dead,* 9.

19. Ibid., 10.

20. *Sala de la Memoria,* Parque por la Paz, Villa Grimaldi.

21. See Roland Barthes, *Camera Lucida: Reflections on Photography* (New York: Hill and Wang, 1981).

22. Marianne Hirsch, *Family Frames: Photography, Narrative, and Postmemory* (Cambridge: Harvard University Press, 1997).

23. Marianne Hirsch and Leo Spitzer, "What's Wrong With This Picture? Archival Photographs in Contemporary Narratives," *Journal of Modern Jewish Studies* 5 (2006): 245.

24. Ibid., 246.

25. Nora, *Realms of Memory.*

26. Hirsch and Spitzer, "What's Wrong," 250.

27. *Sala de Memoria,* Parque por la Paz, Villa Grimaldi.

28. Ibid.

29. Ibid.

30. Ibid.

31. Ibid.

32. Ibid.

33. "Proyectos: Memorias de Vida y Militancia," Espacio Memoria y Derechos Humanos. http://www.espaciomemoria.ar/memorias-de-vida-y-militancia/.

34. Miguel Ángel Boitano, *Memorias de Vida y Militancia,* Espacio Memoria y Derechos Humanos.

35. Apart from the memory of her son's possible fate, it is possible that Lita was shocked by the plane's presence because this project's stated goal is to represent the lives of the disappeared instead of the grim circumstances of their deaths.

36. Memorias de Vida y Militancia: Miguel Ángel Boitano, YouTube, 29 August 2013. https://www.youtube.com/watch?v=-yBpZ1mRfeM.

37. As observed in Lita's reaction to seeing the plane, the project even creates the circumstances for her, as a mother, to break free from focusing on her child's tragic end and to think for a moment about who he was prior to his militancy.

38. "Proyectos: Memorias de Vida y Militancia," Espacio Memoria y Derechos Humanos. http://www.espaciomemoria.ar/memorias-de-vida-y-militancia/.

39. Ibid.

40. Ibid.

41. Ibid.

42. Ibid.

43. Gibson, *Objects of the Dead*, 26.

44. Ibid., 23.

45. Ibid., 2.

46. Ibid., 9.

47. Ibid., 24.

48. *Proyecto Tesoros*, Colectivo de Hijos, http://www.proyectotesoros.org.

49. Ibid.

50. Ibid.

51. Ibid.

52. Ibid.

53. Davis, *Haunted Subjects*, 13.

54. Daniel Miller, *The Comfort of Things* (Cambridge: Polity Press, 2008), 1.

55. Ibid., 2.

56. "People are not fully determined culturally, or parentally; but neither are they free agents who choose who they may become. Through the reinforcement of various influences at particular times, certain traits and styles develop which come to characterize them, not as individuals but as networks of relationships. This produces what I have called, at different times in this book, an aesthetic. I do not use this term to implicate the arts. Rather, it refers to pattern—sometimes an overall organizational principle that may include balance, contradiction and the repetition of certain themes in different genres and settings" (Miller, *The Comfort of Things*, 293).

57. Miller, *The Comfort of Things*, 296.

58. My employ of the term "portraits" here references the schematic Miller employs to order his study, divided into thirty portraits, each of which profiles an individual household, both its occupants and their material possessions, on a random street in London. Miller explains: "By choosing this term I don't mean anything technical or artistic, and certainly I hope nothing pretentious. It simply helps convey something of the overall desire for harmony, order and balance that may be discerned in certain cases—and also dissonance, contradiction and irony in others" (*The Comfort of Things*, 5).

59. Ibid., 27.

60. *Cautiva*, directed by Gastón Biraben (Argentina: Cacerolazo Productions, 2005), DVD.

61. Ibid.

62. For instance, I saw *El año en que nací* in Minneapolis, Minnesota, where it was presented in Spanish with English subtitles in January of 2014.

63. Program, *El año en que nací*, Walker Art Center, Minneapolis, Minnesota, 30 January 2014, 7.

64. Anna White-Nockleby, "Fragmentos del pasado: lo documental en el teatro de una nueva generación," Paper presented at the IV Seminario Internacional Políticas de la Memoria, Buenos Aires, Argentina.

65. Ibid.

66. Program, *El año en que nací*, Walker Art Center, Minneapolis, Minnesota, 30 January 2014, 4.

67. Ibid., 5.

68. Liliane Weissberg, "In Plain Sight," in *Visual Culture and the Holocaust*, ed. Barbie Zelizer (New Brunswick: Rutgers University Press, 2001), 21.

69. Ibid., 23.

Afterword

1. Alicia Kozameh, *Steps Under Water*, 27.

2. Alicia Partnoy, *The Little School*, 26.

3. Jorge Tiscornia, "La llegada," 67.

4. Heidegger, "The Thing."

5. Harman, *Tool-Being*.

6. Estefanell, *Un hombre numerado*.

7. Kozameh, *Steps Under Water*, 75.

8. "Even the most perfect reproduction of a work of art is lacking in one element: its presence in time and space, its unique existence at the place where it happens to be" (Walter Benjamin, "The Work of Art in the Age of Mechanical Reproduction," in *Illuminations*, trans. Harry Zohn (New York: Shocken Books, 1968), 220.)

9. Benjamin, "The Work of Art," 220.

10. Ibid., 221.

11. Richard, *Cultural Residues*, 79.

12. Ibid., 79.

13. Bernardi, "An Angel," 29.

14. Baudrillard, *Fatal Strategies*, 111.

Abuelas de Plaza de Mayo, "Genetic Aspect—The Identity," abuelas.org.ar/idiomas /english/genetic.htm.

Achugar, Hugo. "Historias Paralelas/Ejemplares: La historia y la voz del otro." In *La voz del otro: Testimonio, subalternidad y verdad narrative*, edited by John Beverley and Hugo Achugar, 61-84. Ciudad de Guatemala, República de Guatemala: Universidad Rafael Landívar, 2002.

Agamben, Giorgio. *Remnants of Auschwitz: The Witness and the Archive*. New York: Zone, 1999.

Agosín, Marjorie. *Inhabiting Memory: Essays on Memory and Human Rights in the Americas*. Texas: Wings Press, 2011.

Argento, Analía. *De vuelta a casa. Historias de hijos y nietos restituidos*. Buenos Aires: Marea Editorial, 2009.

Arias, Arturo. *The Rigoberta Menchú Controversy*. Minneapolis: University of Minnesota Press, 2001.

Arias, Lola. *El año en que nací/The Year I Was Born*. Program. Minneapolis: Walker Art Center, 30 January 2014.

Avelar, Idelber. *The Untimely Present: Postdictatorial Latin American Fiction and the Task of Mourning*. Durham, NC: Duke University Press, 1999.

———. "Five Theses on Torture." *Journal of Latin American Cultural Studies* 10.3 (2001): 253–271.

Barratta, Raquel. "La noche de la tijera." In *Cuadernos de la historia reciente 1968 Uruguay 1985: Testimonios, entrevistas, documentos e imágenes inéditas del Uruguay autoritario* vol. 2, 39-41. Ediciones de la Banda Oriental, 2006.

Barthes, Roland. *Camera Lucida: Reflections on Photography*. New York: Hill and Wang, 1981.

Baudrillard, Jean. *Fatal Strategies*. Translated by Philip Beitchman. London: Pluto, 1990.

Becker Eguiluz, Nubia. *Una mujer en Villa Grimaldi*. Santiago: Puhuén Editores, 2011.

Benedetti, Mario. "Prólogo." In *Conversaciones con la alpargata*. Mauricio Rosencof, 5-7. Montevideo: Ediciones de la Banda Oriental, 2004.

———. *Pedro y el capitán: Pieza en cuatro partes*. México: Editorial Nueva Imagen, 1979.

Benjamin, Walter. "The Work of Art in the Age of Mechanical Reproduction." In *Illuminations*. Translated by Harry Zohn. New York: Shocken Books, 1968, 217–251.

Bennett, Jane. *Vibrant Matter: A Political Ecology of Things*. London: Duke University Press, 2010.

Bennett, Jill. *Empathic Vision: Affect, Trauma, and Contemporary Art*. Stanford: Stanford University Press, 2005.

Bernardi, Claudia. "An Angel Passes By: Silence and Memories at the Massacre of El Mozote." In *Inhabiting Memory: Essays on Memory and Human Rights in the Americas*, edited by Marjorie Agosín, 28-50. Texas: Wings Press, 2011.

Beverley, John. "Torture and Human Rights: A Paradoxical Relationship?" *Human Rights in Latin America and Iberian Cultures*. Edited by Ana Forcinito, Raúl Marrero-Fente, and Kelly McDonough. *Hispanic Issues On Line* 5.1 (Fall 2009): 98–109.

———. "Prólogo a la segunda edición." In *La voz del otro: Testimonio, subalternidad y verdad narrativa*. Edited by John Beverley and Hugo Achúgar, 9-16. Ciudad de Guatemala, República de Guatemala: Universidad Rafael Landívar, 2002.

———. "The Margin at the Center." In *The Real Thing: Testimonial Discourse and Latin America*, edited by Georg Gugelberger, 23-41. Durham: Duke University Press, 1996.

Biraben, Gaston, dir. *Cautiva*. Cacerolazo Producciones, 2004. DVD.

Bleecker, Julian. "Why Things Matter: A Manifesto for Networked Objects—Cohabiting with Pigeons, Arphids, and AIBOS in the Internet of Things." In *The Object Reader*, edited by Fiona Candlin and Raiford Guins, 165-174. London: Routledge, 2009.

Breckenridge, Janis and Louise Detwiler. *Pushing the Boundaries of Latin American Testimony: Mata-morphoses and Migrations*. New York: Palgrave Macmillan, 2012.

Bruschtein, Natalia, dir. *Encontrando a Víctor*. Mexico: Centro de Capacitación Cinematográfica (CCC), La Lavandería Producciones, 2004. DVD.

Calveiro, Pilar. *Poder y desaparición: Los campos de concentración en Argentina*. Buenos Aires: Ediciones Colihue, 1998.

Calvo, Adriana. "Campos." In *Ni el flaco perdón de Dios: HIJOS de desaparecidos*, edited by Juan Gelman and Mara La Madrid, 97-115. Buenos Aires: Editorial Planeta Argentina, 1997.

Camiruaga, Gloria, dir. *La Venda*. Santiago, Chile: ADOC, 2000. DVD.

Castillo, Gabriela, et al. "Mano a mano: un lenguaje para resistir." In *Cuadernos de la historia reciente 1968 Uruguay 1985: Testimonios, entrevistas, documentos e imágenes inéditas del Uruguay autoritario* vol. 1, 11-22. Ediciones de la Banda Oriental, 2006.

Centenera, Mar. "El ADN, 30 años al lado de Abuelas para encontrar a los nietos robados por la dictadura." *El País*, 18 June 2017, https://elpais.com/internacional/2017/06/14/america/1497472745_062450.html.

Charlo, José Pedro, dir. *El Almanaque*. 2012; Uruguay, Spain, and Argentina: Guazú Media, Media 3.14, Memoria y Sociedad, Morocha Films, and Chellomulticanal, 2012. DVD.

Charlo, José Pedro and Jorge Tiscornia. *El almanaque de Jorge Tiscornia*. Montevideo: Yaugurú, 2012.

CONADEP. *Nunca más: A Report by Argentina's National Commission on Disappeared People*. London: Faber and Faber, 1986.

Cortiñas, Nora. "Diccionarios." In *Ni el flaco perdón de Dios: HIJOS de desaparecidos*, edited by Juan Gelman and Mara La Madrid, 171-179. Buenos Aires: Editorial Planeta Argentina, 1997.

Crenzel, Emilio. *Memory of the Argentine Disappearances: The Political History of Nunca Más*. Translated by Laura Pérez Carrara. New York: Routledge, 2012.

da Silva Catela, Ludmila. *No habrá flores en la tumba del pasado: La experiencia de reconstrucción del mundo de los familiares de desaparecidos*. La Plata: Ediciones al Margen, 2001.

Dandan, Alejandra. "Son de campos que no hacían traslados aéreos." *Página 12*, 21 January 2013, accessed 7 April 2013, https://www.pagina12.com.ar/diario/elpais/1-212298-2013-01-21.html.

Davis, Colin. *Haunted Subjects: Deconstruction, Psychoanalysis and the Return of the Dead*. New York: Palgrave MacMillan, 2007.

de Arteagabeitia, Rodrigo. *Vicaría de la Solidaridad (1976–1992): Abierta a todos*. Santiago: Gráfica Nueva, 1992.

desaparecidos.org, "Proyecto Desaparecidos: Por la memoria, la verdad y la justicia."

Derrida, Jacques. *Specters of Marx: The State of the Debt, the Work of Mourning, and the New International*. New York: Routledge, 1994.

———. *Demeure: Fiction and Testimony*. Translated by Elizabeth Rottenberg. Stanford: Stanford University Press, 2000.

DGO. "Entrevista a una llave de agua." *Diario de Chacabuco 73*. 23 December 1973. Santiago, Chile: Museum of Memory and Human Rights. Archive.

Dorfman, Ariel. "Código político y código literario: El género testimonio en Chile hoy." In *Testimonio y literatura*, edited by René Jara y Hernán Vidal, 170-234. Minneapolis: Institute for the Study of Ideologies and Literatures, 1986.

Duchesne, Juan. "Las narraciones guerrilleras: Configuración de un sujeto épico de nuevo tipo." In *Testimonio y literatura*, edited by René Jara y Hernán Vidal, 85-137. Minneapolis: Institute for the Study of Ideologies and Literatures, 1986.

EAAF. "History of EAAF." *eaaf.org*.

Edurne Portela, M. *Displaced Memories: The Poetics of Trauma in Argentine Women's Writing*. Lewisburg: Bucknell University Press, 2009.

"ESMA: Entregaron fotos de desaparecidos arrojados al mar." *TN.com.ar*, 15 December 2011.

Estefanell, Marcelo. *Un hombre numerado*. Montevideo: Ediciones Santillana, 2007.

Feld, Claudia. "El 'adentro' y el 'afuera' durante el cautiverio en la ESMA. Apuntes para repensar la desaparición forzada de personas," *Sociohistórica* 44 (2019) Universidad Nacional de La Plata: 1-18.

Finchelstein, Federico. *La Argentina fascista: Los orígenes ideológicos de la dictadura. Nudos de la historia argentina*. Buenos Aires: Editorial Sudamericana, 2008.

Forcinito, Ana. *Los umbrales del testimonio: Entre las narraciones de los sobrevivientes y las señas de la posdictadura*. Madrid: Iberoamericana, 2012.

Fundación Solidaridad. *Dignidad Hecha a Mano 30 años: Handmade Dignity 30 years: 1975–2005*. Fundación Andes, Banco Estado, 2005.

Gandsman, Ari. "'Do You Know Who You Are?' Radical Existential Doubt and Scientific Certainty in the Search for the Kidnapped Children of the Disappeared in Argentina" *ETHOS* 37 no. 4 (2009): 441–465.

Gates Madsen, Nancy. "Bearing False Witness? The Politics of Identity in Elsa Osorio's *My Name is Light* (*A veinte años, Luz*)." In *Pushing the Boundaries of Latin American Testimony: Meta-morphoses and Migrations*, edited by Louise Detwiler and Janis Breckenridge, 87-106. New York: Palgrave MacMillan, 2012.

Gatti, Gabriel. *Surviving Forced Disappearance in Argentina and Uruguay: Identity and Meaning*. New York: Palgrave Macmillan, 2014.

Gelman, Juan and Mara La Madrid. *Ni el flaco perdón de Dios: HIJOS de desaparecidos*. Buenos Aires: Editorial Planeta Argentina, 1997.

Genefke, Inge and Peter Vesti. "Diagnosis of Governmental Torture." In *Caring for Victims of Torture*, edited by James M. Jaranson and Michael K. Popkin. Washington DC: American Psychiatric Press, 1998.

Gibson, Margaret. *Objects of the Dead: Mourning and Memory in Everyday Life*. Carlton: Melbourne University Press, 2008.

Giudice, Pedro. Personal Interview. 12 August 2013.

Gordon, Avery. *Ghostly Matters: Haunting and the Sociological Imagination*. Minneapolis: University of Minnesota Press, 2008.

Grosz, Elizabeth. "Darwin and Feminism: Preliminary Investigations for a Possible Alliance." In *Material Feminisms*, edited by Stacy Alaimo and Susan Hekman, 23-51. Bloomington: Indiana University Press, 2008.

Gugelberger, Georg. "Introduction: Institutionalization of Transgression: Testimonial Discourse and Beyond." In *The Real Thing: Testimonial Discourse and Latin America*, edited by Georg Gugelberger, 1-22. Durham: Duke University Press, 1996.

———. *The Real Thing: Testimonial Discourse and Latin America*. Durham: Duke University Press, 1996.

Guzmán, Patricio, dir. *Nostalgia de la luz*. Atacama Productions, Blinker Filmproduktion, Westdeutscher Rundfunk (WDR), 2010. DVD.

Hansen-Glucklich, J. *Holocaust Memory Reframed: Museums and the Challenges of Representation*. New Jersey: Rutgers University Press, 2014.

Harman, Graham. *Tool Being: Heidegger and the Metaphysics of Objects*. Chicago: Open Court, 2002.

———. *Heidegger Explained: From Phenomenon to Thing*. Chicago: Open Court, 2007.

Heidegger, Martin. "The Thing." In *The Object Reader*, edited by Fiona Candlin and Raiford Guins, 113-123. New York: Routledge.

Hernández, Juan Felipe. "La Química de la Memoria: A Benjaminean Approach." *Journal of Latin American Cultural Studies* 22 no. 3 (2013): 259-270.

Herrera Córdoba, Matías and Lucía Torres, dirs. *El Buen Pastor: Una fuga de mujeres*. Córdoba / Argentina: Cine El Calefón, 2010. DVD.

Hite, Katherine. *The Art of Commemoration: Memorials to Struggle in Latin America and Spain*. London and New York: Routledge, 2012.

Hirsch, Marianne. *Family Frames: Photography, Narrative, and Postmemory*. Cambridge, MA: Harvard University Press, 1997.

Hirsch, Marianne, and Leo Spitzer. "Testimonial Objects: Memory, Gender, and Transmission." *Poetics Today* 27 no. 2 (Summer 2006): 353–383.

———. "What's Wrong With This Picture? Archival Photographs in Contemporary Narratives." Journal of Modern Jewish Studies 5 (2006): 229–252.

Howe, Alexis. "Rethinking Disappearance in Chilean Post-Coup Narratives." Unpublished doctoral dissertation, University of Minnesota, 2011.

Huyssen, Andreas. *Present Pasts: Urban Palimpsests and the Politics of Memory*. California: Stanford University Press, 2003.

Jara, René. "Prólogo." In *Testimonio y literatura*, edited by René Jara y Hernán Vidal, 1-6. Minneapolis: Institute for the Study of Ideologies and Literatures, 1986.

Jara, René and Hernán Vidal. *Testimonio y literatura*. Minneapolis: Institute for the Study of Ideologies and Literatures, 1986.

Jelin, Elizabeth. *State Repression and the Labors of Memory*. Translated by Judy Rein and Marcial Godoy-Anativia. Minneapolis, University of Minnesota Press, 2003.

Jelin, Elizabeth, and Victoria Langland. *Monumentos, memoriales y marcas territoriales*. Madrid: Siglo XXI de España Editores, S.A., 2003.

Jinkis, Jorge. "Ni muerto ni vivo." *Pagina 12*, 3 August 2006, https://www.pagina12 .com.ar/diario/psicologia/9-70866-2006-08-03.html.

Jiménez, Francisca. "Los 36 años de la Fundación Solidaridad." 27 August–3 September 2011, http://www.masdeco.cl/los-36-anos-de-la-fundacion-solidaridad/.

Joyce, Christopher and Eric Stover. *Witnesses from the Grave: The Stories Bones Tell*. Boston: Little, Brown and Company, 1991.

Kwint, Marius "Introduction: The Physical Past." In *Material Memories*, edited by Marius Kwint, Christopher Breward, and Jeremy Aynsley. Oxford: Berg, 1999.

Kozameh, Alicia. *Pasos bajo el agua*. Buenos Aires: Editorial Contrapunto, 1987.

———. *Steps Under Water*. Translated by David E. Davis. Berkeley: University of California Press, 1996.

Laub, Dori. "Bearing Witness or the Vicissitudes of Listening." In *Testimony: Crises of Witnessing in Literature, Psychoanalysis, and History*, edited by Shoshana Felman and Dori Laub 57-74. New York: Routledge, 1992.

———. "An Event Without a Witness: Truth, Testimony and Survival." In *Testimony: Crises of Witnessing in Literature, Psychoanalysis, and History*, edited by Shoshana Felman and Dori Laub, 79-92. New York: Routledge, 1992.

Lazzara, Michael J. *Chile in Transition: The Poetics and Politics of Memory*. Gainesville: University of Florida Press, 2006.

Link, Daniel. "Qué sé yo. Testimonio, experiencia y subjetividad." In *Crítica del testimonio: Ensayos sobre las relaciones entre memoria y relato*, edited by Cecilia Vallina, 118-131. Rosario: Beatriz Viterbo Editora, 2009.

Longoni, Ana. "Fotos y siluetas: dos estrategias contrastantes en la representación de los desaparecidos." In *Los desaparecidos en la Argentina: Memorias, representaciones e ideas (1983–2008)*, edited by Emilio Crenzel, 43-63. Buenos Aires: Editorial Biblos, 2010.

Maier, Linda S. and Isabel Dulfano. *Woman as Witness: Essays on Testimonial Literature by Latin American Women*. New York: Peter Lang, 2004.

Martínez, Virginia and Gonzalo Arijón, dirs. *Por esos ojos*. Uruguay/France: 1997. DVD.

Martorell, Elvira. "Recuerdos del presente: memoria e identidad. Una reflexión en torno a HIJOS." In *Memorias en presente: Identidad y transmisión en la Argentina posgenocidio*, edited by Sergio J. Guelerman, 133-170. Buenos Aires: Grupo Editorial Norma, 2001.

Masiello, Francine. *The Art of Transition: Latin American Culture and Neoliberal Crisis*. Durham: Duke University Press, 2001.

Miller, Daniel. *Material Cultures: Why Some Things Matter*. Chicago: The University of Chicago Press, 1997.

———. *Stuff*. Cambridge: Polity Press, 2010.

———. *The Comfort of Things*. Cambridge: Polity Press, 2008.

Ministerio de Ciencia, Tecnologia, e Innovacion Productiva: Presidencia de la Nacion. "Banco Nacional de Datos Geneticos (BNDG)." 21 December 2013. Web.

Museo de la Memoria y los Derechos Humanos, *Interfaz: Prision Politica y Recintos Carcelarios en Chile 1973/1990*. Santiago: Ograma, 2012.

Nance, Kimberly. *Can Literature Promote Justice? Trauma Narrative and Social Action in Latin American Testimonio*. Nashville: Vanderbilt University Press, 2006.

Nora, Pierre, and Lawrence D. Kritzman. *Realms of Memory: Rethinking the French Past*. New York: Columbia Univeristy Press, 1996.

Pardal, *Naipes "La Gayola."* Centro Cultural y Museo de la Memoria (MUME). Object Reproduction. Montevideo, Uruguay.

Partnoy, Alicia. *The Little School: Tales of Disappearance and Survival*. Translated by Alicia Partnoy, Lois Athey, and Sandra Braunstein. San Francisco: Cleis Press, 1998.

———. "Cuando vienen matando: On Prepositional Shifts and the Struggle of Testimonial Subjects for Agency." *PMLA* 121 no. 5 (2006): 1665–1669.

Penchaszadeh, Victor B. "Abduction of Children of Political Dissidents in Argentina and the Role of Human Genetics in their Restitution." *Journal of Public Health Policy* 13, no. 3 (Fall 1992): 291–305.

Pérez, Mariana Eva. "Manos grandes." In *Re-encuentros: Por la identidad y la justicia. Contra el olvido y el silencio*. Fundación Contamíname, 2007.

Pi, Sofia, et al. *Historias debidas: 11 entrevistas a ex presos políticos*. Montevideo: Ediciones del CIEJ, 2013.

Presidencia de la Nación Argentina. *76:11 afiches: Momentos que hicieron historia*. Buenos Aires: Jefatura de Gabinete de Ministros de la Nación Secretaría de Comunicación Pública, 2011.

"Proyecto." *Memoria Abierta*. http://memoriaabierta.org.ar/vestigios/proyecto.html.

Proyecto Tesoros. Colectivo de Hijos, 7 April 2014, http://www.proyectotesoros.org/.

Quieto, Lucila. *Arqueología de la ausencia*. Photographs. Museo de Arte y Memoria. La Plata, Argentina.

Rasmussen, Yuyo and María Noel Domínguez. "Todo está guardado en la memoria." In *Cuadernos de la historia reciente 1968 Uruguay 1985: Testimonios, entrev-*

istas, documentos e imágenes inéditas del Uruguay autoritario vol. 4, 61-66. Ediciones de la Banda Oriental, 2006.

Ratto, Pablo, dir. *El último confín*. 2004. DVD.

Remedi, Gustavo. "Tell Me How It Happened: Unbinding the Discourse on Memory, the Political Crimes of the Recent Past, and Human Rights." In *Layers of Memory and the Discourse of Human Rights: Artistic and Testimonial Practices in Latin America and Iberia*. Edited by Ana Forcinito. *Hispanic Issues On Line* (Fall 2013): 215–230.

Rey Piuma, Daniel. *Un marino acusa*: *Informe sobre la violación de los derechos humanos en el Uruguay*. Montevideo: TAE Editorial, 1988.

Reyes, Stela. Personal Interview. 13 August 2013.

Richard, Nelly. *Cultural Residues: Chile in Transition*. Translated by Alan West, Theodore Quester, and Jean Franco. Minneapolis: University of Minnesota, 2004.

Rodríguez, Ileana. *Liberalism at its Limits: Crime and Terror in the Latin American Cultural Text*. Pittsburgh: University of Pittsburgh Press, 2009.

Roof, Judith. *The Poetics of DNA*. Minneapolis: University of Minnesota Press, 2007.

Ros, Ana. *The Post-Dictatorship Generation in Argentina, Chile, and Uruguay: Collective Memory and Cultural Production*. New York: Palgrave MacMillan, 2012.

Rosenblatt, Adam. *Digging for the Disappeared: Forensic Science After Atrocity*. Stanford: Stanford University Press, 2015.

Rosencof, Mauricio. *Conversaciones con la alpargata*. Montevideo: Ediciones de la Banda Oriental, 2004.

Sala de la Memoria, Corporación Parque por la Paz: Villa Grimaldi. Object Exposition. Comuna de Peñalolén, Santiago, Chile.

Salama, Mauricio Cohen. *Tumbas anónimas: Informe sobre la identificación de restos de víctimas de la represión ilegal*. Buenos Aires: Catálogos Editora, 1992.

Sanjinés C., Javier. "Beyond Testimonial Discourse: New Popular Trends in Bolivia." In *The Real Thing: Testimonial Discourse and Latin America*. edited by Georg Gugelberger, 254-265. Durham: Duke University Press, 1996.

Saona, Margarita. "Plain Things and Space: Metonymy and Aura in Memorials of Social Trauma." In *Layers of Memory and the Discourse of Human Rights: Artistic and Testimonial Practices in Latin America and Iberia*. Edited by Ana Forcinito. *Hispanic Issues On Line* (Spring 2014): 73–90.

Scarry, Elaine. *The Body in Pain: The Making and Unmaking of the World*. New York: Oxford University Press, 1985.

Seguel, Roxana et al. "Londres 38: Prospección exploratoria. Búsqueda, recuperación y análisis de evidencia biológica y cultural en un centro de detención y tortura." Santiago: Dirección de Bibliotecas Archivos y Museos, Londres 38, Centro Nacional de Conservación y Restauración, 2012, https://www.londres38 .cl/1934/w3-article-93321.html.

Sklodowska, Elzbieta. *Testimonio hispanoamericano: Historia, teoría, poética*. New York: Peter Lang, 1992.

Sodaro, Amy. *Exhibiting Atrocity: Memorial Museums and the Politics of Past Violence*. New Brunswick: Rutgers University Press, 2018.

Sondrol, Paul C. "1984 Revisited? A Re-Examination of Uruguay's Military Dictatorship." *Bulletin of Latin American Research* 11 no. 2 (1992): 187–203.

Sosa, Mercedes. "Cuando estoy triste." *A que florezca mi pueblo*. Universal Import, 1975.

Steinwasser, Marga and María Antonia Sánchez. "Química de la Memoria: Una experiencia de la desaparición." Museo de la Memoria, 1 April 2007, https:// www.museodelamemoria.gob.ar/page/muestras/id/20/title/Qu%C3%ADmica -de-la-memoria.

Strejilevich, Nora. *El arte de no ovlidar: Literatura testimonial en Chile, Argentina y Uruguay entre los 80 y los 90*. Buenos Aires: Catálogos, 2006.

Stoll, David. *Rigoberta Menchú and the Story of All Poor Guatemalans*. Boulder: Westview Press, 2008.

Tandeciarz, Silvia R. "Citizens of Memory: Refiguring the Past in Postdictatorship Argentina." *PMLA* 122 no. 1 (2007): 151–169.

Tavani, Eduardo. "Las marcas de la memoria." In *Las marcas de la memoria: 30,000 detenidos-desaparecidos ¡Presentes!* edited by Eduardo Tavani, 9 Buenos Aires: Instituto Espacio para la Memoria, 2012.

Tiscornia, Ana. "Una memoria, un documento histórico, una obra." In *El almanaque de Jorge Tiscornia*, edited by José Pedro Charlo and Jorge Tiscornia. Montevideo: Yaugurú, 2012.

Tiscornia, Jorge. "La llegada." In *Cuadernos de la historia reciente 1968 Uruguay 1985: Testimonios, entrevistas, documentos e imágenes inéditas del Uruguay autoritario* vol. 3, 65-81. Ediciones de la Banda Oriental, 2006.

———. "Los almanaques." In *Cuadernos de la historia reciente 1968 Uruguay 1985: Testimonios, entrevistas, documentos e imágenes inéditas del Uruguay autoritario* vol. 2, 3-21. Ediciones de la Banda Oriental, 2006.

———. *Nunca en domingo: Penal de Libertad, 1972-1985*. Montevideo: Ediciones de la Banda Oriental, 2014.

Todorov, Tzvetan. *Les abus de la mémoire*. Paris: Arléa, 1995.

Treacy, Mary Jane. "Double Binds: Latin American Women's Prison Memories." *Hypatia* 11 no. 4 (1996): 130–145.

Vestigios. Memoria abierta. http://www.memoriaabierta.org.ar/vestigios/.

Vezzetti, Hugo. "El testimonio en la formación de la memoria social." In *Crítica del testimonio: Ensayos sobre las relaciones entre memoria y relato*, edited by Cecilia Vallina, 23-43. Rosario: Beatriz Viterbo Editora, 2008.

Vidal, Hernán. *Chile: Poética de la tortura política.* Santiago: Mosquito Comunicaciones, 2001.

Vuskovic Cespededes, Ruth and Sylvia Ríos Montero. *Libres en prisión: La otra artesanía. Artefactos creados en dictadura / Chile 1973-1990.* Santiago: Editorial USACH, 2015.

Weizman, Eyal. "Osteobiography: An Interview with Clyde Snow." *Cabinet* 43 (Fall 2011): n.p.

Weissberg, Liliane, "In Plain Sight." In *Visual Culture and the Holocaust*, edited by Barbie Zelizer, 13-27. New Brunswick: Rutgers University Press, 2001.

White-Nockleby, Anna. "Fragmentos del pasado: lo documental en el teatro de una nueva generación." Paper presented at the IV Seminario Internacional Políticas de la Memoria, Buenos Aires, Argentina.

Yañez, Antonia. Personal Interview. 12 August 2013.

Young, James. *The Texture of Memory: Holocaust Memorials and Meaning.* New Haven: Yale University Press, 1993.

Yúdice, George. "Testimonio and Postmodernism." In *The Real Thing: Testimonial Discourse and Latin America*, edited by Georg Gugelberger, 42-57. Durham: Duke University Press, 1996.

www.ingramcontent.com/pod-product-compliance
Lightning Source LLC
Chambersburg PA
CBHW020352270326
41926CB00007B/401